The Writer's Library

The Writer's Library

The Authors You Love on the Books That Changed Their Lives

Nancy Pearl and Jeff Schwager

HARPER LARGE PRINT

An Imprint of HarperCollinsPublishers

HarperCollins books may be purchased for educational, business, or sales promotional use. For information, please e-mail the Special Markets Department at SPsales@harpercollins.com.

FIRST HARPER LARGE PRINT EDITION

Illustrations by A.E. Kieran

ISBN: 978-0-06-302883-8

Library of Congress Cataloging-in-Publication Data is available upon request.

20 21 22 23 24 LSC 10 9 8 7 6 5 4 3 2 1

To Joe Pearl and Megan Muir,
without whom this book, and so much else,
would not have been possible.

Contents

Foreword

by Susan Orlean

I n Senegal, when someone dies, you say that his or her library has burned.

I don't know how I came across this phrase, or what I had googled that led me to it, but as soon as I saw it, I was intrigued, so I scribbled it on an index card and hung it on the wall beside my desk. At the time, I was in the middle of writing about the largest library fire in American history, which occurred in 1986 and nearly destroyed the Los Angeles Central Library. The afternoon I stumbled on the phrase, I was, as usual, puzzling over the fundamentals of my subject. Why did I care—why should anyone care—about a library burning? If books are just paper and ink, and in the modern era can be reproduced easily, why do we feel the loss of even one book so acutely? Why do books seem so human, so personal? What makes them feel almost alive, as if a book is a person sitting right beside us, whispering a marvelous story in our ear? These are the same questions that propelled Nancy Pearl and Jeff Schwager to undertake *The Writer's Library*, asking writers what books whispered most persistently in their ears.

The Senegalese phrase puzzled me almost as much as it fascinated me. Of course, I love books. The books that have meant the most to me have quite literally changed me. But I still had trouble picturing myself as a human library.

Furthermore, I didn't see what death and a library fire had in common. And yet something about the phrase stuck with me, nagged at me. Day after day, I stared at that index card and tried to figure out what it meant. I read everything that threaded a direct line from bound manuscript to human existence. My favorite observation came from John Milton, who declared in 1868 that "books are not absolutely dead things, but do contain a potency of life in them to be as active as that soul was whose progeny they are." I certainly understood that "potency of life": I couldn't bear to throw a book out, even if it was falling apart, and I felt that each book on my shelves had a radiant presence, like a familiar friend. Indeed, books have the capacity to seem more alive than any other inanimate object. They inflect the way we feel and think. For writers, especially, the love of a particular book can be seminal, as Nancy and Jeff learn. For Jonathan Lethem one such book is James Baldwin's *Another Country.* For Maaza Mengiste, *The Corpse Washer* by Sinan Antoon shook her to her core. For Andrew Sean Greer, *Tales of the City* by Armistead Maupin lives and breathes. For an eight-year-old Donna Tartt, her grandmother reading her Charles Dickens's *Oliver Twist* aloud opened her mind to the full force of literature.

But do we in some way resemble books? Do we embody the books we've read throughout our lives? That seemed the harder part of the equation. In the end, the answer made itself clear to me in a heartbreaking way. My mother was responsible for introducing me to the love of books and libraries, and she made sure I was as besotted with them as she was. When I was a child, she took me to the library several times a week, and she treated those visits as a sort of hallowed ritual, and the books we borrowed were as precious as relics. She dreamed of being a librarian. In fact, almost every time we drove home from the library, she punctuated the trip with a long sigh and the announcement that if she could have chosen any profession in the world, she would have been a librarian. The library suited her perfectly, because unlike some avid readers, she didn't yearn to own scores of books. She simply loved consuming them, and she believed that each book she read became part of her, patched into her consciousness. Owning the physical copy of the book wasn't necessary at all.

I knew my mother took pride in the fact that she had indoctrinated me with library love, even though I hadn't ended up fulfilling her dream of becoming a librarian. We often talked about what we were reading, and reminisced about our trips to the library. Then she was diagnosed with dementia. Every time I visited her, it was as if chunks of her memory had been pried loose and fallen away. It was as if the ideas and memories and daydreams and notions that made up who she was were like individual volumes, and over time, they were being pulled out of her internal library and discarded. To borrow the Senegalese phrase, it was as if her library was burning—the essence of who she was and what she remembered, all stored in tidy rows in her mind, was vanishing. Among what was lost were all the stored memories of every book she had read and internalized, gathered over decades, savored and synthesized, now gone, gone, gone.

Never had it been more vividly illustrated to me that we are indeed living libraries. Our consciousness is a soaring shelf of thoughts and recollections, facts and fantasies, and of course, the scores of books we've read that have become an almost cellular part of who we are. In this sorrowful moment of losing my mother, I came to understand that the equation of the human mind and books was correct. At last, I understood how much we all are our books. Their meaning to us doesn't end when we close the last page. What we glean from them alters us permanently; it becomes part of who we are for as long as we live. There is joy in appreciating how much our books are truly alive—on our shelves, on our desks, but most of all in our minds.

The Writer's Library demonstrates how for writers, especially, the books we have read and loved and adored are integral to every atom of our beings. The first books that beguile us, the sentences that inspire us, the characters we feel we know as well as our best friends—Nancy and Jeff show that these make up who we are and what we try to create so that the next readers can fall in love with books just as deeply as we did.

The Writer's Library

Introduction

This book never would have been written had we not met in the spring of 2017, when Jeff was curating an exhibit for the Washington State Jewish Historical Society honoring twenty exceptional women who have made their mark in the state, including Nancy. During our interview for that project, we saw something we liked in each other: a similarity in background, each of us raised in a secular Jewish household whose guiding principles were based on empirical facts, not theology; a love of books and authors, characters and language, and most of all good stories; a shared sense of humor that helped us get through the days of our lives, particularly the darkening days of twenty-first century America; and a basic enjoyment of intelligent conversation. Neither of us would have written this book alone. Without each to spur the other on, we would have stayed home and read.

Having decided to collaborate on a book of interviews with authors, we chose to focus on an essential question that didn't seem, to us, to be adequately, or at least exhaustively, covered in the many interviews each of our subjects participates in every time they publish a new book. That question was, *How does the practice of reading inform the life of a writer?* While, inevitably, our interviews would drift into the subject of our subjects' own work, our primary goal was to get them talking about other writers and other books. Did they come from reading households? What were the first books they read? What books made them realize they wanted to become writers themselves? What did they read for pleasure? What did they read for something more than pleasure—knowledge, instruction, comfort, sustenance? The questions came fast and clear—you'll see them all as you read these interviews. But they all boil down to the same thing: *Why do you read, and how does reading help you write?*

Thus the title, *The Writer's Library.* Not necessarily the writers' physical libraries, but the libraries they carry around in their hearts and minds; the books that have shaped their tastes, their psyches, the subject matter that fascinates them, the craftsmanship that fills them with envy, the stories that have resonated so deeply that they feel like stories they themselves have lived. For in telling us about the books that informed their lives, they would tell us the stories of their lives.

With our general subject settled, we each drew up a list of authors we'd like to include. A long list. Two long lists. *(Too long lists?)* There was considerable overlap, but there were also plenty of differences. Our earliest lists included a handful of foreign writers, but as a way to focus the project, we decided to restrict ourselves to American authors. But American authors who reflect the America we see around us today, from all four corners of the country, from its vast middle, and also those who come here from around the world to be part of the American experiment.

How then did we decide which specific authors to interview for this book? First and foremost, we love them all—as incisive writers, as insightful readers, as people, as conversationalists. Second, they made themselves available to us, not only for the time it took to conduct their interviews but also, in many cases, for the time it took to revise and sharpen their words once we had transcribed and edited our original conversations. (We left the extent of their editorial input up to the individual authors to decide, to make sure they could stand firmly behind every word attributed to them in this book.) If we didn't include your favorite writer in *The Writer's Library*, it was probably because he or she was not available. We desperately wanted to include everyone's favorite writer!

One of the best parts of talking about books with people—especially if those people happen to be writers whom you've admired for a long time—is discovering that you share a love of the same books. This was definitely the case for Nancy when we talked about children's books with Michael Chabon and Ayelet Waldman. Or for Jeff, every time a writer would bring up his favorite authors, Philip Roth and Alice Munro, or his favorite book, *Jesus' Son* by Denis Johnson. But just as exciting for us was learning about unfamiliar authors and books. While we had in common with the writers a knowledge of and, to a greater or lesser degree, an appreciation for the Western canon, which is primarily male and white, we were delighted to discover—through our interviews—a myriad of new (to us) writers, many of them female and people of color, that swelled our to-be-read lists substantially. While the canon still inherently shaped the reading our authors did, it's clear that the Old World Order of literature is changing and will become still more inclusive, which is good news for both readers and writers.

All of these interviews, with one exception, were

done in person. We decided early on that we wanted to talk to people face-to-face, to feed off one another's excitement about books and reading. (The one exception, Donna Tartt, never seemed to be in the same city that we were, and with our deadline looming, we agreed to an email interview—which we think is a delight to read, though we missed the opportunity to experience and draw out her literary enthusiasms firsthand.) Many of the interviews were done in the writers' homes, which proved fascinating for us, and often allowed us the opportunity to glimpse the actual libraries of our interview subjects. We made trips from our home base of Seattle to Portland, Oregon, to Northern and Southern California, to New York and Philadelphia, and also took a long, circuitous drive around New England that left us victim to the vicissitudes of some not very helpful navigational apps and a torrential summer storm—but we maintained our good humor, and our friendship survived stronger than ever.

Here, then, is *The Writer's Library*. We hope you enjoy reading it as much as we enjoyed talking to these wonderful writers—and readers.

—*Nancy and Jeff*
Seattle, Washington
January 1, 2020

Jonathan Lethem

Jonathan Lethem is legendary among his fellow writers for his voracious reading, and also his prodigious habit as a book collector. After dropping out of Bennington College—where his classmates included Donna Tartt and Bret Easton Ellis—following his freshman year, he continued his education, and fed his acquisitive hobby, by working in the used bookstores in Berkeley, California. There, he read everyone from Asimov to Zweig, and began developing his own unique literary style, a blend of high art cut with a pulpy sensibility

that has defined his career as one of America's most acclaimed genre blenders: a writer whose highbrow stew freely mixes in ingredients from sci-fi, mysteries, film noir, rock and roll, comic books, screwball comedy—you name it.

He was born in Brooklyn in 1964, the son of Richard Lethem, an avant-garde painter, and Judith Frank Lethem, a political activist, who divorced when Jonathan and his two siblings were still young. Judith's death, when Jonathan was thirteen, created a void that shaped his world and, inevitably, his work. As he told journalist Jackie McGlone in 2007, "My books all have this giant, howling missing center—language has disappeared, or someone has vanished, or memory has gone." That absence is felt, most famously, in Motherless Brooklyn, about an orphaned, Tourette's-afflicted private detective, and The Fortress of Solitude, about the friendship between two motherless teens; but the sense of loss is palpable, to greater or lesser degrees, in each of his novels. He's written eleven to date, along with three short-story collections, a handful of novellas, and enough nonfiction to fill several volumes.

We met Jonathan at the Four Seasons Hotel in Seattle, while he was in town to promote his most *recent novel,* The Feral Detective. *A hard-boiled broadside against the values of Trumpist America, it is, for want of a better phrase, utterly Lethemesque.*

━━━━━

NANCY: What are you reading now?

JONATHAN: This morning, on the plane, I finished Chelsey Johnson's *Stray City,* which was fantastic, so human. I felt bad for the person in the seat next to me, because I was crying quite a bit at the finale. Maybe I'll pick something out tonight at Elliott Bay Books to read on the way home.

NANCY: Since you're living in Southern California now, have you read *The Nowhere City* by Alison Lurie?

JONATHAN: I love that book. I'm a big Alison Lurie fan, and that's one of my two or three favorites. I always feel like it's a bittersweet thing when you say that some living writer is underappreciated, but I think she is. I think she's a treasure, a writer who does the novel in such a pure sense. In some ways she's more like an English writer. Not that she doesn't have American themes, but that quality of being committed to the traditional novel and fulfilling its terms so beautifully.

JEFF: Speaking of English writers and Southern California, I know you're a fan of Hollywood novels. Have you read Gavin Lambert?

JONATHAN: Oh yeah, *The Slide Area*, which is a book of interconnected short stories. There actually are a lot of good Hollywood novels. It's a substantial genre.

JEFF: Do you have a favorite, other than the obvious choice, *The Day of the Locust* [by Nathanael West]?

JONATHAN: In some ways, as much as *Miss Lonelyhearts* [also by Nathanael West] means to me, I think I feel closer to *The Day of the Locust* for being a little more novelistic, a little less like a T. S. Eliot poem in prose form. I also really like Don Carpenter's *Turnaround*. He has three Hollywood novels, but I think *Turnaround*'s the best one. Also, his final novel to be published, *Fridays at Enrico's*, which I had a hand in helping finish, is partly a Hollywood novel. Carpenter specialized in portraying development: the producer and writer tandem, working together and trying to make something happen. There's a really good Hollywood novella hidden inside the sprawl of *Fridays at Enrico's*. As with a lot of his things, he doesn't write about the myth: he writes about the reality of California, or the West, and he does the same thing with the film industry.

JEFF: You're sort of a legendary book collector. Can you talk about that?

JONATHAN: Sure, yeah. I collect autographed books in particular, partly because you need something to distinguish your pursuit. I worked in used bookstores for fifteen years, and I had access to all kinds of amazing things. And I realized I could collect everything and then my house would be—well, it is a problem anyway. I sort of have two and a half houses and my academic office that are overflowing with books. But I realized at some point that I wanted to have certain limits, and so I mostly collect writers that I think of as not widely collected. There are writers I love who are obvious, but I just don't think of them as *mine* to collect. You know, Philip Roth is great, and I love him, but I don't worry about his first editions. But I have every Don Carpenter first edition, I think two or three of them autographed. I also collect paperbacks. I really like pulp, dime store, the classic pocket-sized paperbacks, and I like Penguins. I like old pocket-sized paperbacks. One thing I collect that often really surprises people is extremely pulpy pocket-sized editions of what they think of as very *literary* writing, like Nabokov or Faulkner or Jean Rhys, done with kind of a lurid, tabloid-y, pulpy paperback cover. I have a big run of those. You know, John Cheever, *The Enormous Radio* with—

NANCY: Or *The Wapshot Scandal*—I remember that pulpy cover!

JONATHAN: Yeah! I really like those. I also collect a lot of the writers who were published in paperback originals. For me, of course, the awareness that that could be a way to have a literary career begins with my fascination with Philip K. Dick. The first ten or so of his forty-odd books, and certainly many of his most important books, were paperback originals, like *Martian Time-Slip.* Then when I got into the Black Lizard reissue writers, and realized how much Charles Willeford and Jim Thompson meant to me, having some of those in their original editions is very exciting for me. And I collect all the Anchor paperbacks that Edward Gorey designed. And I really like double novels. Some of Philip K. Dick's early novels, like *Eye in the Sky*, were published as half of a double. So I've been working for a long time to try to assemble the first hundred Ace doubles, and by now I've got about sixty percent of the first hundred. So a lot of my collecting shelves are taken up with ephemeral things, books that were almost published like magazines; I mean, they're almost disposable.

NANCY: When you were a kid, did you own a lot of books or did you use the library?

JONATHAN: I did use the library for a while. I had a favorite branch of the Brooklyn Public Library, and I'm still very sentimental about that place. But I got into buying books pretty quickly. And I first realized how excited I was by used bookstores when I was thirteen or fourteen. You know, New York City had a lot of retail space that wasn't expensive in those days. So you could putter along with a kind of crapped-out used bookstore forever, because there was not a really big premium on the rent for a storefront. I would hang around with these old bookmen, or sometimes younger bookmen, and just kind of be the kid around the shop and try to apprentice myself to them in some way. I'd offer to take home books instead of money for pay, and that was usually the thing that got me in the door. I was kind of collecting in a weird way—I was *amassing* books, let's say, by the time I was fifteen or sixteen, and was already having space problems and putting things in boxes to hide them away. I had some things on my shelves and some things that were overflow, or "back stock." That's never really stopped.

NANCY: Were you mainly interested in collecting science fiction then?

JONATHAN: Lots of science fiction, yes, and then just writers that I got excited about that I wanted to collect. Always *odd* writers. I remember pursuing—in a way, what I still do—writers that seemed to me that only I knew about. So collecting them wasn't a matter of spending a lot of money. When you found the books, they were practically a dollar, or they'd be given away, but it was really hard to find them. So I loved *Earth Abides*, and then I discovered that George R. Stewart had written this book called *Storm*, and I was fascinated by that. So I was like, *I'm gonna have every George R. Stewart book*, and I did; I put them all together.

There was some moment when I realized there'd be certain books I'll own that I don't even want to read but I just found to be exciting talismanic objects. They were connected to books that I would read. There might be, you know, A. E. van Vogt and Philip K. Dick, and they both conveyed a certain kind of crazy energy to me. And one, I was going to read every word he ever wrote, and it was enormously influential on my writing. And the other, well . . . reading just two or three A. E. van Vogt books was okay. That was fun. But I still like the covers, they still gave me that kind of weird vibe that I was looking for. So it was a lot of science fiction at the outset. There was this painter—really a painter more than a book designer—named Richard Powers, same name as the great American novelist, who did these sort of surrealist-based science-fiction book jackets. They were semiabstract; they looked like the work of a surrealist painter named Yves Tanguy. And I just got obsessed with him. He was so good that it was making me want to read any book he'd done a cover for, and so it was his artwork that led me to Robert Sheckley and Clifford Simak.

NANCY: Oh yeah, Clifford Simak—he could really tell a good story.

JONATHAN: He became a big favorite of mine. And Powers led me to James Blish, who I love. So I collected and I still do collect any cover that he painted because I think, in a way, the Powers jacket was taking me to a stranger place than the writing was. I mean, at its best it would be both. But that's a real place where my love of the visual arts and my excitement about books as objects really came together: I'd identified this painter who was in a way like an auteur. It was like, *Oh, I like all the movies that John Alton was the cinematographer on. I'm just going to see all the John Alton movies!*

JEFF: Or Saul Bass!

JONATHAN: Right! Like, *I'm a big Saul Bass fan. I'll*

go see any movie where he did the titles! Yeah, it was kind of like that. It's really funny—it's like the opposite of "Don't judge a book by its cover."

NANCY: What about the covers of your books? They must be really important to you.

JONATHAN: Sure. I sort of art-directed the early ones. That was possible for a couple of different reasons. One being that, as a new author, I was sort of flying under the radar at the beginning. The publisher and the sales force don't really care if they only give you a five-thousand-dollar advance. You're an eccentric item by definition, and anything that happens is dumb luck. I did have some luck, actually: *Gun, with Occasional Music*, my first novel, found its way, and in fact the reviewer who kind of created that book's trajectory, exceeding the publisher's expectations, said he picked it up because of this jacket that I art-directed.

JEFF: Did you get one of your favorite artists to do it?

JONATHAN: Well, it wasn't that I got my favorite artist to do it. I hadn't heard of the guy, although he's gone on to be an illustrator [Michael Koelsch] that you'd probably recognize. So what I said was, "It should look like an old pulp paperback." My publisher was Harcourt Brace, which was quite a prestigious imprint, and I was thrilled it was going to be a hardcover. But in some way I really had fetishized the idea that I would be published as an ignominious paperback original—that I would have to be rediscovered years later. So I said, "I not only want it to be designed like a pulp paperback but I want the jacket itself to look like an old object." And some of the bookstores, when they first opened the box, returned them to the publisher because they thought it was a damaged shipment. But it really expressed, in a way, my preference for used books over new books. In a way, my thinking was, *Is there a way to publish it "direct-to-used"?* Could I accomplish this? And in a weird way, I did. And there was a reviewer, a very sweet man who was reviewing at *Newsweek* [Malcolm Jones], who pulled it out of the pile quite randomly because the object was arresting to him. I did myself some good there.

NANCY: When did you start reading mysteries?

JONATHAN: The story of my early reading, and the movement from quote, unquote "kid's books," has to do with my mother's shelves. And the switch sort of flips for me with Ray Bradbury on the one hand and Agatha Christie on the other. I think my mother saw that she had a prodigious, insatiable reader on her hands, so she sort of guided me to things that would make sense to a ten- or eleven-year-old who was capable of reading grown-up prose. Yet she knew that the content of a lot of what was on her shelves wasn't going to work for me. Of course I can tell you stories about how eventually I did read *everything* on her shelves, and that created a lot of bewilderment or a lot of fascination, things I had to figure out later. But she was right: Agatha Christie and Ray Bradbury, and also she had Isaac Asimov's *I, Robot*—these things were just instantly vivid for me. I could relate to them and gobble them up. That led me into a lot of other things. And she had a copy of Raymond Chandler's *Farewell, My Lovely* that I came across fairly quickly. That's a little more adult in its ambience, but I could also relate to it, and I figured out that the American crime milieu—rather than those sort of cozy mysteries, with clues and a happy solution—was more going to suit my appetite.

Right around that same time, or shortly after, I wasn't really defying her, but I kept pushing into other parts of her shelves too, and I read a Dosto- evsky novel called *The House of the Dead.* Pretty heavy stuff, but actually it was a dime-store paper- back—I can still picture it, and the title sounded really intense. And I could relate it to things that my grandmother was filling my head with, tales of the twentieth-century nightmares in Russia and Poland

and Germany and the Holocaust. So I was sort of like, *Well, if I can read Dostoevsky, I'm going to read whatever I want,* and I got very pot-shotty, and I was pursuing a lot of different appetites simultaneously. The science-fiction one—I figured out fairly quickly that I liked the poetic, dreamy, surreal stuff like Bradbury, and that led me to Theodore Sturgeon, and then Philip K. Dick and J. G. Ballard. That was more what I was after, rather than something a little harder.

I really like the social critique typical of the writers associated with *Galaxy* magazine, like [Robert] Sheckley, but also C. M. Kornbluth or William Tenn. In a way, that's the atmosphere that Dick begins with, that social satire of the '50s, which I was also developing a taste for in other places. My favorite TV show was *The Twilight Zone*, and the feeling you get from Rod Serling is kind of like those 1950s critiques of conformity and the organization man, and critiques of the Cold War atmosphere and nuclear fear. All of that stuff seemed very germane to me. It also went along with listening to not just Bob Dylan but Phil Ochs and Tom Lehrer and Lenny Bruce.

In a weird way, I felt like I was born out of time, like my cultural clock had a lot to do with the turn from the '50s to the '60s. That's the same atmosphere that other writers that I related to later came out of. Thomas Pynchon is really about that shift from the '50s to the '60s. And Vonnegut. And the Beats. Another book I grabbed from my mother's shelf, *The Dharma Bums*—that blew my mind in a totally different way, and so I thought, *Maybe I'm really into Kerouac*. Well, that petered out, but it still made its imprint. And I got very lucky: I discovered Patricia Highsmith pretty early on. So I had all these different notes that were chiming in.

Then, in high school, I read Kafka's *The Trial*. And that became this talismanic thing for me. I'd been reading a lot of American science fiction with this mysterious, paranoiac, allegorical tone, and here it was being done decades earlier. I began to identify things like J. G. Ballard and Philip K. Dick with Kafka more than science fiction. So I thought, *Who else is like Kafka?* Well, no one, obviously, but it got me on a chase for writers in translation who were thought of as sort of semi-fantastical. Italo Calvino and Stanisław Lem and Kōbō Abe and Julio Cortázar. I started to think there was this constellation of writers—every country has one of these people! Angela Carter!

There's this kind of writing, it has no name, and

of course now people offer all sorts of unsatisfactory names for it. But it's recognizable. I think a writer like Haruki Murakami wrote into this same idea, as I did. I'm writing in English, so you might want to call it science fiction. I'm not going to fight that—I like science fiction—but I think it actually has as much to do with Calvino and a lot of these other things that are in my firmament. Also, crime fiction was an obsession. I was never published as a crime writer, not to the extent I was as a science-fiction writer. But it's a predominant element in my writing life.

JEFF: How old were you when you read *House of the Dead?*

JONATHAN: I would say I was twelve when I read it—and I wanted more Dostoevsky. Then of course I read *Crime and Punishment* in high school. But I was a little intimidated by the mammoth size of his really great works, so I found a short novel called *The Gambler,* which was very influential to me. I really liked it a lot; in fact, I think it sank deeper into me than *House of the Dead.*

I frequently consider this idea of secret genres. An obvious example: the academic satire. There's no marketing category, there's no section in the library for it, but it's a very definite form with very strong formal properties: it always takes place in a semester, and there's got to be the Christmas party where everyone's secrets come out because they get drunk . . . Another one that interests me is the gambling genre. I worked very directly into it with *A Gambler's Anatomy*. That's the Dostoevsky grain coming back again, because when I first read *The Gambler*, it was as esoteric to me as science fiction, the idea that there was a world of people going off to gamble. Gambling is much more common in American life now. There's a great American film, one of Robert Altman's most perfect films, *California Split*, that to me is as influential as any novel on my idea of the gambling genre. I've watched it over and over again.

JEFF: And he, of course, also adapted Chandler's *The Long Goodbye*. While we're talking about Altman, *McCabe & Mrs. Miller* is my favorite of his. You've written about western films, but did you ever read westerns?

JONATHAN: Well, this is a funny thing. Westerns have been really important to me as a film genre, but I haven't read widely in the pulp version of the genre. I love a couple of more literary westerns: *Warlock* by Oakley Hall and *Butcher's Crossing* by John Williams, which I think is even better than *Stoner*—to me, it's his masterpiece. *Little Big Man*—

NANCY: I do have an immoderate love for that novel.

JONATHAN: Great book. Great, great book. And [Thomas] Berger, of course, became very important in my life, later on. I discovered him at age sixteen or seventeen. I began with *Neighbors*, which then would have been a brand-new book. And then, in my twenties—and this gets back to my collecting people who weren't very collectible—I had every Berger book. Later, I became friends with him and got involved in his life in some very interesting ways—that could be a whole other interview. I ended up being the person who scattered Thomas Berger's ashes into the Hudson River. And he left me some very eccentric objects in his will as well as a portion of his literary inheritance, so now every time someone buys a copy of *Little Big Man* I get, like, three cents.

NANCY: Are there books you've lent out of your library that you've never gotten back and you can't remember who had borrowed them?

JONATHAN: Well, one thing is, as a used book hound, I'm always trying to reproduce that magic moment of *finding* the thing I've been looking for. So I let myself copiously overbuy. I stack up copies of books I know I'll want to give away. With some of the less frequently found Thomas Berger books, like *The Houseguest*—which I regard as a great place to start with Berger, and one of his best books—I'll buy any copy of *Houseguest* I find, just to give away. So I inoculate myself against that frustration. I basically don't lend books: I either refuse or I give them away, and it just feels better. And it excuses my otherwise irrational behavior of buying books I already own.

JEFF: Is there a book that you consider your most precious or valuable?

JONATHAN: Well, it's unfair, because I've been an antiquarian, you get the inside line on things that come across the buying desk, and I own a few real treasures. I guess I'll protect myself by saying these could be located in a house in Maine, or perhaps one in California, or maybe in my office on campus, so you can't come and steal them without trying three different locations. It's like three-card monte—you have to break into three buildings. But I own a first edition of *Great Gatsby*. Although it's a very beat-up copy.

Then there are the eccentric items. I really love this one novel by Budd Schulberg, *The Disenchanted*. I got invited to read with him one night, and I brought it with me, so I have a personally inscribed copy of *The Disenchanted*. And the thing about books is they're like time machines. That novel fictionalizes Schulberg's time, as a young man, hanging out with F. Scott Fitzgerald. It's like a living link. In a way, it's a better Fitzgerald item to me than the *Gatsby*, because it touches Fitzgerald, who touches Schulberg, who hands it off to me.

Another one: when I interviewed Bob Dylan for *Rolling Stone*, I did get him to sign *Chronicles*. He even bungled it—he made a weird mistake in his inscription to me. He was trying for something and changed his mind halfway through, which is something you would encounter in his art, right? He started to say "from one writer to another," and then he felt that that was not what he should be saying. So he tried to change it to "from one writer to a *real* writer," and then he got tangled up in that and crossed it out. I can't remember exactly how it ended up. But it's a kind of botched inscription, which is much cooler than having the coherent one that he must have had in mind.

NANCY: With *Dissident Gardens*, I assume much of that came from your family, but were there books that influenced you in writing it?

JONATHAN: Oh yeah. Tess Slesinger's *The Unpossessed*. Christina Stead's *I'm Dying Laughing*, which I think was an unfinished novel that was published posthumously. But in part it's about being expelled from the Communist Party. *The Middle of the Journey* by Lionel Trilling. Those were all really emblematic for me. But also, any time I work with that kind of material and the sort of sprawlingness of it, I feel given permission by some of Philip Roth's larger books, like The American Trilogy [*American Pastoral*, *I Married a Communist*, and *The Human Stain*]. And also, as with *Fortress of Solitude*, I felt a really strong influence of [James] Baldwin's *Another Country*. When I write about New York and the bohemian demimonde that I grew up inside, one of the first books that gave me a way to look at my own world from the outside was *Another Country*, so it was hugely important in constructing both of those books.

JEFF: Many of your books deal powerfully with loss. Are there particular books that have informed your writing about loss?

JONATHAN: Baldwin, I just mentioned. It's suffused with a sense of loss. You know, from *Giovanni's Room* onward, I certainly associate him with that articulation. But also Kafka, although he allegorizes it. There's just such a sense of inexpressible loss and dislocation. I think also William Maxwell, *Time Will Darken It* and *The Folded Leaf.*

NANCY: Or *So Long, See You Tomorrow.*

JONATHAN: Yeah, Maxwell's a poet of writing about loss *abidingly*, just opening one's self to it as a subject. Those are some examples that come to mind right away. This maybe will seem a little more indirect, but Calvino writes beautifully about loss. He disguises it. He writes, maybe in some ways, more the way I do about it, which is that there are these kinds of contraptions, conceptual stories that give way to an awareness of loss in the middle. An apparently silly book of mine, *As She Climbed Across the Table*, that turns out nevertheless to have this sort of, you know, abyss lurking inside it—that's very much under the influence of Calvino, who has a story in *The Cosmicomics* called "The Dinosaurs," which is about when the mammals come, and there's one dinosaur left, and they all ask him to tell stories about his world. You know, I think Calvino, with his relationship to World War II, he lived across such an abyss, such a divide in his experience, and he's writing about it indirectly everywhere. You find it again and again, this mourning of a kind of inexpressibly different world of childhood and of Europe before fascism. He's a huge influence for me.

JEFF: Working in the detective genre, as you did explicitly in *Gun, with Occasional Music, Motherless Brooklyn*, and *The Feral Detective*, how much were you influenced by the holy trinity of Dashiell Hammett, Raymond Chandler, and Ross Macdonald?

JONATHAN: I read all the Hammett books at one point, and he's unbelievably iconic, but he doesn't reach into me the way Chandler does. Macdonald, I believe, not only graduates the hard-boiled detective story to the next level, but he takes a lot of the things that make Chandler one of my life-companion writers, and he extends them. Macdonald is terrifically important to me. In terms of figuring out what I wanted to do with the hard-boiled detective story at the beginning, with *Gun, with Occasional Music*, Macdonald was much more germane, even though everyone thought of it as Chandler-esque. Chandler is inimitable; he writes without understanding what he's doing. You can't model yourself on his structure because, while every book is a tour de force, it's like watching a really drunk guy walk down the street and almost fall, over and over again. Somehow he's on his feet! It's a brilliant pratfall! But Macdonald systematizes the form. He turns it into something classical. He makes it like a sonnet or something. It's so sturdy.

NANCY: A Greek tragedy.

JONATHAN: A Greek tragedy! I was thinking of something like *The Underground Man*, because Macdonald, in the '60s, begins to write about both the counterculture in Southern California and ecological things. Like the oil spill in *Sleeping Beauty*. So you can see me really quite openly imitating Macdonald in the way that the idea of climate change and catastrophe is creeping around the edges of the front story in *Feral Detective*. But also, even more simply, the way he writes in a very scrupulous way about different aspects of this region. There's a handful of good fictional portrayals of the Inland Empire—Susan Straight, Kem Nunn—not many. You find some in Macdonald. He does the whole Southland, Long Beach, Santa Barbara—he goes from place to place trying to figure it out.

NANCY: One last question: I find much of your writing very funny. Do you ever think you're not taken seriously enough as a funny writer?

JONATHAN: I love that question. Thank you. Because let me say this, Nancy, most of the time when I get a hostile review, I think the fundamental misunderstanding is that they think that things I intended as funny are meant to be taken seriously. Reviewers bear down. They don't understand the book is trying to make them laugh. Even in something like *Dissident Gardens*, you know, it's not only a book about the sorrows of disappointed Communists, of the pain between mothers and daughters! The climax of that book is a guy running down the street in a Lincoln costume, getting shot by angry mobsters for selling them a fake gold Krugerrand. So I adore that question. I *do* feel that. But it's the hardest defense to make. "I was trying to be funny" sounds so pathetic. "I meant it as a joke!" You can never really say it, but your question allows me to say it. "Yes, I meant it as a joke!"

Some Books and Authors in Jonathan's Library

James Baldwin, *Another Country*
Thomas Berger, *The Houseguest*
Don Carpenter, *Turnaround*
Philip K. Dick, *Martian Time-Slip*
Fyodor Dostoevsky, *The Gambler*
Patricia Highsmith
Chelsey Johnson, *Stray City*
Franz Kafka, *The Trial*
Alison Lurie, *The Nowhere City*
Ross Macdonald, *The Underground Man*
Haruki Murakami
Kem Nunn
Philip Roth, *American Pastoral*, *I Married a Communist*, and *The Human Stain*

Tess Slesinger, *The Unpossessed*
Christina Stead, *I'm Dying Laughing*
George R. Stewart, *Earth Abides*
Susan Straight
Nathanael West, *The Day of the Locust*

Laila Lalami

We met Moroccan American author Laila Lalami just as her fourth novel, The Other Americans, was being published. This story of the impact of the hit-and-run death of a Moroccan immigrant on a multicultural California community was a finalist for the 2019 National Book Award. Her previous book, The Moor's Account, was a fictionalized memoir of the Moroccan slave Estebanico, who traveled from Spain to Florida in the sixteenth century as part of the Narváez expedition; it was a finalist for the Pulitzer Prize.

Laila was born in Rabat, Morocco, in 1968, more than a decade after the country officially became independent, but while it was still snarled in the cultural confusion caused by four decades of French colonial rule. At Mohammed V University in Rabat, she earned a degree in English, then was awarded a fellowship to study linguistics at University College London. In 1992, she moved to Los Angeles, where she earned a PhD in linguistics from the University of Southern California. She is now a professor in the creative writing department at the University of California, Riverside.

We interviewed Laila at her home in Santa Monica. The setting was perfect for our purposes: one entire wall of Laila's living room is taken over by floor-to-ceiling bookshelves, and as we took our seats on the sofa opposite that wall, we had a perfect visual representation of Laila's reading life.

NANCY: What do you read when you read for pleasure?

LAILA: It varies. The term "literary fiction" is interesting to me. When I was growing up, before I was a professional writer, I never heard this term or thought about it. Either a book was good or it wasn't good, and that was it. I certainly came to my love of literature more through what would be considered "genre" today. I started out reading comic books and then got into adventure stories, then the big epics and historical fiction. When I was a teenager, I went through a whole period where I was reading romance. I got into so-called literary fiction when I was maybe fourteen or fifteen. Adult fiction was really what it was. Now I do read what is considered literary fiction a lot—but it's not a criterion for me to decide whether to read a book. Instead, I ask myself what's the conceit? Is it interesting? What does it have to tell me about the world? Is it fresh? Is it something I haven't seen a million times before? That's really how I decide what I'm going to read.

JEFF: Most of the books on your shelves are in English. Do you read mostly in English?

LAILA: Now I do. My French books are all on the top shelves, including those I brought with me from Morocco years ago; the Arabic books are in my office. When I was growing up, I was reading exclusively in Arabic and French, but now 99 percent of what I read is in English.

NANCY: Growing up in Morocco, were there many American books available to you?

LAILA: That's actually a really interesting question, and it's going to require a really complicated answer. Morocco was a French colony between 1912 and 1956, and during their forty years of occupation, they disrupted the entire educational system. One of the goals of French education in Morocco, as it was in all the colonies, was to train a class of clerks that could run the state. That's the kind of school my dad went to.

Even though Morocco was already independent by the time I started going to school, the children's literature that was available was still in French. People say to me, "Well, what's the big deal? You get to learn another language. You're bilingual. That's enriching; everything should be fine." The problem is that in a situation like that, if you're not French, but everything you're reading, the world of the imagination, the world of books, is exclusively populated by French people with French concerns, you feel you don't belong there. So even though I was a big reader, I didn't really see myself in books. My whole family were readers. Everybody read. That's all we did. And so yes, I did come to my love of literature through French.

There were some titles that were translated from English, like the Enid Blyton books, and we got some other American titles, but not that many. The vast majority of what I read as a child was French.

I only began reading English when I took it in high school. One of the first books that we were ever assigned was *Of Mice and Men* [by John Steinbeck], because it was very short. In my third year, I had this phenomenal literature teacher, and she assigned *The Woman Warrior* by Maxine Hong Kingston, which I thought was amazing. So every year the notion of American literature expanded for me. I loved reading in English.

NANCY: How did you happen to major in English in college?

LAILA: In Morocco it's sort of like the New York City high school system, where you have to specialize very early on. You're either in the arts or the sciences, and I was on the science track—math, physics, and all that. When I finished high school, I was supposed to sit for medical school exams. Medical school in Morocco is seven years, and it starts right after high school; you do undergrad and grad at the same time. I didn't turn in my paperwork on time, so I didn't get to sit in for the exam. I had no other idea of what I wanted to do. I was one of those kids who was kind of okay at, like, five different things, and so I thought, *Well, I love reading. And I do* *pretty well in English. So I'm just going to major in English.* I remember when I told my parents, my dad was devastated.

JEFF: He was looking forward to having a doctor in the family.

LAILA: Yeah! Or an engineer. Something that, you know, pays the bills. And all of a sudden I'm going to major in English. So that was when I committed to studying the language and reading literature.

NANCY: You mentioned Enid Blyton's books for kids. Were British books widely available? More available than American titles?

LAILA: Earlier I mentioned that French was how I was introduced to literature. The French government had a vast system of cultural centers, including libraries. So if you wanted, you could join the French cultural center. For a fee, you could get a card, and you could borrow books from the library or watch movies at the center. That's what my sister and I did all summer. It was a little cultural hub. The British did the same thing in all the major cities in Morocco. So when I was an undergrad and I needed to do research on an assignment, where was I going to find all that information? It was going to be at the British Council library. So I started borrowing books from there. That's how I really started being exposed to not just British literature but also British politics and culture. The undergraduate English curriculum included classes on both American and British civilizations. For example, in American civilization they taught us about the Constitution, the Revolutionary War, things like that. We weren't just reading the literature. But I took courses on both British and American literature.

NANCY: Many American embassies around the world sponsor what they call "American centers" or "American spaces." Was there one in Morocco?

LAILA: There was! And again, we're going to get into history—the American cultural centers were called Dar America, which means House of America. There were Dar Americas all over the Middle East. These were open during the Cold War and were still in operation during the late 1980s, when I was in college. But in 1989 the Berlin Wall came down. And people in Washington were like, "We won! There's no need for these cultural centers anymore." So in the '90s, they started closing them, and of course now we know that was not necessarily the best move, because, as I said, it was like a little hub where you could actually go and read books and have that little space to watch movies. I remember when we studied *Death of a Salesman* [by Arthur Miller] in college and the Dar America had the version with Dustin Hoffman; we sat there, all these Moroccan students, and we watched it. I used to go there all the time.

NANCY: Is there a particular characteristic of Moroccan literature that sets it apart from, say, French or Arabic literature?

LAILA: Moroccan literature, as a result of colonialism, is a dual-expression literature. You have, for example, Tahar Ben Jelloun, who writes in French. Driss Chraïbi also wrote in French. Fatema Mernissi, who did her PhD here in the US, wrote in English and French. But there are others, like Leila Abouzeid and Mohamed Choukri, who write in Arabic. As a result of emigration from Morocco, there's a large Moroccan diaspora in the Netherlands, and there are authors who write in Dutch. I know of at least one Moroccan novelist who writes in Italian. I've been thinking perhaps Moroccan literature is no longer a national literature but rather a transnational one.

JEFF: What were the important books to you when you were in your formative years, when you were becoming a passionate reader of adult literature?

LAILA: Tahar Ben Jelloun's *The Sand Child*. And I also love his poetry: there's a book called *Les Amandiers Sont Morts de Leurs Blessures*. I remember loving that.

JEFF: What does that translate to?

LAILA: *The Almond Trees Have Died of Their Wounds.* Also Mohamed Choukri's book *For Bread Alone.* In nonfiction, there's Fatema Mernissi. She's a major figure in feminism, and she was extremely significant to me as a fifteen-year-old girl. I remember she used to have a monthly column in the magazine *Women of Morocco,* which is how I discovered her work. I had just started reading adult fiction, and it was very important to me to read Moroccan writers at that age because I had been so immersed in French lit.

JEFF: Were there French books you particularly appreciated, or did you always feel "other" from them?

LAILA: Well, I read them. But once you have that realization of, *Oh, this [Moroccan] story is actually about people like me,* you're naturally more drawn to that. So, at that point, I think I was just really looking for stories that were more inclusive.

JEFF: Were there any American books you were drawn to?

LAILA: As a teenager, I would say not really. The Americans that I read around that time would be crime novelists, like Rex Stout, Patricia Highsmith, Stephen King, people like that. It wasn't what you would call literary fiction.

NANCY: When you were in England studying, did you get into English writers?

LAILA: The abiding memory I have of that time was that it was right after the fatwa [against Salman Rushdie] and we couldn't get the book [*The Satanic Verses*] in Morocco. But I was already leaving to go to England, so when I arrived in London in 1990, one of the first things I did was get *The Satanic Verses* and read it. And I remember thinking, *This is it? This is what this whole controversy is about?* It was insane to me. That's how you know that the fatwa itself was politically driven and not necessarily motivated by what was actually in the book. Because there were plenty of other people who had written things that were equally "offensive" and hadn't gotten into that sort of trouble.

NANCY: Do you think your interest in feminism was a natural outgrowth of your divided upbringing?

LAILA: Yes, because growing up it seems normal to you to think that this is how the world works—you don't question it because that's how you live. Think about Margaret Atwood's *The Handmaid's Tale*. One of the reasons that the book hits such a nerve with readers is that the people who are in it are still questioning, but in another generation everyone would accept what was happening as perfectly normal. When you're growing up in something like that, you don't really question the life you're living. You don't question that you're talking in Moroccan Arabic, but when you walk into a bank, you're actually speaking in French, even though you're both Moroccans. There's this code switching, where in a business environment, we're going to speak French, or when you go into a job interview . . . It's just a very bizarre situation. But it was our daily life, so it was only later as I became an adult, and I read more, particularly Edward Said's *Orientalism*.

NANCY: I was going to ask about him.

LAILA: I read him when I was in England, and he had a profound influence on me. That book is easily misunderstood, particularly right now. It's one of those books that really talks about the reservoir of knowledge that is created by a colonial power seeking to represent the Other in a particular way. I feel like now it's being used in sort of cheap ways. People say, "Oh, this is Orientalist," but they don't really think through exactly what it is they're implying. Lately I've noticed there's a lot of laziness around this term.

JEFF: It's an easy label.

LAILA: Right. "Orientalist" doesn't mean it's a white person writing about a brown person. It means it's a person with power doing it to a person without

THE WRITER'S LIBRARY · 43

power as a means of justifying subjugation. So it's a little more complicated, and I feel like it's become one of those cheapened clichés.

NANCY: Do you think the way you read books now has been influenced by *Orientalism*, by the way Said looked at the world or tried to understand the world?

LAILA: Yeah, I think part of the reason that book is so seminal is that it really articulated for all of us who are from the colonies how we were perceived by the outside world. So, for example, growing up in Morocco, we got all the French magazines, and we would see ourselves represented in horrifically simplistic ways. I will never forget, when I was a teenager reading *Elle* or *Marie Claire*, one of those magazines, and they had a feature about Islam, and they had this illustration of a glass of milk with a fly in it. And it said, "If a fly falls into your milk, dip the other wing. Allah says so because on one side is the poison, the other side is the cure." It was ridiculous! Another illustration was a woman with a black eye, and it was, "Allah gives you permission to correct her." This is how they're looking at us! When they look at my mom, my dad, my family, these are complex human beings, just as complex as those people were, and they're reducing them in this way! In this women's magazine, which is supposed to be about makeup and lifestyles! You always felt, when you read, the sense that there's going to come a moment, and you're going to turn the page, and suddenly you're going to discover you're the Other.

James Baldwin said that when he was growing up he used to love western movies. And he would cheer for the hero, and it took him a long time to realize, "Oh no, I'm not the cowboy, I'm the Indian." It's that experience. You're reading, and there comes a moment in the text where you realize, *Whoa! I'm not the audience for this. This is somebody else.* And I think that's what Edward Said's great achievement was: articulating for us how all of this is connected to the desire to subjugate us, to keep us supporting this empire, and serving it with our economy, with our bodies, with everything.

JEFF: When I was growing up here in Southern California, there was a chain of coffee shops called Sambo's.

LAILA: When I was growing up there was a French brand of hot chocolate called Banania, with a super-racist illustration. It was sold all over North Africa. And we bought it and drank it.

When people ask me "Are you a political writer?" I think that really says more about how you view the world. Do you view yourself as outside these tensions I have lived with my whole life? The fact that you're outside of them, you're the one who needs to be more aware of your role in these tensions.

JEFF: It's the ultimate white privilege, to be able to ignore politics.

LAILA: Yes!

NANCY: I want to ask you about *The Moor's Account.* I was thinking how important it must be to you because it explains so much of what you've been saying.

LAILA: That book changed so much for me both as a person and as a writer. I remember very clearly the moment I had the idea for it. I was reading a book called *We Are All Moors,* about the stereotypical representation of the immigrant, and how it comes from sixteenth-century Spain. And the author very casually mentioned that a Moroccan slave named Estebanico, who was brought here to the US in the sixteenth century, was considered the first black explorer of America. And I thought, *Wait a minute, why haven't I heard about him?* And so I got the [Alvar Núñez] Cabeza de Vaca book [*Narrative of the Narváez Expedition*] and as soon as I read it I knew I had to write this novel, because I could see immediately the gaps in this story and what it's leaving out. I could see that Cabeza de Vaca had intended the book for the king, so he was presenting history in a particular way for his own benefit. And I knew I could subvert all of that into fiction. The reason I say it changed a lot for me is because, as a writer, I had never written historical fiction, so it was a huge challenge, getting the voice right and all of that. But also, personally, because this is a book that a lot of Moroccans heard about and read, it opened me up to a whole lot of new readers. A really transformative book.

NANCY: When you were working on it, did you read a lot of historical fiction?

LAILA: Yes, lots. Lots.

NANCY: Were there books that particularly helped you?

LAILA: Of course. I reread *Beloved* [by Toni Morrison], because it's based on the real-life case of a woman named Margaret Garner. I read [Morrison's] *Song of Solomon.* She's so good at choosing the right detail that can really illuminate an entire scene. I loved Geraldine Brooks's novel *Caleb's Crossing,* which is about a Native American man attending Harvard. It's just so interesting that early in Harvard's history they had a student like that and the next one was, like, a hundred years later. I loved Amitav Ghosh's Ibis trilogy, the one that includes *Sea of Poppies.* I read a ton of historical fiction and also did a lot of research.

I also read [V. S.] Naipaul, who is one of those problematic writers. But part of the reason I read him was because he writes about the cross-cultural encounter, and he writes about journeying into a different country and what happens when people from different races and cultures encounter each other, and he does it in a way that is very candid, even abrupt. Oftentimes, he's openly racist, openly sexist. And yet at the same time, I study him for the sentences and for what he has to teach me about effective prose. In ten words he can do so much. Of his books, I would say *A House for Mr. Biswas* is the tenderest. Everything after that, as he gets older, he gets grumpier, and more racist, and ever more grumpy. He really did get worse as he aged.

Ann Patchett's *State of Wonder* was also about a journey into a deeper territory, and she's also a really, really beautiful writer at the level of the sentence.

NANCY: What about the other Salman Rushdie books, like *Midnight's Children*?

LAILA: Oh, I love *Midnight's Children*.

NANCY: Me too. And I was thinking at the level of the sentence.

LAILA: Yes, so playful. One thing I love about Rushdie's writing is how he opened the way for making the English language more welcoming to people who are not native speakers of English, and to really enrich English by opening spaces within the sentence for other languages to kind of mix with English. I think because he does it, it's making it easier for readers who have been exposed to his work to read someone like Luis Alberto Urrea, who does it a lot with Spanish, and not be like, *Oh my God, there's three words of Spanish. What am I going to do?* He really opened the way for a lot of writers who come from other language cultures to play with English and have it actually work for them.

NANCY: Another book by him that I really loved was *The Moor's Last Sigh.* There aren't a lot of books in English that feature Moors.

LAILA: And he's actually really good also with historical detail.

NANCY: Yes, I thought so. I hoped so.

LAILA: Have you read his *Imaginary Homelands*?

NANCY: No, I didn't read that one.

LAILA: It's an essay collection. Really, really good. That reminds me, I should teach that book.

NANCY: Can you talk about what you teach?

LAILA: I teach at the University of California, Riverside. We're a Hispanic-serving institution, and we're also the most diverse campus out of the ten campuses of the UC [system]. Many of our students are the first in their families to go to college, and what I notice over and over is that they're not used to seeing themselves [in books] either. For many of them, literature is this lofty thing. And often my job is basically to make it clear that literature has something to do with their lives; that it's part of their lives. I agonize so much about which books to assign—you have no idea. And when I find something that works, I tend to go back to it.

In nonfiction I often assign James Baldwin's *Notes of a Native Son* and *The Fire Next Time*. I teach Didion's *Slouching Towards Bethlehem*— the opening essay is set in Riverside, which is a landscape my students are familiar with, and it's interesting to hear their response to that particular piece. Recently I've taught Valeria Luiselli's *Tell Me How It Ends*, and I think that's been a really good experience too. My students read about how the current administration is handling refugees and immigrants, but often they're not aware that this was how the state was treating people at the border long before Trump came along.

What else am I teaching in nonfiction? Memoir I always find so hard. I've taught *The Glass Castle* by Jeannette Walls and *Men We Reaped* by Jesmyn Ward and *A Border Passage* by Leila Ahmed.

Sometimes I'll teach a graphic novel. I've taught *Palestine* by Joe Sacco. I've taught *Persepolis* [by Marjane Satrapi].

In fiction, it just depends. I taught one of my favorite books, *Waiting for the Barbarians* [by J. M. Coetzee] recently. My students loved it, but they also thought it was a little weird. The whole foot-washing thing didn't quite work for them. I also taught his novel *Disgrace* once. I teach Toni Morrison's work regularly.

JEFF: One writer we have to ask you about is Paul Bowles. As a Moroccan, how do feel about his work? How do you feel he represented the Moroccan people?

LAILA: It's interesting, because he's proof that you can live in a culture for forty years, be surrounded by people from that culture, have relationships with them, friendships, sexual relationships, and yet still perceive yourself to be superior to them. If you look at how he writes about Moroccans, they're all basically semi-savages. At the level of craft, however, I think he's a very strong prose writer. "A Distant Episode" is just an incredible short story. Just incredible. I've taught it too. *The Sheltering Sky*, of course—most of it happens in Algeria. But it's still tagged as though it's about Morocco. He's a very touchy writer for me, because when you read his work as a Moroccan, you see yourself only in negative ways. It's just a very difficult reading experience.

NANCY: Are there any Moroccan writers you'd like to translate into English, to help them reach a larger audience?

LAILA: You know, I would love to do that. I think in other countries that is considered completely normal, that you work as a novelist and you translate. Here in the US that's not the case, I guess because many American writers are monolingual. I would love to do it. I just haven't gotten around to it. In fact, a few years ago I pitched a translation to the New York Review Books Classics—I had just done an introduction for them for *Season of Migration to the North* [by Tayeb Salih], and I said, "How about I do a translation for you of Driss Chraïbi's first novel, *The Simple Past*?" They said, "Why don't you translate fifty pages and we'll see?" So I worked on that and I sent it to them, and I never heard back from them about it.

NANCY: Do you feel pressure as a Moroccan American writer to always include Moroccans or Moroccan Americans in your books?

LAILA: Well, I enjoy writing Moroccan characters, and

I feel they are so absent from so much of the fictional landscape, I feel it's almost my mission to keep them there. Having said that, with this new book [*The Other Americans*], I have four Moroccan characters and five who are not, and actually that was really fun to do.

JEFF: What do you think about the argument that writers shouldn't write about characters of different races? That they don't have the right.

LAILA: People talk a lot about the right to tell stories. And I think we really need to shift the conversation to the responsibility that comes with writing these stories. I welcome people writing about characters from different backgrounds, but there's so much homework you have to do, and you can't be lazy about it.

I think there needs to be more effort if you're going to write from a different perspective. I remember thinking through these questions when I was working on *The Moor's Account*. The primary sources I had on indigenous people were all from white conquistadors, so of course I knew that those sources were biased because often the purpose of these writers was to portray Native Americans as savages. That is literally what they called them, "the savages." I was trying to write historical fiction that was as factual as possible, so I needed to figure out how to handle expressions like this in the sixteenth century. I had to figure out how to communicate this without seeming like I'm agreeing with it. Do I put it in dialogue versus narratives? There are all kinds of choices you face as a writer. And I think the first step is just being aware of it. Being aware that you are writing about other people and that means you have to work at understanding them if you're going to write them.

JEFF: And the larger the platform you have, the more responsibility you have.

LAILA: You're right. It's interesting, talking about indigenous people, but *Blood Meridian* by Cormac McCarthy is a rough read. The way he writes about Natives in his books is problematic.

JEFF: Well, go back to Shakespeare—you've got Othello and you've got Shylock in *The Merchant of Venice*. You can't have two more problematic characters.

LAILA: And people still read them, and study them. That's the thing, when you talk about "Orientalism," you can't just say it's a label. It's much deeper than that. You can have a work of art that's amazing but is going to include those elements of racism, because our lives are like that. None of our lives are free of racism.

Some Books in Laila's Library

Leila Ahmed, *A Border Passage*
Margaret Atwood, *The Handmaid's Tale*
Geraldine Brooks, *Caleb's Crossing*
J. M. Coetzee, *Waiting for the Barbarians*
Amitav Ghosh, Ibis trilogy
Tahar Ben Jelloun, *The Sand Child*
Maxine Hong Kingston, *The Woman Warrior*
Valeria Luiselli, *Tell Me How It Ends*
Toni Morrison, *Song of Solomon* and *Beloved*
V. S. Naipaul, *A House for Mr. Biswas*
Ann Patchett, *State of Wonder*
Salman Rushdie, *Midnight's Children* and
    Imaginary Homelands
Edward Said, *Orientalism*
Tayeb Salih, *Season of Migration to the North*
Jesmyn Ward, *Men We Reaped*

Luis Alberto Urrea

Luis Alberto Urrea was born in 1955 on a personal and cultural borderline between Mexico and the United States. His mother was an Anglo-American from Staten Island, New York, who was wounded while serving in the Red Cross during World War II. When she met Luis's father, who was born in Sinaloa, Mexico, he was the head of security for Mexico's president. Luis's childhood was spent in Tijuana, where he was born, until he was three years old and the family moved to San Diego, where his father's

diminished prospects and resulting anger created a family situation of continual conflict. At times, Luis's psyche was his parents' battlefield, as they waged family war to make him American or Mexican. All this, while dealing with the inherent racism of San Diego in the 1960s and 1970s, shaped, in Luis, a rebellious and sensitive soul inevitably drawn to artistic heroes and creative pursuits.

He was accepted into the University of California, San Diego, where he studied creative writing. His father's death, under violent and mysterious circumstances in Mexico, where he had gone to raise money for Luis's graduation gift, inspired an essay that found its way to visiting professor Ursula K. Le Guin, the legendary science-fiction author who became his friend and mentor. Still, it wasn't until 1993, when he was in his late thirties, that he published his first book, Across the Wire: Life and Hard Times on the Mexican Border. Since then, he has written more than a dozen books, including poetry, nonfiction, novels, and short stories, in genres ranging from sci-fi to mystery to magical realism. His 2004 book The Devil's Highway was a finalist for the Pulitzer Prize in nonfiction, and his most recent novel, The House of Broken Angels, was a National Book Critics Circle Award finalist in 2018.

We interviewed Luis at his hotel in downtown Portland, Oregon, which he was visiting following an appearance at a literary festival. Afterward, Nancy and Jeff headed to Powell's Books, one of the country's largest bookstores, to have a look around, and lo and behold, Luis and his wife, Cindy, had the same idea.

━━━━━━━

NANCY: Were you encouraged to read as a child?

LUIS: Well, my family was exactly split between the US and Mexico. My mom was a blue-blood New Yorker from a very sophisticated, very literate family. She knew one of Hemingway's wives, and her best friend was the editor of Paris *Vogue*, while my father was a Mexican military man. And they were at war, a constant culture war. I was Louis to her, Luis to him. My father was striving to make me more Mexican all the time, and I think he sensed the United States was winning, because I read comic books, which he hated, in English, and I was reading books in English, and that music that I listened to, that rock and roll, which he detested, was in English, so he was always stepping up the Mexican-ness. And my mother did not like the fact that I spoke with a Mexican accent.

JEFF: How was the war resolved?

LUIS: When we moved to the United States from Tijuana, my mom decided that she could win the war by introducing me to "true" literature. Not those Batman comic books or *Mad* magazine—in her opinion they were trash, as were the stupid TV shows I watched. She began her campaign with Dickens, *Oliver Twist.* I was a little kid in grade school, and my mom would read to me every night before I fell asleep. She'd begin reading and she'd get so carried away she'd become British and start speaking in a terrible British accent, and I remember thinking, *What's wrong with my mom? She's speaking really weirdly.* I knew what she was reading was English, but it was something beyond me, and I think in some way she was working voodoo on me, like dangling a bait: *This is what you could have,* she was saying silently. Pretty canny psychologically. It's stuck with me since I was seven. I've never forgotten it.

What cemented it for me is that I would fall asleep to this, and I would—I can still see it when I think about it—I would see waves in the ocean, with words on them, white waves, with these words as she read them. I think she got a little frustrated with me and Dickens, so she switched to Mark Twain. And that was it, man. It was *Tom Sawyer.* And I was just astonished. Growing up in San Diego and Tijuana, we didn't have big rivers, so I didn't know what the Mississippi was, but it all seemed fabulous. This old man, this dead American, who had probably in my mind been dead maybe a thousand years—I didn't know—had written this thing that was so graspable and contemporary and funny, that it was as though he was right there with us. He stepped into the room. I'll confess it to you, because now we can put it on the record, that my first erotic realization in life was Becky Thatcher.

NANCY: Tom's friend Becky?

LUIS: I was hot for Becky Thatcher, man. And there's that scene when Tom Sawyer chews her piece of gum that she'd been chewing. I lost my mind! I remember lying there, and I thought, *What? He's got her gum in his mouth?* First of all, I didn't know you could do that, and I never even thought something like that could be in a book. I remember saying something to my mom, like, "Um, I was distracted, Mom. Could you read that again?" I was like, *Whoa!* So I really wanted to be Becky Thatcher's boyfriend, really badly, and many, many, many years later, my wife, Cindy, and I took our daughter to Hannibal, Missouri, and we were walking around the Twain house, and I realized across the street from his bedroom is Becky Thatcher's bedroom, and I was having some hot flashes just remembering it. Then my mom followed Twain with *The Jungle Book* [by Rudyard Kipling], and that was it, I went crazy. I was Mowgli. After that I wanted to read about young males doing outrageous things, which led me to space opera—which kind of disappointed my mother, let's face it. Andre Norton's *Storm Over Warlock* was my go-to book. There was this young lad with two psychic wolverines and a hawk, and he fought the giant ant men who invaded from space. I read it over and over. That was me.

NANCY: Your mother sounds like she would have made a good librarian.

LUIS: There was no library in our neighborhood, so every week we'd go to the library in downtown San Diego on the bus. Two buses. She was smart enough to make a little ritual of it. So we'd get off the bus and go to Woolworth's first, have a hot dog, and I'd have an orange soda, and then we'd go to the pet section, and I'd look at the parakeets, and I'd look at the goldfish—it had to be exactly the same way every week—and then we walked to the library. She was pretty cool. Basically, I think she was just sick of me—"So go enjoy yourself," she'd say. "But don't go in the bathroom. There are very bad men in the toilets." I'd say, "Oh, okay, Mom." I would max out my library card every Saturday, and I'd come home feeling like a millionaire. And she let me get whatever books I wanted. She rarely looked. And I would read those books, and I felt as though the universe was mine. I didn't like taking them back. I wanted to keep them but couldn't. So when I could get books, it was amazing.

NANCY: Did you own a lot of books?

LUIS: My mom got me two sets of books, one of novels for kids. I remember they were bound in a dark brown fake leather with gold titles. That's how I read *Robinson Crusoe* [by Daniel Defoe], which I couldn't understand, and *Black Beauty* [by Anna Sewell], all those books. And the other was kind of a pale green set of hardcovers that had *One Thousand and One Nights* and other classic stories, which led me to be crazy for mythology. I was an indiscriminate reader. I just wanted to read, read, read. Part of that, you know, had to be a benefit of living in that scary, ethnically volatile barrio in southeast San Diego.

JEFF: What was that like for you as a biracial kid?

LUIS: It was a troubled neighborhood, and it was very much a war between brown, black, and white. And in those days, fortunately, there weren't the weapons they have now, but there were knives and things. Brass knuckles. I was in this odd position of being, you know, an Irish-looking white boy who spoke Spanish. And nobody quite knew what to make of me, so they figured, "Let's just beat him up." At that time, I wanted to be a priest, and I'd come out of my Catholic school in my stupid uniform, and you could hear the bugles sound, and they'd come—for me. So it was much better to stay in the apartment with Batman and Ray Bradbury than to be outside.

NANCY: Did you read Spanish in those days as well?

LUIS: One of the things that was driving my father mad was trying to fight the literary battle, right? He had learned English in a beautifully literary way. He memorized the dictionary. Five pages a week. Word by word. And then he would make me give him English tests. I remember sitting at this kitchen table in our terrible little apartment with him and saying "Okay, Dad, what is an aardvark?" He was trying so hard, and you know, it's probably no shock to anyone that Tijuana was not a literary center in those days. I'd say it was within the last fifteen years that we got our first public lending library. There weren't bookstores in those days. You know, this was probably 1963, 1964, something like that.

Anyway, my father had been scouring Tijuana for something for me to read in Spanish, to solidify my Mexican-ness to him. And he found something, and it was from Spain, paperback, double volume edition, of Homer. *The Iliad* and *The Odyssey*, translated into Spanish; but my father didn't quite get it. He came home—he was given to these elaborate male gestures—and slammed it on the kitchen table, and he told me, "Luis, study these in their original Spanish!" I've laughed about it for sixty years. It was just so pure and beautiful. And even then, I knew, *Wait a minute. That's Greek. I've got these over here—*

NANCY: In those pale green leather—[Laughter.]

LUIS: Finally he took me deep into Mexico several times. Total immersion. To wash the gringo out of me. Then the only thing to read was in Spanish. I think it did the trick for my dad. He was always concerned that I wasn't Mexican enough. I was Mexican American and that wasn't going to do. The battle in my house was that I was entirely American and entirely Mexican, and both of my parents were language fascists. I hated it, because I couldn't pass the test no matter what it was. Now I'm grateful for it, and I realize my parents' marriage was like a strange dance. A novel. It was like a Richard Yates novel.

NANCY: Jeff and I are huge Richard Yates fans.

LUIS: I love him too. I wish he were more of a headliner still. I love all the short stories. *Revolutionary Road* was a little beyond me, I think. But the stories—

NANCY: *The Easter Parade* is a killer novel.

JEFF: Probably my favorite novel is *A Good School*. But the stories—I agree. I probably read them every two years. Just amazing stories.

LUIS: You know, I read everything. And in college, when I knew I was going to be a writer, I wrote every sort of thing. I didn't know you needed to specialize. It was the '70s, at Cal [University of California, Berkeley]. We had a lot of poseurs in the writing program. Poets would dress like poets: black turtlenecks. I remember I was astonished because some of them would hold their cigarettes European style. And I remember thinking, *You're all weak!* Because no one seemed to be from a working life, and certainly nobody else had been born in Tijuana, and nobody had come out of the barrio.

JEFF: What sorts of things did you want to write?

LUIS: In those days I wanted to be a science-fiction or fantasy or horror guy. My mother was so upset that I had such bad taste. There was a liquor store near our home that sold those seventy-five-cent paperbacks, Fawcett Crest.

NANCY: Ace Doubles.

LUIS: Ace Doubles! Oh my God. The best thing ever. You'd read one whole novel and turn it upside down and read the other one. I remember I came home once with Hunter S. Thompson's *Hell's Angels*. That was probably the most trouble I got in with my mother. Just endless diatribes about my love of distasteful and vulgar things. Those opening paragraphs describing those men going out on the run—I'd never read anything like it.

NANCY: Were there other writers besides Hunter Thompson that blew you away?

LUIS: Charles Bukowski. *The Days Run Away Like Wild Horses Over the Hills.* It was one of those books that just gave me free rein. Like *Trout Fishing in America* by Richard Brautigan. It was like a passport into the land where I wanted to live. So I went to the bookstore, and I was looking around, and I had fallen in love with Stephen Crane, the poems, and I had totally been freaked out by Bukowski because I thought, *I didn't know you can say that stuff.* So I went over to the poetry area, and I look on the shelf, and there's Leonard Cohen's *The Spice-Box of Earth*, and I thought, *Leonard Cohen, whose songs I love, has a book? What?* And I picked it up, and next to it, *The Lords and the New Creatures* by Jim

Morrison, and I pick that up, and next to that was *Tarantula* by Bob Dylan, and next to that was *In His Own Write* by John Lennon, and I was holding all of these, and that's when the angels of blue collar rock and roll spoke to me, because it was just ridiculous, biblical, that epic moment where light comes out of the sky, and angels sing some high C, and I think, *These guys typed! It didn't just happen. Right? They actually sat down.* And that led to *Beautiful Losers* by Leonard Cohen. I thought, *This man. Singer-songwriter. A poet. And he writes dirty novels?*

NANCY: I know you were great friends with Ursula Le Guin. How did that come about?

LUIS: When I was almost done with college, my father died. He died bringing me a graduation gift from Mexico. I was his first kid to go to college. It was a big, gruesome, awful experience—he died at the hands of the Mexican cops, and they kept his body and held it for ransom. What he was bringing me was a graduation gift of cash, and I had actually gotten the cash, because someone had snuck it out of my father's pocket and passed it through to me. I had to spend my gift to buy the corpse back. So, you know, the border revealed itself in its worst guises. And I didn't know how to process that, except I was writing all the time, and I wrote a piece about it, and my English professor at UCSD [University of California, San Diego] had brought in Ursula Le Guin as a visiting professor, and he gave her the story. And that's what started my real life as a writer.

JEFF: Were you familiar with her work before that?

LUIS: Yes, especially the Earthsea novels. And the early stuff, like *The Word for World Is Forest* and stuff like that. I think *The Left Hand of Darkness* was beyond me at the time. Anyway, she read my story and told my professor that she needed to meet me. "Bring him to the apartment," she said. The school apartment in La Jolla. So he said, "Ursula Le Guin wants to meet you." I was like, *Oh, no.* He said, "In fact, she wants you to join her workshop, but she needs to talk to you first." You know, as a writer now, I see all the symbolism. It was nighttime, and we went to this apartment, and you'd go up the stairs, and there was a light on, you're going toward the light. Like a *Led Zeppelin IV* inside album cover, going toward the magus with the light. And we knocked on the door, and this tiny woman opens the door. She was smoking a pipe in those days, and she had a highball or some kind of whisky in her hand, and I thought, *This is the coolest person I've ever seen in my entire life.* And she said, "Luisito, come in!" She sat down in this little armchair and turned sideways towards me. "Tell me about yourself, Luisito."

I was smitten. I'd never seen anybody like this. She was several steps beyond my mom, who seemed so exotic to me. And Ursula was so kind. She said, "I just want to tell you that I'm going to buy this story for an anthology." "What?!" "Yes. Is that all right?" "Yeah!" I didn't even know what it meant. She had to teach me what manuscript format was. And the workshop was astonishing. David [Brin] was in the workshop. And Kim Stanley Robinson was around. And she brought Toni Morrison to meet us.

NANCY: What about reading? Did she suggest books to you?

LUIS: Ursula coached me through so much, and she was very, very firm. But so kind. And she told me, "Luisito, it's time for you to read feminists. You better start reading women. Let's get with that." She'd give me these insane bits of wisdom, because she was convinced I was actually going to do this thing—I was actually going to write—and she would tell me these things, like "I want you to remember something," and I said, "What?" And she said, "Invariably, when men write about women, their characters in some part of the book will stop before a mirror

and say, 'My God, my breasts are magnificent.'"
And I just was dying, you know? And I didn't know
if she was serious or not. And she smacked her hand
on the table, and she said, "We don't do that!" I said,
"I'll remember. I will remember."

NANCY: And, by golly, you have!

LUIS: I try to! I always think of Ursula reading what I
write.

JEFF: So who are some of the women writers who've
influenced you?

LUIS: Oh, Diane Wakoski. As soon as she said it, I was
thinking, *Okay, let's go to the bookstore,* and in the
bin of discarded paperbacks, there was *The Motorcycle Betrayal Poems.* And I picked it up, and that
dedication: "Dedicated to all the men who betrayed
me, in hopes that they fall off their motorcycles and
break their necks." I thought, *I think I love her.* It
was just the right book because it was accessible.
And then I thought, *The best thing I can do is sign
up for a feminist literature course.* Just get guided
into this stuff, because Ursula says so. I was the only
guy in the class.

JEFF: Great way to meet girls.

LUIS: Really! And we read Olive Schreiner. A lot of
Doris Lessing. All kinds of great, great authors.
And it was a great gift to me, because I was just

naturally drawn to boy stuff because I was a boy. I had unfortunately discovered Robert Ludlum, and I thought, *This is great literature. These wild plots are brilliant!* Not. [Laughter.]

NANCY: When you were a kid, did you wish there were books that reflected who you were, what your life was? Or didn't it even matter?

LUIS: I never thought about the ethnic side. I'll tell you. I was drunk on the possibilities of what these people were doing; I was in it for the sensation. My personal world wasn't that much fun, though I think I was always seen as this fun, mad, crazy kid, especially when I got to junior high and high school. We left the barrio, and we moved to this white, working-class, Anglo suburb, and that's where I saw my father crushed under the heel of California. He was still somebody, whether he was in Mexico or what I call Diet Mexico, the barrio, but then when we left . . . That was hard to watch.

My mother won the war. It was her world we were living in. So I escaped constantly. She was furious with me for never turning off the TV. It was like religion. I would get *TV Guide* and I would plan out my entire week by what time the giant ant movie would be showing. I was reading magazines, like *Famous Monsters of Filmland* and *Mad* magazine, but we also subscribed to *Look* and *Life* and *National Geographic.* I read all the time. I was always finding some other world, because the one I was in, I couldn't deal with. And my family was coming apart. All of that. So yeah, I don't know, maybe I was trying to find myself. I don't know. I was really taken with heroic guys doing stuff. And I think Ursula taught me that I could also be impressed and identify with heroic women doing things. Her message to me was always about humanity.

Being raised in Southern California in those days, there was no such thing as Mexican or "Hispanic" literary culture. Nothing. And I went all the way through high school, all those years, not a mention of any Latin American anything. The only thing that was ever mentioned was *Don Quixote.* We never read it. We never saw it. And the teachers would pronounce it *Donkey Hoatie.* Right? And I honestly thought it was about a donkey, like a kid's book, about a donkey named H-o-a-t-i-e.

JEFF: That would be a great book to write.

LUIS: I know. Donkey Hoatie and his adventures. Imagine my shock when I finally learn that this is one of the greatest novels in history. Then I got to college, and lo and behold, this universe I had not known fell upon me. It was Borges, Cortázar,

Neruda—that was from a girlfriend who gave me *The Heights of Macchu Picchu*. I had never even heard of this guy. Carlos Fuentes, then Gabriella Mistral and Alfonsina Storni, and late in the game, [Gabriel] Garcia Marquez.

JEFF: So what do you read now?

LUIS: I stoke the furnace with poetry. I read a lot of poetry. I especially love Japanese poetry. Haiku means a lot to me. If you were to go into my writing room, there's basically two solid walls of poetry books. I love Mary Oliver, of course. Neruda was really important to me. B. H. Fairchild. You name it. They're all in there. I got—I just picked up a Clemens Starck book—Oregon poet. Jane Hirshfield.

NANCY: We love Jane.

LUIS: I love her too. I finally met her at Bread Loaf, and everybody there knew I loved her, but I was too shy to talk to her. I'm often too shy to talk. After I did a reading, she came up to me, and I was like, *Oh God*, and I backed up against the wall, and she said, "Why haven't you spoken to me?" And I said, "You're Jane Hirshfield, man!" And she was so cool. And she said, "You know what we need to do? We need to take a Greyhound bus somewhere, far away, sit side by side and write in our notebooks the whole time." And I was like, "Oh man, yeah. Let's do that,

Jane." Yeah, I love her. I think she's so brilliant. And her prose is brilliant too. She's got that piece on liminality ["Komachi on the Stoop: Writing and the Threshold of Life"]. Writers are always on the edge of two worlds. It's just fantastic.

And I love mysteries. A lot.

NANCY: Mysteries or thrillers? Or do you not make a distinction?

LUIS: I used to be a thrillers guy. But I don't get thrilled anymore. Even now, reading mysteries, as soon as the bang-bang begins, I'm bored. And I often don't finish them. Except for Lee Child. I finish every one of his.

JEFF: Since you grew up in Southern California, are you a Ross Macdonald fan?

LUIS: Yeah, all the family stuff. I never read detective fiction except some Raymond Chandler when I was a kid. But my mom's family is related to Dashiell Hammett. I was a big Robert B. Parker fan as well. When I got the appointment to teach at Harvard, I went to my library in Claremont and I said to the librarian, "You got anything about Boston?" I didn't know anything about Boston. I thought Boston was south of New York—that's what I knew. And he said, "Looking for Rachel Wallace?" I said, "What? Looking for Rachel Wallace?" I said, "Does she write about Boston?" He said, "No, it's a mystery by Robert B. Parker." He gave me *Early Autumn* and *Looking for Rachel Wallace*, said, "Check these out." And I lost my mind. I read everything. I couldn't stop reading Robert B. Parker. And when I got to Boston, I sent him a note, and I said, "I just want you to know, I've gotten this job at Harvard, and I love your stuff so much that I am making the freshmen read Spenser mysteries instead of all this highfalutin stuff. We're not going to do Dickens. We're going to do Spenser." And he wrote me back and said, "Dickens who?" [Laughter.] And he said, "It seems to me I better come meet your students." I was like, "You're kidding." He said, "No," and we picked a date, and what I'll never forget about him is I was waiting for him, to take him to the classroom, and I was wearing jeans, white running shoes, and a Harris tweed coat, and he walked up to me in jeans, white running shoes, and a Harris tweed coat. And he said, "I approve. You've got style."

JEFF: Before we started taping the interview, you mentioned Bigfoot a couple of times.

LUIS: Oh, I'm a Bigfoot fan. I am a believer.

NANCY: I thought you were talking about a foot fetishist.

LUIS: No. Sasquatch! I'm waiting for him to show up.

They're allegedly quite active around us right now. I was in Bend [Oregon] giving a talk, and I said, "Well, I'm always looking for Bigfoot." And one of the women in the audience said, "You want to see Bigfoot?" And she told me the exact location, because a lot of people around here have seen him.

There's a new book called *In the Valleys of the Noble Beyond* by John Zada that's about a search for Bigfoot. It's incredibly literary and kind of transcendent. He's totally taken with this myth of Bigfoot and trying to figure out what it's all about, and he comes up to the Pacific Northwest and goes up into British Columbia, into the rain forest, staying with indigenous people and ecologists, and he's frustrated because he never finds it. But he's with people who talk about it openly. It's an amazing book, and what really killed me about it is that he talks about more philosophical things. Like, what if this is an expression of something ineffable? What if it doesn't matter if it exists or not? And there's this beautiful passage I'm going to use in my writing classes, where he starts pondering the fact that we think we're solid, but we're not, we're sparkling. We're little universes of sparkling—we just don't know it. What if we see and know so little of what's around us? What is image? What isn't? What is fantasy? What isn't? It's just an amazingly well-written book, and he never loses his faith in this thing existing, and some of the Indian people are saying, "You're crazy." And some are going, "Of course." And he says, "Well, why has nobody seen it?" And they're like, "We've seen it for ten thousand years. What are you talking about? There's hundreds of thousands of people who've seen it. We know." And they all tell him, "If you're looking for it, you will never find it." And he's trying to figure this out. Is this like elves? Is this like fairies? Is this some personification of something? Is it real? It's real. We're made of electrons. It's real.

Some Books and Authors in Luis's Library

Jorge Luis Borges
Richard Brautigan, *Trout Fishing in America*
Charles Bukowski, *The Days Run Away Like Wild Horses Over the Hills*
Leonard Cohen, *The Spice-Box of Earth* and *Beautiful Losers*
Julio Cortázar
Jane Hirshfield
Rudyard Kipling, *The Jungle Book*

Ursula K. Le Guin, The Earthsea Trilogy
Pablo Ncruda
Robert B. Parker, *Early Autumn* and *Looking for Rachel Wallace*
Hunter S. Thompson, *Hell's Angels*
Mark Twain, *The Adventures of Tom Sawyer*
Diane Wakoski, *The Motorcycle Betrayal Poems*
Richard Yates, *The Collected Stories of Richard Yates*
John Zada, *In the Valleys of the Noble Beyond: In Search of the Sasquatch*

Jennifer Egan

*J*ennifer Egan's Brooklyn town house has a steep
staircase that winds its way up four floors, each of
which is lined with overflowing bookshelves: mostly
novels, but one large, low shelf is filled with the
children's books she read with her two teenaged sons
when they were younger, and another is full of plays
that belong to her husband, theater director David
Herskovits. On the top floor of the house—literally
on the floor—are multiple foreign editions of each of

the books she herself has written, which an assistant is organizing to donate to local libraries.

Born in Chicago, Jenny spent her formative years in San Francisco following her parents' divorce and remarriages. Bouts of loneliness during a gap year in Europe led to a desire to write, and when she returned, she got a BA in English literature from the University of Pennsylvania. She returned to Europe to get an MA from Saint John's College at Cambridge.

Her first book, the short-story collection Emerald City and Other Stories, was published in 1993, followed by the novel The Invisible Circus in 1994. Her second novel, Look at Me, came out a week after the 9/11 attacks in 2001, causing a stir because it dealt, in part, with an Arab terrorist planning an attack on the US. But it was A Visit from the Goon Squad, her 2011 novel of interconnected music industry stories, that cemented her status as one of America's most acclaimed writers, as well as earning her the Pulitzer Prize for Fiction. Her most recent book, Manhattan Beach, is set primarily during the World War II era, on the Brooklyn waterfront not far from where she lives.

Jenny is the current president of PEN America,

the US branch of the international organization that
defends free expression and the freedom to write. Our
interview took place at her dining room table, where
we talked about books under the watchful eye of one
of her three cats.

—————

NANCY: Were you a big reader as a child?

JENNIFER: I think I was. I learned to read pretty
early. My mother is a huge reader, and to this day,
my relationship to reading is very connected to her.
My biological father was also a very smart guy, and
a reader, but I don't think we talked about books so
much. My mom taught me to read; she actually found
a tutorial in the *Chicago Tribune*: "How to Teach
Your Child to Read." I think I was maybe three or
four, pretty young. But you hear about writers who
were very precocious and were reading Tolstoy at
age ten. That was definitely not me. I liked all the
things that you would expect, like Nancy Drew. I
loved comic books. The Little House on the Prairie books [by Laura Ingalls Wilder] were huge for
me. I found those to be a really encompassing world,
and I definitely turned to reading as an escape. My
parents divorced when I was very little, and after
my mother and stepfather moved to San Francisco,

I would go back to Chicago to visit my father and stepmother. I started doing that at age seven, which was hard because I was still so young. I remember reading the Little House books at night in the summers when I would visit Chicago, and people yelling for me to come down to dinner, and me pretending I didn't hear, trying to read a little longer.

I was an indiscriminate reader. I liked everything. We would go to the library every week and I would take out a bunch of books. I would read one and I always thought it was the best book I'd ever read, and when it ended I was so unhappy, and I would hate the next book for like one chapter and then I would think, *No, this is the best book I've ever read!* I just liked being transported. And really almost anything could do it. I loved mysteries. Ghost stories. I loved whodunits, I loved Agatha Christie. It's so funny—I started reading her to my kids, expecting her books to be amazing. They're not! I don't know how I thought that.

JEFF: How old were you when you were reading Agatha Christie?

JENNIFER: Probably a tween. Every time I finished one, I was flabbergasted! The killer was always the last person I would've thought of. Now I can tell from page one. I remember these Ellery Queen ten-minute mysteries. I loved those. I thought they were electrifying. So reading was always a pleasure, for sure, but I would not say I was a sophisticated reader. It never occurred to me that I could become a writer. No one in our family did that, so there wasn't any mystique around "the writing life" for me. I hadn't thought much about the fact that there *were* writers. I do remember a writer visiting my school once when I was in third or fourth grade, and it seemed as unbelievable as someone descending from the clouds. I thought, *You wrote a book?!* It was shocking that a human being could do that. She had one piece of advice for us, which is the worst writing advice anyone can ever give anyone: "Write what you know."

JEFF: Your novel *Look at Me* is largely set in Rockford, Illinois. Is that where your father lived? Were you writing what you knew?

JENNIFER: My parents lived in Chicago, but my grandparents lived in Rockford and my mother grew up there. I do love to write about *places* that I know. I know Rockford pretty well from a child's perspective. That's the way I draw from my experience. But not in terms of people, or even events. I rarely write about an event that I've experienced. For example, when I was working on my novel *The Keep,* which involves a prison writing class, I considered actually trying to teach in a prison. And I thought, *No, because that'll actually make it harder for me to write about it.* But the places are important. If there's some kind of memory element to the place, that always helps. Not nostalgia per se, but the intensification that can come along with memory, the way it sifts through impressions and leaves you with what is most arresting.

NANCY: Did your love of the Laura Ingalls Wilder books lead to a love of historical fiction in general? Is that what led you to write *Manhattan Beach*?

JENNIFER: No, I wouldn't say so. I haven't read all that much historical fiction. I was more interested in the place and atmosphere of wartime New York. That's really how it started. That basic curiosity pulled me into all kinds of research, for years, at the beginning of which I was still writing other books, and that research eventually suggested certain characters and milieus. I was thinking of New York during World War II, which led to the waterfront and the Port of New York. By place I mean more than that. An environment, let's say. For example, the punk rock scene in San Francisco in the late '70s [which was one setting in *A Visit from the Goon Squad*]. I witnessed that very much as a bystander, but I really did see it, and I had been thinking for a long time, *I'd really love to use that.* But it's not like I can just decide to do it. It needs to intersect with another idea. It needs to be animated, and that doesn't happen just because I decide it will. It has to wait its turn. I'm sitting on other environments, actually. I really want to write about New York in the nineteenth century. That's my next big historical idea, but there's no idea yet!

One way I start is by collecting books, and keeping them all together in a particular place, and that makes me feel like I'm starting to grow a creature in a lab. I sort of put these books together and then I can feel my thoughts starting to run through them. Sometimes even before I really get into reading them. I just know they're there. I did that for *Manhattan Beach.* I have this gigantic bookshelf with books from that era, like John O'Hara's *BUtterfield 8* is there. All kinds of waterfront books, some very technical. A study of merchant sailors from the 1930s. *A Merchant Marine Officers' Handbook.* It was almost like that bookshelf was an externalized portion of my brain that I could access by just looking at all those books.

JEFF: So have you started with Edith Wharton for nineteenth century New York?

JENNIFER: Well, I started with Edith Wharton when I was a teenager, and she's been a huge touchstone for me, especially *The House of Mirth*. I just wrote an introduction for the new Scribner edition, which is coming out in January. Her New York novels are absolutely superb. *The House of Mirth* is one of the best American novels ever written. So it's nice to have an excuse to revisit all of those. But it's not really the Gilded Age I'm interested in; I want to go back a little further. We'll see, but one person I read recently for the first time was Fanny Trollope.

NANCY: Oh, right, her *Domestic Manners of the Americans.*

JENNIFER: So good. I mean, she was hilarious. Her descriptions of Americans are unbelievable. Picking their teeth with knives. There was a huge problem with spitting. Which is interesting, because I encountered that when I went to China in 1986 as a backpacker. I actually got ill while I was there, and I rarely get sick, but with everyone spitting everywhere, it's no surprise. It's just so unhygienic. This is exactly what she was complaining about. There were a lot of really bad sicknesses. There was typhoid, and it would sweep through towns in the Ohio Valley, but the men would not stop spitting because they all chewed tobacco. It's fascinating.

So that's 1820s, early '30s. That may be a little too early, but what I'm really trying to do is get a better sense of the century. I want to figure out where I want to pause in the structure of New York's growth and evolution. I don't know the answer yet. But it's so much fun to read and try to figure it out.

JEFF: What are you reading to help make that decision?

JENNIFER: There are some great mysteries and whodunits from the nineteenth century I've been reading, although you know who did it pretty early. It's a little like Agatha Christie, though much better, because it's a lot about character. But there's no surprise in who did it. And Louisa May Alcott, who wrote *Little Women*, wrote horror and mysteries as well; I need to get some of those. The Wilkie Collins mysteries are spectacular. I just revisited them. *The Woman in White* is one of the best thrillers I've ever read. There's a great bookstore called Freebird [Books & Goods] on Columbia Street that specializes in old books about New York. I've been going there for years, and that store was essential to my research for *Manhattan Beach*. It has a lot of guides to New York for tourists. I keep going and buying all these books that I really haven't had time to read and stockpile them on the bookshelves. That's kind of fun too.

JEFF: Going back to your childhood: you read indiscriminately—

JENNIFER: And liked indiscriminately—

JEFF: And liked everything when you were young. You said you read as an escape. Do you remember the first book you read that made you look at literature as a more serious pursuit?

JENNIFER: As a teenager, I loved a bunch of books that now I can't even classify. I read *Rebecca* [by Daphne du Maurier] at eleven, and my mother basically said, "There's no living with you. Just finish this!" Because I was so overwrought. And then another book that preoccupied me unbelievably was *The Magus* [by John Fowles]. Later, he revised it because it was so incomprehensible. Has anyone else ever done this? He rewrote it and republished it because people were so confused by the original. And the revised version made no more sense than before! [Laughter.] But I read it again and again. It's funny; it's also very gothic, like *Rebecca*. It has twins. There are doppelgängers. I'm a sucker for that stuff. Then Richard Adams's *Watership Down* took over my life. I got a rabbit. I named it Hazel. Someone just wrote something in the *Times* about *Watership Down* and how it's deeply good and we can learn from it. Maybe so. Another one was *Shōgun* [by James Clavell]. A lot of these were popular, commercial books my mother was reading. It's so funny, because she and I barely spoke while I was a teenager. I loathed her, and I think I was pretty loathsome too. But somehow there was still a conduit for book recommendations, because we were still reading a lot of the same books. *Ordinary People* [by Judith Guest] was another one I remember loving. So I don't know how to classify these, or what I'd think of them now, but I was reading adult, commercially successful books, let's say.

I reached a point in high school when I was really a delinquent in certain ways. I was very socially self-conscious and very eager to fit in, and all of that was so distracting. Sometimes I think about how much more I could've read if I hadn't been like that. I remember arguing with my mother, because she thought I was being a slacker and not reading good enough stuff. But then somehow in the middle of all of that I stumbled on *The House of Mirth*. I had never heard of it. I remember reading it at my grandparents' house, and it was a different order of engagement. That was a formative encounter for me as a reader, when I understood that sometimes the great books have that designation because they are truly extraordinary.

NANCY: When you found a book like *Rebecca*—and I love the idea of you being so overwrought, I can just picture it—did you then go on to read all of du Maurier?

JENNIFER: I don't think I did. I remember that summer. My stepfather was working in Hawaii, so we were living in Hawaii. That's how I remember when this was.

JEFF: Like that book *Reading Lolita in Tehran* [by Azar Nafisi]: *Reading Rebecca in Hawaii.*

JENNIFER: With an avocado tree! We got there and thought, *Amazing! We'll have avocados.* After a week it was like, *I never want to eat another avocado.* The tree was huge, and it would drop these gigantic, soft, horrible avocados everywhere. Anyway, that's where I read it. No, I remember that summer I was really interested in reading about drugs. A lot of books about heroin and things like that. From the library. I was eleven.

NANCY: Do you remember any of those books?

JENNIFER: I remember reading technical books about what the different families of drugs were. I remember reading one called *The Junkie Priest* [by Daniel Egan]. The priest wasn't a junkie. He was helping so-called junkies. So no, I did not go on to read all of Du Maurier.

JEFF: What about Edith Wharton? When you read *The House of Mirth*, did you read her other books?

JENNIFER: I did not. I have gone on to read a lot of Wharton, and she was such an uneven writer. It's really surprising. I think about that a lot. As far as I can see, unless I'm missing something, she wrote three great books, all set in New York. And then she wrote some really crappy ones, including a later one set in New York called *Twilight Sleep* that's sort of depressingly bad in that it uses some of her old devices, but not well. But, you know, Wilkie Collins did the same thing. In some of his later stuff, he used the same tricks as he used so beautifully in *The Woman in White*, but just not well. It's a cautionary tale.

But anyway, no. I often don't go on to read more books by the same person immediately, and I think there's something a little self-protective about that, because it's rarely as good or the same. I tend to wait and sort of let the book be its own thing. The exception was books that were meant to be consumed in quantity, like Nancy Drew, where they're essentially the same book again and again. But *The Custom of the Country* and *The Age of Innocence* are also really great. I still think *The House of Mirth* is the best, but you can argue that.

NANCY: She did write a very funny short story called "Xingu," which is about a group of women who get together to talk about books.

JENNIFER: She published lots of stories, and I want to read more of her New York stories. I'm not as familiar with those. I'm excited to discover those.

NANCY: What about Henry James?

JENNIFER: At that time, I didn't read Henry James. Later I did, of course. I just reread *Washington Square* in the last couple of weeks. So great. That's an interesting book because it was published I think in 1880, but it's narrated as if it were the 1860s, and it's talking about the 1840s, so the setting is actually contemporary with Frances Trollope. James is very focused on how New York had changed, and in fact, his narrator talks about how there were still streets with no houses at the time the book is set. James's *The Golden Bowl* is one of my favorite books, although I feel I need to reread it. There comes a point where saying it's one of your favorites doesn't really mean anything if it's been too long since your last reading. I think I'm reaching that point with *The Golden Bowl.* But I also reread *Portrait of a Lady* in the last few years, which really held up—in fact, I loved it more than I did the first time.

And James and Wharton are such different writers. Liking Wharton does not mean you're going to like James, and liking early James doesn't mean you're going to like late James. Another James that I really loved was *What Maisie Knew*. As a child of divorce, I felt like he was way ahead of his time in understanding the strange complicity that a child ends up having with separated parents: an oddly adult relationship that's age-inappropriate, and how compromising it is to the kid. James really got that.

JEFF: What about high school? Did you read much then?

JENNIFER: What was I doing in high school? Smoking pot! I wasn't reading a lot. I don't even remember what I read in high school. Honestly. I went to a big public high school. I remember we read *Moby-Dick*, which I thought was the worst book I had ever opened in my life.

NANCY: Me too.

JENNIFER: I have no memory of it, just of the trailer where the class was held where we read it.

JEFF: Did you read Salinger in high school?

JENNIFER: I don't remember if I read him then. I remember reading him in New York as a young person and loving *Nine Stories*. I do remember in high school reading, like, Richard Brautigan, sort of Beat people, a little bit. Kerouac. And high school is the time to read him for sure, because he does not hold up. Let's see. Who else along those lines? I was very enamored with the world of music. You know, record albums were sort of like books. They had a lot of pages and notes. I approached those with energy and excitement, and I remember poring over those Patti Smith records. My friends and I worshipped her. We went to her concerts; we knew every lyric. It's so amazing—I introduced her at an event recently, and I thought, *Wow, this is really strange that I get to do this.* But in terms of what books was I actually reading? It's like a blank. I don't know.

JEFF: Well, when you're smoking a lot of pot, things don't stay in your brain quite the same way.

JENNIFER: Lost years! What was I reading? I was doing a lot. Those were intense years.

JEFF: When was it that you started thinking about being a writer?

JENNIFER: I took a year off between high school and college, and that's when I kind of figured it out. Partly because I'd wanted to be an archaeologist and I gave that a try at the beginning of the gap year: I paid to go on a little dig in Illinois, and I realized, *Oh my God, what was I thinking?* It was hot. It was boring. What I'd loved about archaeology, meta-phorically, was the idea of digging and sort of learn-ing about human life. But the act of digging and finding tiny shards of things meant nothing to me.

JEFF: So much more pleasant to do it in a book.

JENNIFER: Yeah. And before that I thought I wanted to be a doctor, and again, I think I had a very meta-phorical idea about that. Honestly, that was about cutting people open and knowing what was inside them. But then I got very squeamish, so I didn't like that idea anymore. Anyway, I had never been to Europe, and I was dying to go. I got a backpack and flew to London, and got a Eurail pass. It was actually kind of hard, because my mother and step-father's marriage was ending, so it felt like running away, which is never a great way to travel. And being alone . . . This is something I try to explain to kids now—I was just at a high school yesterday talking about this—but they cannot fathom that being alone really meant *being alone*. They don't know what that was like! No cell phones. No internet. So I felt really alone, pretty raw during that trip. I had some great times, and a lot of times I remember with af-fection. But there was this scary underside, where I was having panic attacks and feeling like something really bad was going to happen, and I didn't know what was going on, and I thought maybe I had blown out my brain on drugs.

Somehow in the course of those tremendous lows and highs, I realized that writing was an essential component of experience for me, whatever that experience was, and I think that's what really made me understand that I had to do it. It wasn't that I thought I could necessarily write well; I just knew that I had to do it. It came much more from a feeling that it was an essential part of my relationship to the world in an almost spiritual way, or as close as I get to that. Storytelling gives life meaning. Quite literally. We dream at night. We synthesize our experience into remarkable texts that are full of symbolism and complexity and all kinds of referents and meanings and incredible landscapes, and that's what writing is for me, I guess. That synthesis.

NANCY: When you were in Europe, during that period, did you read? To help you escape?

JENNIFER: I did. Amazing how much it helped. The particular thing I remember reading was a book of short stories by Dickens. "A Christmas Carol" was one of them. Talk about a culture clash. I remember specifically being in Italy in summertime and being very scared and reading Dickens, and he helped! He's like catnip. Those nineteenth-century writers are so absorbing. So reading was a help.

NANCY: What about Mrs. Gaskell?

JENNIFER: Not then.

NANCY: Because she would be so calming, sort of soporific.

JENNIFER: I wasn't that sophisticated a reader yet. Those nineteenth-century Brits—I would say I certainly model myself on them now. Gaskell, without a doubt, is super great. And *Middlemarch* may be the best novel written in English. So I adore all of those, but I didn't discover them until later.

JEFF: When you thought about being a writer, were there writers whose work really resonated with you in a way that you said, "I want to do that"?

JENNIFER: I don't know if there were. I don't have a memory of thinking that, but maybe I did. It's so easy to make up answers, but I truly don't know. It really had a lot more to do with a recognition of what made me able to live than any idea of what I might contribute—if anything! But when I got to college, I do remember that I was immediately trying to do things that were experimental. I got to Penn in the early '80s, and semiotics ruled the day, so I immediately tumbled into that and became very enamored of it—I think way too much, in that I read too many texts about texts, and not enough of the texts I was reading about. I did get to those later, but it felt a little like the cart before the horse.

So I think it was semioticians I was emulating, or someone like [Samuel] Beckett. I remember reading *Murphy* in college and thinking, *Oh, this is really cool—he's sort of deconstructing the novel.* What I probably should've been doing was reading more novels rather than trying to deconstruct them. Later, I remember seizing upon writers that I wanted to emulate. A specific one I remember was Ethan Canin's book of stories *Emperor of the Air*. That book was so encompassing for me. I really felt like I wanted to do what he was doing.

JEFF: Was it the voice of Ethan Canin that appealed to you so much?

JENNIFER: I think it was the voice, especially the way he often used older narrators, which was interesting because he was a very young man. Also, *The Mysteries of Pittsburgh.* Michael Chabon and I are about the same age, and I remember when that came out, the kind of vividness, the overwhelming sensory quality of the language. I remember just being very swept away. And that happened with some other people. Joyce Carol Oates. But that was after I moved to New York, so we're missing, like, six or seven years there. I don't know whom I was copying, if anyone, in those years.

NANCY: What do you like to read now?

JENNIFER: A lot of what I read is driven by what I'm working on. I love that feeling of having a project. So right now it's nineteenth century, but I was already reading a lot of that. Over the last few years, I read both of Trollope's big series, the Barchester and the Palliser series. I love the nineteenth century. The novel did so many things then, and it's funny we now think of nineteenth-century fiction as "conventional." Whoever says that has not read a nineteenth-century novel anytime recently, because they're pretty crazy books. I just love the freedom and the looseness and the confidence. The kind of eclecticism, the way so many strata of society were present.

JEFF: What about contemporary writers?

JENNIFER: I'm going to be interviewing Zadie Smith at the 92nd Street Y in a few weeks, and I really like her work. I'm revisiting some of it, and I had never read *NW*, so I just started that. It's spectacular— maybe her best so far.

JEFF: Looking back at specific books of yours, do you remember what you were reading when you wrote them? For example, *Look at Me*, which Nancy and I both love.

JENNIFER: *Look at Me*. Okay, let me think about that. A lot of [Don] DeLillo. He's been a huge inspiration for me. I remember specifically reading *Underworld* while I was working on *Look at Me*, and knowing consciously that this was what I wanted to do. My work before *Look at Me* had been pretty conventional. So it was really a case of doing what you were asking, earlier, if I had done: choosing a writer—DeLillo—and emulating. Also, [Ralph] Ellison's *Invisible Man* was a revelation for me, using stream of consciousness and experimentation as a way of revealing internal states.

With my first novel, *The Invisible Circus*, Robert Stone was an influence. Also, Jean Rhys and James Salter and Joyce Carol Oates. Meanwhile, the first wave of academic studies of the '60s were just coming out. Todd Gitlin's book *The Sixties* had a big impact on me. In college I'd read his *The Whole World Is Watching*, which deeply influenced my thinking about that period.

NANCY: What about when you were writing *A Visit from the Goon Squad*?

JENNIFER: [Marcel] Proust for sure. I had read some Proust as a younger person. I think I got through *Swann's Way*. But all the stuff about time, I was like, *What a bore. Who cares?* Then I found Proust again in my late thirties and I felt very differently about the subject of time. Proust only lived to be fifty-one, but I think people aged so much faster then. And now I'm feeling the impact of what he felt about time passing in a way that I couldn't, even in my late thirties.

So Proust inspired *Goon Squad* pretty directly: I was finishing *In Search of Lost Time* when I started working on *Goon Squad*. And then the other thing was serialized TV. I had a period where I watched *The Sopranos*, and that got me thinking about serialization, which ultimately just led me back to the real serialists: the literary ones. My gateway drug was TV, which I kind of no longer watch. I don't have time and there's so much of it, and I'm tired of how much time even publishing people spend talking about it. *You're in the publishing industry! Stop talking about television!* So anyway, an interest in serialization, and then excitement about the structure serialization invites, all of which I was awakened to through *The Sopranos*—that combination led to *Goon Squad*.

Then for *Manhattan Beach* there was a massive quantity of reading, not just research but contemporary literature from the period I was interested in. Lots of crappy detective fiction, racist, sexist . . . Actually, that made me remember something I learned in college, when I took an American Civilization class with Janice Radway: we used works of fiction as cultural artifacts, which is a fascinating and useful thing to do. When I was working on *Manhattan Beach*, almost nothing was better for yielding up cultural touchstones and collective memories, suppositions—habits of life and mind. It's all baked into fiction. So I read a lot of fiction from the '20s, '30s and '40s, and it didn't matter if it was good or bad.

JEFF: Pulp fiction?

JENNIFER: Pulp fiction, and also stuff with literary aspirations that may or may not have been fulfilled. One writer I discovered was Maritta Wolff, who wrote some interesting books, one in particular called *Night Shift*, published in 1942, about the demimonde in, I think it's a midwestern city. What I liked about that book was that she was honest about what actually took place sexually in women's lives, as opposed to what was *supposed* to be taking place— which was nothing, for single women anyway.

Also, a lot of sea literature, which is a genre unto itself, and became very exciting to me as I was working on *Manhattan Beach*. I mean, Patrick O'Brian. Oh my God. Soap operas at sea! They're so good. Except I finally had to stop because they weren't even in my period. Maybe I'll have an excuse to go back to O'Brian now.

Each of my books is pretty explicitly in conversation with other books. And I tend to try to stay in that reading conversation while working on whatever I'm working on, because I don't want to lose the connection. Even through the page proofs of *Manhattan Beach*, my husband saw me reading yet another crappy detective novel, and he said, "Your book is done! Why are you still reading these?" I kept exhaustive lists of expressions, local color, businesses, addresses; this document was hundreds of pages long, full of details that I pulled from books and organized systematically. And I was still making adjustments when the novel was in page proofs.

JEFF: One last question on *Goon Squad*: Was the literature of rock and roll a reference point—beyond liner notes, which I'm a big fan of too?

JENNIFER: There were some rock and roll books that helped me. One in particular: *So You Wanna Be a Rock & Roll Star*, by Jacob Slichter, who was the drummer for a group called Semisonic. I thanked and acknowledged him in *Goon Squad* because his memoir was what first alerted me to the importance of pauses in rock and roll songs. I really owe Jake a debt. We ended up meeting after *Goon Squad* was published, and he was wonderful. Very well read, and writing another book.

JEFF: What about DeLillo's *Great Jones Street*, about the fictional rock star Bucky Wunderlick?

JENNIFER: I haven't read that. I discovered DeLillo around the time of *White Noise*, and by the time I was working on *Goon Squad*, I was trying to move away from him, which was important to do because he'd been so important for *Look at Me*. I've found that trying to do new things also means moving away from my heroes. It's bittersweet but necessary: like eventually having to move out of your parents' house.

Some Books and Authors in Jenny's Library

Richard Adams, *Watership Down*
Ethan Canin, *Emperor of the Air*
Agatha Christie

Wilkie Collins, *The Woman in White*

Don DeLillo, *White Noise* and *Underworld*

Daphne du Maurier, *Rebecca*

Ralph Ellison

Judith Guest

Henry James, *Washington Square* and
The Golden Bowl

John O'Hara, *BUtterfield 8*

Jacob Slichter, *So You Wanna Be a Rock &
Roll Star*

Fanny Trollope, *Domestic Manners of
the Americans*

Edith Wharton, *The House of Mirth*

Maritta Wolff, *Night Shift*

T.C. Boyle

"*What fun we will have!*" *That was the response
from T.C. Boyle to our interview request—and
in person, Tom (as he's known to all friends,
acquaintances, journalists, and librarians) is nothing
if not fun. In years past, both Nancy and Jeff had
interviewed Tom, but this meeting had the added
attraction of taking place at his Montecito home, which
was designed by Frank Lloyd Wright and narrowly
escaped destruction in the fires and mudslides that
plagued Santa Barbara County in 2018.*

Tom's career stretches more than forty years, from his first book, the short-story collection Descent of Man in 1979, to his latest, Outside Looking In, a historical novel about Timothy Leary's experiments with LSD. In between, he has written some of American fiction's most wide-ranging, incisive, and downright entertaining work, exploring issues like immigration and social disparity in Los Angeles (The Tortilla Curtain), man's troubled relationship with the environment (A Friend of the Earth), historical figures from Frank Lloyd Wright (The Women) to Alfred Kinsey (The Inner Circle), and epics that focus on flawed characters pushed to their limits by events beyond their control (World's End, Drop City, and The Harder They Come). Between novels, he has remained committed to short stories, publishing nine collections that touch on multitudinous aspects of American life.

Tom's reading—and the library that's scattered throughout his house—is as varied as his writing, and provided endless grist for the mill of our interview.

―――――

NANCY: What are you reading now?

TOM: My next novel deals with animal consciousness, so I've been reading a lot about that, including

Carl Safina's *Beyond Words: What Animals Think and Feel.* Next up is the new Frans de Waal book [*Mama's Last Hug: Animal Emotions and What They Tell Us About Ourselves*].

NANCY: Those stories about animal emotions are so moving.

TOM: They are. There's something in this material that breaks my heart, and I'm not sure what it is. There are seven and a half billion of us, and I love us all, but enough already. The animals just—it tears my heart out. The cruelty. The *L.A. Times* had a picture on the front cover a couple weeks ago of some tenderhearted animal rights people going out to the Farmer John's slaughterhouse in downtown L.A. at dawn when the trucks are coming in with the pigs in them. And they've got a long stick with a sponge on it and they're giving the pigs water. And here's the picture of the pig, his head is out, and he's drinking water. They're going to be in the slaughterhouse in half an hour, but nobody bothers wherever the hell they're coming from to give them water! And they want water, and they have hope. They don't know! I mean it's just so horrifying.

NANCY: What recently broke my heart was *Voyager*'s last words on Mars, where he said—I'm already anthropomorphizing—it said, "My battery is failing and it's getting dark." And the NASA engineers played back the song "I'll Be Seeing You."

TOM: Well, that's the future. See, I'm still in the past of being an animal and loving animals, but the future of course is precisely that. The machines will have emotions. And by the way, I hate them all. Every single damn machine there is, they are my enemy, they make us enslaved to them, and then they break.

JEFF: As you talk about your strong feelings for animals, I think of your novels *A Friend of the Earth* and *When the Killing's Done*, where that really comes through.

TOM: I think I could've been perfectly happy as a field biologist. That was one of the joys of writing *When the Killing's Done*. I met them, became friends with them, they took me on their rounds, spent nights on the island—it's fascinating to me. Though one small problem with it as a profession is, you have to take math. [Laughter.] So here I am! Fascinated by all creatures and everything that has to do with creatures.

NANCY: Is there another novelist or fiction writer who's writing about animal consciousness in a way that you admire?

TOM: Let's go all the way back to Albert Payson Terhune—*Lad: A Dog* and all the rest. Those are the first books I ever read. All his wonderful books, and also *Big Red* [by Jim Kjelgaard] and *Lassie Come Home* [by Eric Knight], where you're in the mind of the dogs. I just loved those.

JEFF: Do you have a dog now?

TOM: Yes. She's out in the guesthouse with my wife now. She's a puli and she's six years old. She's my constant companion.

NANCY: Speaking of your wife, does she write?

TOM: No, God bless us. I can't imagine writers marrying other writers. There's your enemy, right in bed with you. [Laughter.]

NANCY: Do you have any favorite books about marriage? I see you have a copy of John Updike's *The Maples Stories*.

TOM: Yeah, that's good. Updike is one of my heroes. I have read, oh, probably three-quarters of his books, and that's saying a lot, since he wrote six thousand books. Yeah, *The Maples Stories* I love. It's one of the books that comforts me that I'll reread occasionally.

NANCY: Your new book, *Outside Looking In*, is about Timothy Leary, his disciples, and the experiments they did with LSD.

TOM: Well, I'm writing about this because I'm fascinated with the idea of animal consciousness, *our* animal consciousness, and is it possible to expand it?

LSD has come back into fashion again, and I wanted to remember what it was like. Does it allow you to see God? Is there God? And if so, is God simply a miswiring of the neurons? Is it something that basic? I wanted to explore that. I was a hippie, I knew all about that era, and so does everybody else. But how did we get there? For most of us, Timothy Leary was a preposterous clown on TV in a robe, drearily chanting things. Who is this old guy? But to go back and see him as he first was when he started doing this: a charismatic, handsome, and powerful guru, who believed in what he was doing. As a former druggie myself, I been there, I done that, I know just what that is all about and how seductive any kind of drug can be, even though LSD is not physically addictive. And it's also the whole notion of cutting down your editing brain so that all the sense impressions flow in. Is that God?

NANCY: There's a great description of an LSD trip in the book. Pretty mind blowing.

TOM: I've got a wonderful surprise for you, Nancy. I put two tabs in your Pellegrino. [Laughter.]

NANCY: Can you give us some to go? [Laughter.]

JEFF: What are the important books of that era, the ones that informed *Outside Looking In* but also informed you?

TOM: *The Electric Kool-Aid Acid Test* [by Tom Wolfe]. I reread it for *Drop City* and again for this book. It remains one of the most brilliant and hilarious books I've ever read. I don't know how he does it. He's really not a journalist. He's a novelist. He's so great! So that was certainly one, and then of course all the usual books about psychedelics.

NANCY: Like [Aldous] Huxley's *The Doors of Perception?*

TOM: Yeah. I reread that for this book as well. Huxley was huge in that circle in Cambridge in those days. When Huxley was dying, he had his wife shoot him up with LSD, twice. Wow! Personally, I'd rather just die in my sleep. You know, it's extreme.

JEFF: How important is it to you to stick to the facts when you're writing a historical novel like *Outside Looking In?*

TOM: Well, in my first novel, I began with a little note, which addresses your question. [Reading:]"As the impetus behind *Water Music* is principally aesthetic rather than scholarly, I made use of the historical background because of the joy and fascination I find in it. And not out of a desire to scrupulously dramatize or reconstruct events that are a matter of record. I have been deliberately anachronistic, I've invented language and terminology,

I've strayed from and expanded upon my original sources. Where historical fact proved a barrier to the exigencies of invention, I have with full knowledge and clear conscience reshaped it to fit my purposes." [Chuckles.]

JEFF: That answers my question.

TOM: Yeah. So I look back on my twenty-eight books and I realize a lot of them are historical novels. I find the odd bits of history, like *The Road to Wellville*. Why do we eat corn flakes? Or Doctor Kinsey, who invented sex; well, where did that come from? I'm fascinated by the actual history. So, too, in this book, this commune and the disciples and all of this. That's all true to fact, and that's crazy enough. That's fascinating enough. So I want to give you the real history, because I love it. But still the apologia stands.

I got to know E. L. Doctorow years ago, and the first time we read together, somebody asked him that question, and he said, "What you have to realize is that novelists study history for a purpose, and the purpose is to make a novel. To make art." It's a kind of warning to so many would-be novelists or beginning novelists who get so fascinated with the history that they forget they're writing a novel. They try to be too scrupulous with the history. I think I'm getting it both ways. I'm invading the history and inhabiting characters to see where the story will go from this given set of historical facts, which is not to say that I can't violate them if I want to. I wrote my Frank Lloyd Wright book [*The Women*] because I wanted to know about this house and I wanted to know about the architect. And the facts are true. If you've never heard of them, those facts are true. But on the other hand, it's fiction. I could've had him run down by a railway car when he was eighteen if I wanted to. And reconstructed by plastic surgeons. I mean, I could do anything. But I love the history, so I'm giving it to you straight . . . ish. [Laughter.]

NANCY: Someone once said that history gives you the facts, and fiction gives you the truth of the facts.

TOM: I like that.

JEFF: What are your favorite historical novels?

TOM: Well, of course John Barth's *The Sot-Weed Factor* was huge for me, especially in the beginning of my career, when I was writing *Water Music.* Thomas Berger's *Little Big Man.* There are so many. I mean, it's hard to remember. It's like when people say, "What are your favorite books?" Every day it's different.

NANCY: When you were a kid, did you read biographies as well as all those dog books?

TOM: I'm from a working-class family; I'm the first ever to go to college. My father was educated only to the eighth grade. I think I was probably ADD. We didn't have that term in those days. I like to joke that what we did have was a back door. I spent winter and summer basically outdoors with this crazy hyperactivity. My mother read to me, my mother taught me how to read, because I had trouble in school. I was too crazy, you know? So as far as being a bookish kid, no. I was just roaming in the woods and playing sports with the other kids and running wild all the time. But I remember reading comics, and the comics that I most liked were Donald Duck. And the Classics Illustrated. *The Odyssey.* I'd never heard of *The Odyssey*, but here it was in Classics Illustrated. And what we got in school, I was completely turned on. My eighth-grade teacher, Donald Grant, was an amateur actor, and he would read aloud to us on Fridays. "To Build a Fire" [by Jack London] and stories like that just sent chills through me.

JEFF: You're a great performer of your own stories.

TOM: I love to read in public—it's one of my great joys—and to record my own books sometimes, I just love doing it. Because it's a way of connecting personally with the audience on the deepest level with the first voice they heard reading aloud to them, which, oh God bless us, we've all had in our early times. People don't understand. It has to be theatrical, it has to be in the dark, and people have to be comfortable, and there can be no movement or no distraction, because you're casting a spell. It's thrilling for me to become an actor. I've never been an actor in a play, but I'm the actor of my own stories. And for most of my career, until I wrote the story "Chicxulub," I would only read funny things, because it's physiologically impossible to fall asleep and laugh at the same time. "Chicxulub" is a grueling, terrifying story, and I began to read it to audiences, and I just felt this incredible power, because there's a point in that story that is so horrifying nobody moves. I've read it to as many as fifteen hundred people at a literary event. I'm looking out into the blackness. You know how you go to the concert, somebody sneezes, a chair, a burp— nothing! Absolute horror. And the power of that—I feel what great actors must feel: that they've got you! So I do read that one once in a while, hoping to recapture that feeling. I mean, people have slideshows, and they tell jokes, and the authors are interviewed onstage and all of that. That's fine. But I believe in the power of the story and the power of the word. Again, under the right conditions, and let the story talk for itself. And I know that not all authors want to do this—they're introverts, why would they want to do this? But I love doing it.

NANCY: When did you start reading seriously? Was it in high school?

TOM: In high school, I was trying to find my way in life, and we would pass around books like *Dracula*, that sort of thing. It wasn't until I was seventeen and got to college that I began to really read deeply in the authors who were then current. Flannery O'Connor, I discovered her as a sophomore. I'd gone to SUNY, Potsdam, as a music major, flunked my audition, but there I am. It's a college, and I declared a history major because I'd done well in history. I didn't know exactly why, but it was because I was a good writer. Second year: Flannery O'Connor, *A Good Man Is Hard to Find*. Also, John Updike's stories. What blew me away was, here's a story by O'Connor that is a sitcom, very familiar, and then it turns grim on you, as grim as it could be, and has this moral dimension, this whole thing about the ethics of human beings and religion and so on, and I became kind of addicted, and became a double major in history and English. Junior year I blundered into a creative writing classroom, so thank God for liberal arts education. It's there so you can figure out who you are and what you can do. So it was huge for me.

JEFF: When you were reading Flannery O'Connor, did you have a moment when you said, "This is what I'm going to be"?

TOM: No, but I think it certainly shoved me on that road.

JEFF: Was there a writer who made you think, *I am of this tribe?*

TOM: Robert Coover. Robert Coover's first book, *Pricksongs & Descants*. I was having notions of being a writer and fooling around with that and kind of writing fragmented narratives, and Coover came along and showed it to perfection. And before this, of course, were the existentialists and the absurdist playwrights. I loved the absurdist playwrights, for obvious reasons. And I think that that's something to do with how I developed also.

JEFF: Interesting. You were talking about O'Connor's humor and about how it will suddenly take a turn. Your books do that a lot: they'll have some comedy in them and then they'll suddenly get very dark.

TOM: The best comedy is grim, isn't it?

JEFF: Who are your favorite comic writers?

TOM: Certainly Kingsley Amis. *Lucky Jim* is the funniest book in the history of bookdom. I love E. B. White. You know who else is funny who I've always loved? Kazuo Ishiguro. He can be very funny, in *The*

Remains of the Day, for instance—which is one of the greatest books ever. It manages to be funny and everything else, and kind and passionate and great. Coover. [Donald] Barthelme. And [John] Barth. [Gabriel] Garcia Marquez. All the writers I really loved had that streak of wicked humor. Günter Grass.

NANCY: Is there a writer who you think is underappreciated these days?

TOM: Me! [Laughter.] No, no. I don't know. One thing that struck me is that the books and authors who were so huge and so important to me, in the late '60s, early '70s, some of them have vanished completely. John Gardner, for instance. I read everything; I loved him. Boom! Gone! I don't even think he's in print. I reread *Grendel* recently. It's as brilliant now as it was then. Totally holds up. I don't know if anyone in America except me has read it in the last twenty years. It's amazing how quickly the years go by, and how our culture is so obsessed with the new, which is fine, but without remembering what's out there from the past.

NANCY: Was there a book that when you read it you said, *This is a book I should've written*?

TOM: Hundreds of them.

NANCY: Like what?

TOM: Hundreds. Denis Johnson's *Fiskadoro*. God!

What an incredible book. The aforementioned Ishiguro with *[The] Remains of the Day. Love Medicine!* Louise Erdrich. These books are just transformative and so beautiful and individual and great. Of course I wish I had written them.

JEFF: What about a book that you connected to so much that you almost felt like you had written it, only this person got it down on paper first?

TOM: Hard to come up with one off the cuff, but I'm sure—*Moby-Dick.* All my years at sea were wasted because he got there before me. [Laughter.] Nah, I don't know. It's hard to say. But certainly you read great stuff by great writers and you wish that you had done it. *One Day in the Life of Ivan Denisovich.* So one year we were up in the mountains; it's snowy and it's Christmastime. My children were relatively young—twelve, nine, and six or something—and that was their Christmas story. So we're reading it.

JEFF: Thanks, Dad.

TOM: It gets even better. We're reading it and I paused and my youngest son said, "Well, Dad, I mean, why aren't they allowed to have belts?" And my daughter knew the correct answer: "Too much fun." [Laughter.]

JEFF: Do you generally prefer short stories versus novels? Or are you an equal opportunity—?

TOM: Yes, and I'm one of the very rare ones. In the preface to my *Collected Stories*, I quote Stanley Elkin, this thing that was completely shocking to me as a young man at Iowa. Stanley came several times—he's the best reader ever, he's hilarious, I loved him. And now it's the Q&A, and a student raises his hand earnestly: "Mr. Elkin, you wrote this great book of stories, *Criers & Kibitzers, Kibitzers & Criers.* Why don't you write another book of stories?" He said, "No money in it! Next question!"

But, you know, I didn't care about that. I cared about being an artist. And I've had a wonderful rhythm that's good for me, and productive for me, to go from stories to novels, because I write so much in the stories about what's happening now, but I can't address that when I'm locked into a novel, especially one set in a different period. It's great for me, and I'm in a period now, after *Outside Looking In*—I've written six new stories, some of which have been in *The New Yorker* and *Esquire* and elsewhere. That's the start of the next collection, but first is another novel. Then I'll have a second period of story writing, because if you're exclusively writing stories for a longer period, longer than six months, eight months, you begin to lose steam and lose the ideas. This way, whatever you tell me today, or whatever I read in the newspaper, I can clip out, I can jot it down, usually a single sentence, and then when the novel is done, and I have a little bit of mental rest, then it's time to do the stories.

JEFF: Do you have a preference in reading? Do you spend most of your time reading novels or stories?

NANCY: Or nonfiction?

TOM: All three. For me, it's really hard to read somebody's novel when I'm writing a novel, because it's a long-distance marathon, and you can't have somebody else's voice sneaking in or changing your tone. The hardest thing is to get the tone over a year or a year and a half, or however long it's taking you. So generally I'm not reading novels while writing a novel. I wait until I'm writing stories, because then it doesn't matter. Because each story is going to be totally different and from a different point of view, and in two weeks it's going to be over. There are exceptions, though. Upstairs right now is one of my old editions of Faulkner's *Sanctuary*, which is second in my mind to *Light in August* as my favorite Faulkner, and I just cracked it, because I'm starting a new novel, and already thirty pages in it's not exactly what I want. So I read Faulkner and get reinvigorated and I love it. But other than that, I try to avoid reading novels when I'm writing a novel.

JEFF: Who are the short-story writers that you most value?

TOM: [Tobias] Wolff. I love Toby. I love his longer works too. Even *Old School*, which allegedly is a novel, but of course it's part of this wonderful autobiographical series of his life. I just love him, and he's one of the best story writers.

JEFF: What about Cheever? I read that he was your teacher at Iowa.

TOM: John Cheever was my professor for one semester, and I got to know him, he was very kind to me, but of course very sad and very drunk at all times. And I was such a punk and so obsessed with metafiction and the wild and the stuff that we talked about earlier that I didn't really admit that Cheever belonged in the world. He was just this old guy who wrote some stuff in *The New Yorker* years ago. Then I realized, more than almost anybody—John O'Hara does it too—he brings back what it's like to live in an era. Story by story, from his whole life, and it's just so beautiful. And he was an exquisite writer in terms of his phrasing, which is more Shakespearean and biblical than what I would use.

JEFF: Did you read the biography—

TOM: Blake Bailey. He's a genius. I can't wait for

his Roth biography. Of course it might be a wait. Another sixty years—I don't know. His biography of Richard Yates was my favorite biography of all time. I've read it maybe two or three times, and I love it because it makes me feel so good that I'm not Richard Yates. [Laughter.] He was utterly miserable every second of his life from birth until death, and that really inspires me. It makes everything great.

NANCY: We talked about John Gardner earlier. There's been a lot of discussion on Twitter recently about *On Moral Fiction.*

TOM: Really? Now?

NANCY: Yes.

TOM: People must be using it in their classes.

NANCY: Somebody said, "I just read *On Moral Fiction* and I feel like I can never write another word." I was curious what you thought, because online it was pretty much all negative.

TOM: First, my Gardner story: Met him once, in my first year at USC, around '78 or '79, when he came to give a reading. And since I was the only writer there, I spent some time with him. And he was dynamic and amazing and he never shut up, and he was brilliant and so on. And when I first met him, he said something about my book, which was my first collection, my first book of stories, *Descent of Man.* And I said, "Oh, having read *On Moral Fiction*, I don't think you're going to like it much." He gave me a little look and said, "I like a lot more than I let on." [Laughter.]

So, as with all how-to books about writing, it's completely bogus. It's how he views what should be written. Okay, great, it's interesting because we love him, to read it and to think about it, but it has nothing to do with actually writing your own books. In fact, any rules that anyone ever presented to me, I immediately use every resource I have to turn it all on its head and make something great that makes fun of it. How-to manuals are preposterous. You learn to write by reading deeply and not necessarily copying your favorites, because it's a dissimilar process, but to see what they're doing, to read it over and over, and see how it's put together and what it means. It's like a movie that you love. You're blown away by it. There it is—the music, the sound, the color. But then when you see it the second time, then you see this camera angle or this shot or how this is done—then you see a larger way into it. And I think that's how you learn to write. By doing that with texts. Certain books and authors will fascinate you. You don't know exactly why. And if enough of them do, you have your own take on everything that you've ingested, mentally.

So I love John Gardner, I love *On Moral Fiction.* He was a provocateur. He got everybody standing up in the days of metafiction and let it all hang loose, and that's great. But really there are no strictures whatsoever. As soon as you start having strictures, then you have a kind of uniformity, and that's antithetical to what art is. You just let it fly! You are an individual. This is why books—I'm not boring you, am I?

NANCY and **JEFF:** No! [Laughter.]

TOM: Just checking. [Smiles.] It's why books are the most unique art form. Because as the three of us know, it's a one-on-one relation between you and the reader. The reader is a participant in the art. Okay, maybe a movie has the same thing. But still, there it is. That's Meryl Streep's face, that's what the director is giving you. In the book, you are filming the book in your mind, and so is everybody else in their own way. Which is, again, why an artist cannot succeed by trying to think, *Well, what's going to sell?* Maybe hacks do that. But I never had that thought in my mind. My thought is, *Wow! This is a great thing. Let's find out what it is.* Then I make something, and if people like it, hallelujah! And if they don't, well, what am I going to do? I'm not a mind reader. And I wouldn't care anyway.

Some Books in Tom's Library

Kingsley Amis, *Lucky Jim*
John Barth, *The Sot-Weed Factor*
Thomas Berger, *Little Big Man*
Robert Coover, *Pricksongs & Descants*
Louise Erdrich, *Love Medicine*
John Gardner, *Grendel*
Kazuo Ishiguro, *The Remains of the Day*
Denis Johnson, *Fiskadoro*
Flannery O'Connor, *A Good Man Is Hard
  to Find*
Carl Safina, *Beyond Words: What Animals
  Think and Feel*
Albert Payson Terhune, *Lad: A Dog*
John Updike, *The Maples Stories*
Tom Wolfe, *The Electric Kool-Aid Acid Test*
Tobias Wolff, *Old School*

Susan Choi

We first met Susan Choi at a coffeehouse down the street from Seattle's Elliott Bay Book Company, where Jeff was about to interview Susan onstage as part of her book tour. Nancy was a big fan of Susan's 2003 novel American Woman, a fictionalized retelling of the Patty Hearst kidnapping saga, while Jeff had just read and loved her new novel, Trust Exercise, a dazzling and stylistically complex story about high school theater kids, a charismatic but predatory drama teacher, and the damaging aftereffects of abuse. The conversations, *both private and public, were a pleasure, and before the evening was over, we asked Susan if she'd do another interview for this book.*

Susan was born in Indiana in 1969 to a Korean father and a Jewish American mother. Like the kids in Trust Exercise, *she ended up at a performing arts high school in Houston, Texas. From there, she got a BA in literature from Yale and an MFA in creative writing from Cornell. Her first novel,* The Foreign Student, *was published in 1998 and won the Asian American Literary Award for Fiction.* American Woman *came next, in 2003, and was a finalist for the Pulitzer Prize. In 2019,* Trust Exercise *won the National Book Award for Fiction.*

We caught up with Susan again at the Bread Loaf Writers' Conference in Middlebury, Vermont, where she has taught summer classes in creative writing for many years, and where we had the following conversation.

———

NANCY: Did you grow up in a family of readers?

SUSAN: Not particularly. My father was an immigrant from Korea, so English was not his first language, and reading is not really his first passion. He's a mathematician. My mother did some writing and book reviewing at one time. But we didn't have many books in the house. It wasn't a house full of bookshelves holding the reading histories of my parents, although my parents bought me piles of books.

NANCY: Did you visit the library too?

SUSAN: I remember my school library. Mostly I remember it because when I had chicken pox, the librarian had a special pile of books for the kids who got chicken pox. Books about chicken pox. But I don't have really strong memories of using the library much after that.

JEFF: Do you remember your favorite books from back then?

SUSAN: Yeah. I still have most of them, actually. Strangely. Or dorkily. I kept so many of my books, hoping that my children would like them, and for the most part they just don't turn out to be the books that my children like at all. And also, there have been books that I loved that I've reconsidered. I loved The Chronicles of Narnia [by C. S. Lewis]. I was really excited when I started reading them with my son, and I got about halfway through rereading them and I said, "Let's just stop." And we did.

NANCY: How come?

SUSAN: The racism, which I hadn't noticed as a child. The duplicitous, swarthy, turban-wearing bad guys.

And the good and noble, blond-haired, blue-eyed white people. The bad guys were all from the south, where it was hot, and where people lied, and the good people were all from the north. I thought, *Oh, I don't remember this.* And my son was also a little like, "I'm not sure I like this."

JEFF: Any others you can think of?

SUSAN: *The Borrowers.* I loved *The Borrowers* by Mary Norton, and I'm still disappointed that I haven't gotten either of my kids into it.

NANCY: I love *The Borrowers*!

SUSAN: So good!

NANCY: Arrietty!

SUSAN: Arrietty, I know! With her big pencil and her little journal; she'd hold that pencil the size of a pepper grinder, and loved writing. Oh, I love *The Borrowers.* I loved The Chronicles of Prydain, the Lloyd Alexander series. I loved those. Could not pay my kids enough to read those books. I loved The Dark Is Rising, the Susan Cooper series. Could not pay my children to read those books. I think they both read the first one.

NANCY: *Over Sea, Under Stone.* That was my favorite, actually, but I loved them all.

SUSAN: Yeah, me too. So those are the sort of big ones for me. I mean, I'm saying this because I can picture them on my shelf. *Little House on the Prairie* [by Laura Ingalls Wilder], of course. I still have my original boxed set, minus one that someone lost. I'm still really mad that it's gone. I loved those books too. And those I read to my kids.

JEFF: You have two boys?

SUSAN: Yeah.

JEFF: So do you think it's a gender thing? That that's why they're unable to appreciate so many of them?

NANCY: Maybe *The Borrowers*, but not The Dark Is Rising [series]. That has boys in leading roles.

SUSAN: It's funny. I don't know if it's a gender thing necessarily. My younger son doesn't like fantasy. He doesn't like superhero stuff. He had no interest in the Percy Jackson books [by Rick Riordan]. I always thought he would've really liked *The Borrowers*, but I never dragged him to it. They have their own reading tastes.

NANCY: Sounds like you read a lot of fantasy when you were a child.

SUSAN: I did. Although I never thought of it as fantasy. And now the preponderance of these supernatural series for kids, they just all seem the same. I tried to read the Harry Potter books when they came out, and I simply could not get into them.

NANCY: Did you ever want to write it?

SUSAN: Oh, when I was a kid all I ever wanted to write was fantasy. All of my early efforts at fiction were terrible rip-offs of these books. I wrote a whole series of books about little, tiny people. It's so embarrassing. They were called the pinheads, so that was my original twist on *The Borrowers*. My people were even smaller, and it changes everything if they're even smaller.

NANCY: They can't hold that big pencil!

SUSAN: They can't hold that pencil! And when I was little, I wrote stories in which creepy things happened. Probably influenced by The Dark Is Rising. But once I started writing as an adult, I never would've done well at it.

NANCY: Was there a book that you read when you were a teenager that made you want to be a writer?

SUSAN: Wow. God, that's such a great question, and I don't think I have a specific answer. I went through a really weird reading period as a teenager. I think about this now because I have a teenager, and I have a preteen, and it felt to me then, and it still feels to me today, there's amazing children's literature and then there's this weird drop-off, where you're in this abyss going, *What do I read now?* There are all of these adult books, you can read the adult books, but there don't seem to be that many books for that age group.

Actually, you know what? *1984* [by George Orwell] was a huge book for me. I don't think I read it and thought I want to be a writer, because I already wanted to be a writer. I remember actually trying horribly to emulate *1984*, a dystopian, futuristic, blah blah blah.

NANCY: *1985.*

SUSAN: It wasn't quite that. But, you know, I was really influenced by *1984* and *Brave New World*. Those were both books I remember reading as a teen. It's all coming back to me. Ray Bradbury. I remember *Something Wicked This Way Comes*. I was really into that. I recently reread *Fahrenheit 451*, and I was surprised by how dull I found it. It was just such a slog. I'd forced it on one of my kids, who sort of tolerated it. I noticed him not loving it, and I was like, "What? It's a great book." And then I read it and [thought] *A Wrinkle in Time* [by Madeleine L'Engle] was a really big book for me. It was another one that I reread recently and went, *Oh, not so great, actually.*

JEFF: Do you remember the first serious non-genre adult novel that really drew you in?

SUSAN: It's hard to remember what happened between *1984* and, like, Virginia Woolf. It's funny. I attended a performing arts high school at which we didn't do a ton of reading of literature, and that really kind of cut my legs out from under me when I got to college. I just didn't have enough of a foundation to even know what sorts of literature I liked. And I really floundered. In high school we read so many plays. Lots and lots of great plays.

JEFF: Do you remember what plays were important to you?

SUSAN: Oh yeah. I was proud of myself because I got through a bunch of Shakespeare that was assigned to us. You know, we read [Anton] Chekhov. I remember thinking that I really liked [Eugene] O'Neill. I'm not sure if that was a real liking of O'Neill or if it had to do with the fact that I really loved the movie *Reds*. Do you remember that?

JEFF: Jack Nicholson was so great [as O'Neill].

SUSAN: Nicholson was *so* great as O'Neill, so I thought I really liked O'Neill, but I think I was just having a reaction to the movie. I mean, I also tried to read *Ten Days That Shook the World* [a nonfiction account of the October 1917 revolution in Russia by John Reed that inspired *Reds*] but never finished it. I remember really loving Carson McCullers. Really loving

The Heart Is a Lonely Hunter. That was one of the few books I read in high school that made a huge impression. I know I read her play *The Member of the Wedding* more than once. I think I even had to perform a monologue from it.

NANCY: What was it about Carson McCullers's writing that attracted you?

SUSAN: I wish I could remember. The impression I have in my mind of *The Heart Is a Lonely Hunter* is of a sprawling tapestry of strange and interesting people, and all the interconnected lives. I don't even remember the plot. But I remember being impressed with the novel's scope. Not as a writer. As a reader. And you know, in my late teens, early twenties, when I was a college student, I remember reading [Salman Rushdie's] *The Satanic Verses* and being really blown away by it, again, because of this huge, sprawling tapestry effect of so many characters, so many things going on, such a world to enter into. I remember being terribly influenced by it, trying to write in that mode of what [literary critic] James Wood later called hysterical realism, when he was being kind of mean to Zadie Smith. So many characters, so much stuff going on, so busy. I remember trying to write like that and sort of thinking that was the way you did it.

JEFF: Were there other writers who wrote in that same genre that you were particularly drawn to?

SUSAN: This is such an interesting exercise, because it's really hard for me to remember what I read back then. I'm almost going visually, trying to remember what was on my bookshelves.

JEFF: I totally remember what I read back then. I can't remember what I read two weeks ago.

SUSAN: I've started keeping lists because I forget. It's funny. I remember—this is the inverse of the question you asked—I remember not being at all impressed by *The Catcher in the Rye* [by J. D. Salinger]. I read it as a teenager and thought, *What is the big deal?* Also, [F. Scott Fitzgerald's] *The Great Gatsby.* I wasn't at all impressed by *The Great Gatsby.* Boring. But those are two novels that I think are amazing now. And I reread *Gatsby* probably annually. I read *Tender Is the Night* recently because I wasn't sure I'd ever finished it. I was like, *Oh dear. I've read* The Great Gatsby, *like, fifty times and maybe never read* Tender Is the Night. It was great. And *Catcher* I reread in the past year because I was thinking of giving it to my son. And then I didn't. After I read it, I thought, *I'm not sure.*

JEFF: Not who you want your son modeling himself after?

SUSAN: It was more that it just had so much depth I didn't remember. Like Holden Caulfield ending up in an institution. He has suicidal ideation, as we would call it now. There's that remarkable scene, where he goes to visit that teacher who comes on to him. There was just a lot that really flew over my head when I was sixteen, and rereading that book, I was really blown away by how good it is. I mean, everything, all of Salinger's stuff is so good and weird. So many layers.

NANCY: Do you think Franny was pregnant in *Franny and Zooey?* Because I've never been able to decide.

SUSAN: That's such a good question. I haven't read *Franny and Zooey* recently, but lately I've been involved in a long debate about "A Perfect Day for Bananafish": Is it about molestation? Since revisiting it as an adult, I've thought that's what this story is about.

JEFF: Really? With the little girl on the beach?

SUSAN: I suspect that he exposes himself to her. Isn't that what the bananafish is? Seymour goes upstairs and shoots himself, and it's his honeymoon. But yeah, it's an amazing story, because it's so accessible and readable and engaging. Even charming. And then this thing happens, and really you have no idea why.

JEFF: I've never heard that interpretation before. I can't imagine Salinger would've agreed with it.

SUSAN: No, probably not. I didn't come up with that all by myself. I remember the first time someone said, "Well, you know, Seymour's a pedophile." And I was like, "What? That's horrible. He's just having a lovely time on the beach with this child." "Well, then, you know, what's the bananafish about?" And I said, "Oh, it's just whimsical." But I got more and more uncomfortable. And I went back and reread it, and I couldn't get it out of my mind. And because of how shocking the suicide is, that was the thing that made me think maybe so. But you're right. I doubt that Salinger actually would've been pleased with that interpretation.

NANCY: Getting back to *Gatsby*, what was it that you saw in this later reading? I'm always interested in rereading and how we re-experience books.

SUSAN: I do remember it was one of the very few literary novels that I was made to read in high school. Which ruined it for me, I think. As those exposures often do. And I can't remember when I first came back to it. I know that by the time I was writing my second novel, *American Woman*, I was so obsessed with *Gatsby* that I had a copy of it that fell apart, because I actually had it spread out on the floor just trying to figure out how he paced the scenes, from the *it's hot, hot, hot, so hot, are you hot enough?* Remember when the train conductor was like, *Wow, it sure is hot.* But from the beginning of the heat wave to the end—because the heat wave is what makes them all go to New York, then people quarrel, then it all comes out: the thing with Gatsby and Daisy. They drive back in different cars; Myrtle gets run down. The whole momentum of that sequence of scenes is so amazing to me. I was trying to do something similar, and just figure out how to make the scenes succeed each other in a way that was utterly organic—that was something that I started looking at after I read it a bunch of times.

But I think what turned it around for me, whenever it was that I first reread it, was just the ravishing prose. I think that accounts for why I didn't like it as a teenager: I didn't have much of an eye for ravishing prose. I was more of a content reader. And I didn't like the people. Of course that's totally valid, because the people are deplorable, all of them, including Nick. Nick is a total asshole. He's so self-justifying. He puffs himself up. That whole line about how "I am one of the few honest people I've ever known." I'm like, *Oh my God. You're kidding.* But now I'm even more impressed with the book, because the writing is so extraordinary. It's all about the writing for me now.

NANCY: So when you think about the contemporary books that you love, is it the writing that draws you to them?

SUSAN: Yeah, yeah, it is. Because although it's fun to read a great story, so many stories are so similar. I won't give negative examples, but I've been reading as much as I can while I've been up here [at Bread Loaf], and I've thought of that, because it's really the difference between are the sentences wondrous in some way and pleasing, or are they just conveying information?

NANCY: Can you think of a wonderful book where the writing is secondary to the plot?

SUSAN: Theodore Dreiser. I don't think Dreiser is a very interesting prose stylist at all. But I found *Sister Carrie* to be a remarkably compelling book because of the window it gives you into history, and poverty and life in this country in a certain socioeconomic sphere.

And then take somebody like Henry James: I remember the first time I read an entire book by James, in college. This wonderful professor of mine made us read *The Bostonians*, and I'd never gotten through a single book by James, and *The Bosto-*

nians just blew me away, because it has it all. Amazing story, and also incredible social commentary, but also these unbelievable sentences. It's like reading Shakespeare, once you get your ear for it. You're like, *Okay, I think I'll make it through this sentence.*

JEFF: Do you think we ruin books by writers like James or Fitzgerald or Salinger by forcing kids to read them when they're not old enough to appreciate them?

SUSAN: Maybe. My kids are now eleven and fifteen. It's easier to figure out what my eleven-year-old should be reading because there's a lot of new writing and a lot of old, good writing for preteens. But for my fifteen-year-old, I'm totally confused. To me, it feels like he's in this very liminal space as a reader, where the things he's given to read in school, while some of them I think hit the mark, many seem really premature. When he was in middle school, he was given *Lord of the Flies* [by William Golding], and I thought, *I didn't read this book until I was out of college.* I think you can read it as a kid and get what's going on, but you don't really appreciate it. The prose is so surreal and almost hallucinatory, and I doubt he appreciated that at twelve when he was slogging through it to figure out what was going on.

But there are these very rare examples of books that I feel hit the mark, like Sherman Alexie's *The Absolutely True Diary of a Part-Time Indian*. I read it and I said, *This seems like right on-target for his age*. Very straightforward prose. A great voice. The prose wasn't blowing me away so much as the voice really captured me.

Interestingly, Amy Tan's *The Joy Luck Club*, which my son read in ninth grade, and I reread it, and I thought—not to in any way denigrate *The Joy Luck Club*, which is a fine book—but I thought this is a great book for ninth graders. And he totally got that book. And could really connect with it. But there are other books that I think have more going on in terms of literary stuff that I do think are. . . . I don't know if they're ruined, but you have to hope there's some second visit to that book. But why is that going to happen necessarily? For me, it happened because I'm a writer.

NANCY: You co-edited *Wonderful Town: New York Stories from The New Yorker* with David Remnick. Who are the short-story writers you admire most?

SUSAN: Well, Alice Munro. She's maybe my favorite writer. She's a true short-story writer. That is her form.

JEFF: What is it you like so much about her?

SUSAN: It's hard to articulate. I mean, I teach her work. Everything about her stories is compelling. I don't know how she does it. Her characters are utterly real and believable. They're not wild and wacky in any way, but they're so compelling. She has such keen insight into the way people are, and the way people are with each other. It's remarkable. She never, ever errs on the side of including something that isn't absolutely necessary. And she's so good at leaving things out of her stories. Left on the cutting room floor. Look at all the moments she doesn't show you. She has such incredible control that way.

You can reread her stories again and again and again, and they reward rereading. They never get old.

NANCY: Anyone else?

SUSAN: I don't really think anyone's in Alice Munro's league. Tolstoy's dead. I don't really know who would be competing with her at this point.

NANCY: Are there any younger writers who have caught your eye?

SUSAN: Kirstin Valdez Quade is really interesting, and I liked her debut collection [*Night at the Fiestas*] a lot. I thought it was really strong. I was surprised it didn't get more attention. Tessa Hadley is somebody else whose collections I've enjoyed. Oh, also, I have to mention Donald Barthelme.

JEFF: Why him of all the writers of his generation?

SUSAN: What he does with language is so much fun. And funny. I started reading his short stories when I was a teenager, when I didn't really have a lot of formed ideas about what stories were supposed to be like, so I didn't recognize how unusual they were. I just thought they were so fun to read. I didn't know he was a postmodernist. It wasn't until I got to college that he turned out to be associated with all these other writers, who I turned out not to really like at all.

JEFF: Is there a writer or a book that you would like to see rediscovered?

SUSAN: Yes! I have a quick answer for that. I have been amazed for years that this book called *The Wars* by Timothy Findley—do you know this book? He's a Canadian writer. This novel called *The Wars* is just totally unknown in this country and is canonical in Canada. And I read it because one of my best friends is Canadian and she was visiting from Toronto and left it at my house, and I picked it up and read it, and it's just—I mean, I haven't read it in a while, but I read it, I reread it, I taught it. I keep saying, "Those people at New York Review Books should reissue this!" It's the perfect book for them. I can't believe it's not in print. A former literature professor of mine who's Canadian said, "Oh, I don't think anyone got out of high school without reading that book. That was one of the major books in terms of identity."

Another one is *Almost Transparent Blue* by a Japanese writer named Ry Murakami, and the reason I know this book is because I lived in Japan for a short time in my childhood. I think my parents would be horrified if they learned this: You asked if I grew up in a reading household, and there weren't a lot of books around, but this book washed up in the house. I was nine, and it was in English, and there was not a lot around in English, so I read it, and it was, as I recall, full of all sorts of depravity, sex and drugs. But I remember it stuck with me for more reasons than just those. I remember it being a really strange and fascinating book. And I read it when I was way too young. But I think it's set on an American military base in Japan, and it was somehow about this interface between Americans and Japanese after the Second World War. I remember it being a world I hadn't realized existed. And it's still on my mind as a world that not that many people have written about. That postwar Japanese world, and the American presence there. I remember the book itself so vividly; it was this tiny, bright blue paperback.

NANCY: When you were a child, did you look for yourself in the pages of a book?

SUSAN: You know, I don't think it occurred to me to do that for a really long time. I think one of the reasons I felt so shaken by the Narnia rereading was because it wasn't just that it was overt racism in the book; I felt this shock of recognition! I remembered thinking blond hair and blue eyes and pale skin and snowy mountains and green forests and the north were all good. And so tantalizing. I grew up in the Midwest, which is flat, and always had this longing for a chateau in the Alps or something, and when I read that, "To Narnia and the North!" they say, as they gallop off, fleeing from the brown people. I thought, *Oh my God. Is that partly where that came from, that all of the books that I read when I was a kid privileged these pale-skinned, blue-eyed, blond-haired people in these storybook Northern European environments?* So I felt like, *Well, who wouldn't want that?* I don't remember encountering a single fictional character when I was a young reader who was Asian. I mean, who was non-white, let alone Asian. I really don't remember a single book.

It's such a different world now. A better world. Linda Sue Park. I've read all of her books. They're so good. And they're remarkable too, because I read her book about colonial Korea, and I thought, *This is how my father grew up.* And I couldn't believe that there's a children's book that's actually legitimizing the fact that the world that he's told me about existed. I don't remember encountering books that felt that way to me, or it even occurring to me that I should, when I was a kid. I thought of books as a portal to some better place, where all the pretty people live in nice landscapes with interesting things happening to them.

NANCY: I don't know which is sadder, that you didn't find them or that they weren't there.

SUSAN: Yeah, it is sad. It also never occurred to me that people like me would be in a book.

JEFF: When you're working on a novel, do you read differently?

SUSAN: It used to change my reading a lot. But not anymore. It's a lot easier now for me to switch back and forth between writing and reading, and there's less bleed between the two. Which is nice, because it's a lot easier to keep reading what I want to read without feeling, *Oh no, this is going to deform my voice.* I mean, it still happens occasionally. After I read Rachel Cusk's *Outline,* I did feel for a few weeks that everything coming out of my writer's mouth was in this kind of very similar tone, this sort of flat, affectless kind of mesmerizing tone.

NANCY: How do you choose what to read?

SUSAN: You know, it's very arbitrary. I tend to have a lot of books around that I haven't read, and so a lot of it is visual, like they're lying around. I do yoga in my room, and sometimes, as I'm upside down looking at the bookshelf, I see something and think, *Maybe that's what I should read next.* Right now I'm reading *The Summer Book* [by Tove Jansson] because it was recommended to me last summer by someone here at Bread Loaf. I bought it when I got back home and had no interest in it, really, but when I was packing to come up here, I thought, *I bet something about being up at Bread Loaf is going to put me in the mood to read this book that was recommended to me by somebody at Bread Loaf, so I'll bring it.*

Sometimes something just triggers the desire to read a certain book. I was talking to a colleague the other night, an older colleague; we were continuing a conversation we'd been having about polio and summer camps. My kid's at summer camp, and this colleague is in her eighties, and she said, "Did you know one of the reasons there are so many summer camps in the Northeast is because of the polio epidemic? Families needed to get their kids out of the city." I didn't know that. I was shocked, because I didn't grow up in the Northeast, and the summer-camp culture is really foreign to me. She said that Philip Roth's novel *Nemesis* was about this. Roth is one of these writers who every couple to three years all I want to do is read a novel by him, and I read it, and it's great, and then the feeling passes. And then a few years later I'll read another, and so the last book of his I read was *Everyman*, which I thought was really fantastic, but I haven't had the desire to read anything by him since, and then the other night when she said this, I said, "Ah! It's time. I want to read *Nemesis*, because I haven't read it." So that's a funny thing, where I'm really in the mood to read *Nemesis*, but I'm almost done with *The Summer Book*. I have about thirteen pages left, which I'll probably read after we finish talking. So what am I going to do?

JEFF: I love *Nemesis*.

SUSAN: Did you read *Everyman*?

JEFF: I did. I liked it, but I didn't love it as much as I loved *Nemesis*.

SUSAN: *Everyman* was one of those books that I had on my bookshelf for years. I had no interest in it. I thought, *I don't know, Philip Roth, the aging male body. I don't know if I care.* And then, I don't know what—it might have been a chance comment that someone made, someone that I know and like, who said, "I really liked it." So I took it on a trip a few years ago and I just sat in the hotel room sobbing at the end of that book. I thought it was really good.

When Roth died, I was really stricken. I hadn't been aware of the fact that I had been harboring a fantasy that someday I would get to sit across a table from Philip Roth and talk to him. I met him once: "Hi, it's nice to meet you. Great fan of your work." But I wasn't aware of the fact that I was sort of walking around thinking, *One of these days, I'm going to get to talk to Philip Roth. Like actually talk to him.*

JEFF: And now it can never happen.

SUSAN: No, it can never happen.

Some Books and Authors in Susan's Library

Lloyd Alexander, The Chronicles of Prydain (series)

Sherman Alexie, *The Absolutely True Diary of a Part-Time Indian*

Donald Barthelme

Theodore Dreiser, *Sister Carrie*

Timothy Findley, *The Wars*

F. Scott Fitzgerald, *The Great Gatsby*

Henry James, *The Bostonians*

Carson McCullers, *The Heart Is a Lonely Hunter*

Alice Munro

Ryu Murakami, *Almost Transparent Blue*

Mary Norton, *The Borrowers*

Linda Sue Park

Philip Roth, *Everyman*

J. D. Salinger, *The Catcher in the Rye* and
    "A Perfect Day for Bananafish"

Andrew Sean Greer

When we knock on Andrew Sean Greer's front door, we're greeted by the author, his husband, David Ross, and also Olive, their tiny black pug, who'll join us on the sofa for our interview in Andy's cozy San Francisco living room. Andy is especially happy to see Nancy again: she's interviewed him twice for her television show, and she was the chairperson of the jury that awarded him the 2018 Pulitzer Prize for Fiction for his comic novel Less, about a gay man's odyssey of avoidance on the eve of his fiftieth birthday and his ex-lover's wedding. When Jeff asks to see the actual Pulitzer Prize, Andy explains there's no statue or trophy—just a crystal paper weight, with which he smilingly poses for a photo.

Andy and his twin brother, Michael, were born in Washington, DC, in 1970, and grew up in nearby Rockville, Maryland. At Brown University, he studied with metafiction pioneer Robert Coover and Edmund White, the gay novelist whose 1982 novel A Boy's Own Story paved the way for a generation of young gay American writers.

Andy's first two books, the story collection How It Was for Me and the novel The Path of Minor Planets, earned good reviews and respectable sales, but it was his third book, the novel The Confessions of Max Tivoli, that first brought him wide attention, inviting comparisons to Proust and Nabokov by no less an authority than John Updike, and a place in the Today show's book club. Three novels later, Less earned him a Pulitzer Prize and a place in The Writer's Library.

NANCY: What are you reading right now?
ANDY: I just finished rereading *Le Grand Meaulnes* [by Alain-Fournier].
NANCY: Did you read it in English?

ANDY: Yes.

NANCY: So did I. I read somewhere that John Fowles called it the greatest European novel about adolescence.

ANDY: I'd forgotten how amazing it is. This English edition is called *The Lost Estate*.

NANCY: When I read it in college, the translated title was *The Wanderer*. It's weird that the title isn't consistent from edition to edition. I've never reread it, though. Maybe I should.

ANDY: The first time I read it I thought of it as a magical fantasy, and this time I read it as a realist memoir. I don't even know what's wrong with me. It's a totally different book now.

NANCY: Because you're a different person now!

ANDY: I guess so. I read it ten years ago, when I was thirty-eight. That should be old enough to understand a novel. But maybe I read it in a fever. Maybe I just spent more time with it this time? Or is it that I'm more and more nostalgic for childhood and so I understood all those details differently? Michael Chabon used to say it was his favorite book.

NANCY: It won the Prix Goncourt [France's most important literary award].

ANDY: Did it? Like a hundred years ago? [Laughter.] I'm leaving for a week to stay at a cabin north of here to try to escape life and work on a book. So I went to a used bookstore and bought a pile of books. I've been reading Ellen Gilchrist, whose writing is just so charming and distinctive; her writing doesn't sound like anybody else's. And I bought *The Little Sister* [by Raymond Chandler]. I hadn't read it before, which is amazing to me because I thought I'd read everything by him.

JEFF: That's his Hollywood novel. Lots of movie-studio stuff going on.

ANDY: I even read a second-rate Chandler last week called . . .

JEFF: *Playback*?

ANDY: Yes—

JEFF: That's second-rate Chandler.

ANDY: Even that has its charm, you know.

JEFF: It's the last book he finished. *Little Sister* is better than *Playback*.

ANDY: Good. I was hoping that was the case.

JEFF: And there's a movie of it with James Garner that's just called *Marlowe*. Bruce Lee is in it.

ANDY: Wow. As a heavy? I'll watch that even though I never like any of the movies made from Chandler's books.

JEFF: Well, except *The Big Sleep*.

ANDY: Except *The Big Sleep*. The first one.

JEFF: So how do you choose what to read? What goes on in your head as you're—

ANDY: Right now I'm reading for the book I'm writing, so I'm a bad reader, in a way. If I find a book that I'm actually enjoying that doesn't make me want to write, I have to put it down.

NANCY: Really?

ANDY: Yeah. I'm trying to think of a recent one . . . Maybe that's one reason why some books like *Le Grand Meaulnes* didn't mean that much to me when I first read it, and now it seems extraordinary. I think it just depends on what I'm working on and whether it gets me excited.

JEFF: So a book you're reading makes you want to write something now. Inspiring you . . .

ANDY: And it's always about ways or modes of storytelling. So like even last night—here's an author you probably wouldn't expect me to like: Lawrence Ferlinghetti. I was at a reading of his latest book last night, and because he's too frail—he's 100, I think—Armistead Maupin and Maxine Hong Kingston read from it. It was so fantastic! There's one small section that Kingston read that's in italics, two pages—it's the only part of the book in italics—listening to it, I said, "Oh, that's a very clever way of highlighting to the reader, sort of secretly, that this is the heart of the book. I'm not going to actually say it; I'm going to do it in a typeface." And I was like, "That's so interesting! I'm filing that away. That's the kind of thing I'm looking for." It happens in unlikely places.

NANCY: So, *Le Grand Meaulnes*—what are you taking from that?

ANDY: This is why I like old books. Because they all tend to use a particular device, which I remember from my childhood: "There was this guy I met, and here's this story he told me." Which is always the right way to tell the story. Instead of "I recall," it's "A guy told me."

JEFF: Like [W.] Somerset Maugham.

ANDY: Always. Or Joseph Conrad. Even [Nathan] Zuckerman in Philip Roth. It's not always clear why this other character is necessary, but it is necessary, often just for the writer to get into the story. Often these techniques are ways the author is trying to get to an important climax without deflating it with sentimentality, and they don't know how to—you can't go at it directly or it just feels like a soap opera scene. And luckily, in books, we don't have to show the scene. We can skip ahead and remember it, kind of cool it down a little bit, and therefore get it to the right temperature to serve it . . . That was an awful metaphor.

JEFF: I was just admiring that metaphor!

ANDY: You know, you're trying to get it not too hot. You're trying to get it the perfect temperature for the reader so that they don't roll their eyes or miss it entirely.

NANCY: When you're reading, are you always reading as a writer? Can you ever separate who you are as a writer from who you are as a reader?

ANDY: Sometimes.

NANCY: Is that good, or not?

ANDY: Actually, Chandler is a good one, where I'm happy to go through the books and not learn a thing because I find it such a pleasure. Which is why I was excited to find one I hadn't read. Or an Agatha Christie, you know? I almost bought one yesterday, because there's a ton I haven't read. And I like every one.

JEFF: Bubblegum fiction!

ANDY: Yeah! And she just does it so well. Or [P. G.] Wodehouse.

NANCY: Wodehouse I get more out of.

ANDY: Not sure I learned a lot from Wodehouse— though maybe I did for *Less*. It seems pretty Wodehouse-y. Yeah. But at a certain point I gave myself permission to read exactly what I wanted to and not have to be—I'm not very conversant in contemporary literature. I don't find myself reading serious contemporary literature for pleasure.

NANCY: Why?

ANDY: I'm too close to it somehow. You know, people who are super dorks about coffee, for instance?

JEFF: We're from Seattle. We know a few of those.

ANDY: So you're like, "Hey, let's go to Seattle's Best." And they're like, "No, we won't be going there." But I look at *old* books, and they're a pleasure. Like Muriel Spark is just a pleasure. I've been giving out *The Driver's Seat* to people. To my friends who aren't big readers. They're like, "What should I read?" I'm like, "Well, here's a slim little book that you'll love."

NANCY: I love that. Because it always worries me that nobody's still reading those great old writers like Muriel Spark, or Eudora Welty.

JEFF: John O'Hara.

NANCY: John O'Hara. Have you read him?

ANDY: I've never read John O'Hara, although I have a full collection of his writings on the shelf.

NANCY: You have to read *Sermons and Soda-Water*.

ANDY: I have that!

NANCY: They're three novellas. And the epigraph to the collection is from Lord Byron: "Let us have wine and women, mirth and laughter, sermons and soda-water the day after."

ANDY: My singing group in college had a room and that was painted on the wall.

JEFF: *Sermons and Soda-Water* is pure pleasure.

NANCY: Totally.

JEFF: The voice in that book is just—

NANCY: Andy, you'd love it for the voice.

ANDY: That's what I usually try to find, is those voices. When you look at older books, the ones that are alive—some have fallen to the wayside, but often we're left with the best of them. Not always.

JEFF: Yeah. I feel like O'Hara has fallen to the wayside, and he should be up there with the best of them.

NANCY: Are there any books that are out of print, or forgotten, that you'd like to see resurrected?

ANDY: One of my favorite books is Lillian Hellman's *Maybe*, which is just nuts. But it's fascinating, it's so ambiguous and strange and angry and barely makes sense until you think, well, everyone's drunk. It's out of print, and I've tried to get the New York Review Books to bring it back. I said I'd write an introduction. But they haven't bitten yet. I haven't tried in the last year, though. Maybe I could now.

JEFF: You're a Pulitzer Prize–winning author now.

ANDY: I should try again.

JEFF: Do you have favorite San Francisco books?

ANDY: *Tales of the City.* Having just seen Armistead [Maupin] last night, reading Lawrence Ferlinghetti, I suddenly had this sense of this long tradition being handed down in some way. The city doesn't, at the moment, feel that vibrantly artistic, but last night it did.

NANCY: It's like time collapsing. It's been so long since *Tales of the City* came out, but Lawrence Ferlinghetti goes back so much further.

ANDY: He knew Beckett in the '40s—it *was* time collapsing! And you know, there were people there who talked to me about reading Armistead's stories when they came out every day in the *[San Francisco] Chronicle.* And there was a gay couple who came up to me and said how much they loved *Less*, and I was like, "Well, you've read Armistead's books, right?" And they said, "No, we don't know those." I said, "You have to." Because I'm imitating part of that in *Less*. It's part of San Francisco history. That's why Less lives in a house up the little stairs, just because that's where they live—a different neighborhood—in *Tales of the City.*

NANCY: Were there other gay writers who influenced you? What did you read in college that helped you navigate your identity?

ANDY: Because there was no internet of any kind, coming out was looking for any answer about what this was supposed to be. There had been a moment in the '70s of publishing gay male authors and some [gay] women. And there's this trove of works that were about that world, like *A Boy's Own Story* by Edmund White, who I later became friends with. And Andrew Holleran and Ethan Mordden. But those books, often they felt so mournful in a way that I didn't. So I read them with great interest, but it was hard to imagine myself on these dark piers at night in New York City. It just didn't quite jibe with what I was experiencing, which was—I mean, I was full of anxiety, but it was mostly about trying to get a date. I didn't feel existential angst, because time had passed, and it was the late '80s I'm talking about, and I was doing okay. I was in a sheltered world with lots of queer friends.

I remember the first book where I was like, *Oh, this is what it's like.* It was a comedy by Joe Keenan, who was a writer on *Frasier.* But he wrote a bunch of novels that are farces. It was called *Blue Heaven*, in which two men who are trying to scam the Mafia are a couple, and it's barely mentioned that they happen to be two gay men. And I had never read a book where that happened. It's a plot point in that they have to pretend not to be gay, in all kinds of funny ways, but they weren't worried about being gay, because it was written by Joe Keenan, a funny guy living in New York City, and that was not something he thought about anymore. That touched me, moved me, and I never forgot it. I wrote a musical version of his book when I was at Brown that was put on the main stage, and Joe Keenan came and he hated it. And we've been in contact since via Twitter, and he just—

JEFF: He's forgiven you.

ANDY: He's forgiven me, but I mean it was really terrible! [Laughter.] I was nineteen—of course it was terrible! Because, yeah. Which is a surprising answer, right? That that would be the one that stuck with me. And often, other books like *Memoirs of Hadrian* [by Marguerite Yourcenar], which I found more moving than *The Swimming-Pool Library* [by Alan Hollinghurst]. Which, I think was because I'm a prude. [Laughter.] I think I'm a prude. *Swimming-Pool Library* was so gorgeous. I just didn't relate to what they were doing. Proust I found very moving even though his depiction of homosexuality is as sort of strange monsters in the world, and then by the end of the books everyone turns out to be gay, so . . .

JEFF: I have to admit I could never get through Proust.

ANDY: Sorry I gave it away! [Laughter.] I have over time paid a lot of attention to gay writers. Michael Cunningham meant a lot to me and later became a friend of mine. Colm Tóibín almost never writes about being gay, but there's something about *Brooklyn* that feels to me like a gay man telling the story of the struggle of identity, and expectation, and that kind of thing. I don't know. So I think that's an abstract way of thinking about it. Or Jeanette Winterson—like, here's another way to do this entirely. Her memoir [*Why Be Happy When You Could Be Normal?*] I thought was just—

NANCY: Amazing.

ANDY: Amazing.

NANCY: My copy of that is just swollen to twice its size because of all the Post-it notes I used to mark my favorite sentences.

JEFF: Do you write in your books?

ANDY: Yeah, yeah. I do, and I certainly dog-ear them. And if I have a pen handy, I underline the things where I think, *You have to learn from this.*

JEFF: So they're not sacred objects that can't be defaced?

ANDY: Some books are sacred. In fact, *The Washington Post* sent someone to take a picture of me and my library, and they said, "Why don't you hold your favorite book?" And Jonathan Lethem gave me a copy of *Rebecca*, with a red cover with a silver thing around it, and it's like, *What a great book. What a beautiful edition!* And Jonathan gave it to me at a moment when I didn't know him that well, and it felt really special to me.

NANCY: What were the books that mattered most to you as a child?

ANDY: The Oz books I loved. I didn't start reading science fiction until a little later, so as a kid—the bookshelf we had was really old-fashioned. It would be sort of *Railway Children* kind of things, you know? It was like *Five Little Peppers and How They Grew.* I don't think I liked that. You know, like, the Great Brain books?

NANCY: Oh, those are wonderful.

ANDY: I loved all of those. The Narnia books, and it was funny that I didn't think of genres. No one separated it for me, so I would go in and out of anything.

JEFF: The Encyclopedia Brown books?

ANDY: Oh, I absolutely read Encyclopedia Brown. Those were so good! I loved all of those, and the *Two-Minute Mysteries*, even though I never solved them.

NANCY: Were your parents readers?

ANDY: Oh yeah.

NANCY: And you had lots of books in your house?

ANDY: Yeah, my parents both grew up in the rural South. Pretty poor. My mom really poor. And the library was their way of seeing another world. My mom became an experimental chemist—I don't know how she figured that out. My dad taught himself German—his father was in World War II, and if they were caught in enemy territory, they had a kit that was like a chocolate bar, a cyanide pill, and a German dictionary, and my dad taught himself German from that. They both taught themselves things. So for them, books were the most amazing thing on Earth. More than movies, which were intangible, books could change you. So we had a great library. They were great fiction readers.

I mean, I had a really nice childhood. And you can't imagine how proud my mother is of me. When I called her the night I won the Pulitzer, she couldn't believe it! That was the greatest thing that could've happened in her life, that her son would win the Pulitzer Prize. My dad is a big collector of my books in other languages. He's taking a Czech class right now.

JEFF: So he can check up on *Less* in Czech and see how your translator did?

ANDY: Yes! [Laughter.] But they were both so supportive of me being a writer, and they certainly wanted us to read as much as possible. I think it would've been upsetting to them if we hadn't been readers. It wouldn't have made sense. And my nephew—my twin brother's son—is a big reader, which is a relief to all of us.

JEFF: Did you always know you were going to be a writer?

ANDY: I always knew I wanted to be a writer. I was naïve enough not to ever question whether that was possible. I was incredibly naïve. Like, a lot of things adults told me as a kid I believe to this day. Like, "People are decent at heart," and like, "Do what you're passionate about." That kind of stuff. That they don't really mean. So I believed I could be a writer; no one told me I couldn't be one. I never dreamed of doing anything else. I can't do anything else.

JEFF: Was there a book where you read it and thought, *This is what I want to do?*

ANDY: I don't know. I know when I was ten was the first time I started imitating a book I read, because it was the first time—this is not quite answering your question—it was the first time I recognized that an author had made certain decisions in writing a book, and it was *Watership Down* [by Richard Adams]. I won't get this right, but it starts with something like, "The primroses have just begun to fade," and however many pages later, it ends with, "The primroses have just started to bloom." And I was like, *What?!* There's, like, a path! He did that! On purpose! Every other book felt like it was just a fable everyone knew. And this book, I was like, *Someone wrote this in this way on purpose so that I would feel this.* I was reading like a writer, I think, and so I tried to imitate it by writing my "novel" of ten pages, which was a total rip-off. And then, when I was sixteen, I wrote a *Wuthering Heights* rip-off, because I loved that book so much. I didn't understand that the structure of it is so crazy that you can never imitate that book.

NANCY: How important is plot to you? Both as a reader and a writer?

ANDY: I like things to happen. I like structure. Also, I like to feel like I'm in good hands. I want the author to know where he's going.

JEFF: So with *Less*, you knew where he was going? And where he'd end up?

ANDY: Well, it has structure. When you get to the end, the world is round, so the reader knows where we're going. So actually, that's enough. And then there's other thematic movements. I wouldn't say there's a plot. It's not like searching for a missing diamond or something.

JEFF: It's episodic.

ANDY: It sure is. I based it a lot on *Pnin* [by Vladimir Nabokov], which I love. I was reading lots of Nabokov twenty-five years ago, and I remember how disappointed I was with *Pnin* when I first read it. I was like, *Oh, this just doesn't add up to anything.* And as you get older, you find that more interesting, and that it actually is structurally sophisticated, and that the language is so funny. And because it's lighter than a lot of his other books, or lighter *feeling*, as a twenty-year-old you might dismiss it, but now I like it much more.

JEFF: Well, it's so dry, the humor, and I think as a twenty-year-old it's hard to pick up on dry humor about a middle-aged immigrant.

ANDY: I didn't find it funny. Or clever. I really liked clever, which now, I couldn't care less about. It's a relief.

JEFF: The chapters that make up *Pnin* were originally published as short stories in *The New Yorker.* How do you feel about short stories as opposed to novels?

ANDY: I stopped reading a lot of short stories because I was looking for novel structures, and you can't find them there.

JEFF: You have a book of stories, though. To be honest, I haven't read it.

ANDY: No one's read it, and it's from a very long time ago. Some of those stories I wrote when I was twenty-three. I haven't looked back, but, I mean, every story is a different style. I really didn't know what I wanted to do yet.

JEFF: You were finding yourself.

ANDY: Yeah, totally appropriate.

JEFF: It's amazing that you got them published at twenty-three. I wrote a lot of stories at twenty-three that no one would want to read.

ANDY: I don't know how it happened.

NANCY: Did you get an MFA?

ANDY: I did. I went to the University of Montana. I graduated in '96.

JEFF: Was William Kittredge there?

ANDY: Yes, he was my professor. Really amazing, and a really kind guy. And weary of giving advice to students. But the weird thing was, for some reason the MFA program there got very popular just when I applied. So suddenly—he had been teaching, sort of, farmhands for decades, and then all these out-of-towners showed up, and he had to pull himself up to meet different kinds of stories than he'd been talking about before, and he was really good at it. He really had a knack for advice. He gave me really good advice, which I didn't want to hear.

NANCY: What did he say?

ANDY: The last story in my collection is very different from all the others. It's a straightforward, plainly written story about a gay man and a lesbian who get married in the '50s as beards for each other, and it's about their marriage. I wrote it as kind of a joke. Everyone kept complaining about my ornate stories, and I was like, *All right, I'll give you what you asked for*, and Bill was like, "No joke—actually this is what you're good at, I'm sorry to say."

JEFF: Were you out at the time?

ANDY: Yeah, yeah, yeah. But I was trying to be very clever, and this was not clever, it was just moving. And he's like, "Hey, kid, you've found your sweet spot, and you have to do *this* now." And he sent it to Richard Ford, who was editing an issue of *Ploughshares*, and I remember coming home to my little apartment and the answering machine being like, "This is Richard Ford," and that was breathtaking to me.

NANCY: How did you end up in Montana? You grew up on the East Coast, didn't you?

ANDY: I was living in New York City. I was miserable. I couldn't hack it. I applied to MFA programs—it was the only way out I could imagine. And I only got into two. I got into University of Alabama, Tuscaloosa, and the University of Montana in Missoula. And my mother, who was dying for me to get out of New York, flew me to visit them. Which I now see what an extravagant thing that was to do. And they were so lovely in Tuscaloosa, but I went to Missoula, and I was, like, *Holy shit. I have never been in a landscape like that.*

NANCY: That boundless sky.

ANDY: I almost had a nervous breakdown. I didn't know what was going on! I mean, it was sucker season [fishing season for suckerfish], it was May or something. So gorgeous. They put me with another student, David Gilbert, who is a novelist, and we got along so well, the two days I was there. We're still great friends; we're going to hang out in Italy together this summer. It was just fantastic. It was fantastic to go there. It opened up a whole new world of books that I was not thinking about, you know: Raymond Carver, and Richard Hugo's poetry. And there were a lot of young men there who were expecting to have a hard-drinking, couple-pack-a-day-smoking, carousing writer's life, which I think they had briefly. And the women were often not quite taken seriously in our group but were frequently the better writers. They didn't sit up with a bottle of whisky the night before and make a masterpiece. They worked really hard for weeks, which is actually what the job is.

NANCY: Do you remember any of those people?

ANDY: Well, many of them did not continue. Which happens with a lot of writers. There's a writer, Amanda Eyre Ward, who was my friend—she's a popular writer in the Jennifer Weiner kind of way. She's been popular since the moment she got out of there. She's just a hard worker. She was not respected in any way. J. Robert Lennon—John Lennon—was there, and he was a superstar.

NANCY: Did you read his book *The Funnies*?

ANDY: Of course I did.

NANCY: That's a wonderful book. In a way, that reminded me of *Less*.

ANDY: If you want to talk about someone whose every book is different, it's John. I was thinking about *The Funnies* the other day. It's actually taken me to my forties to be able to write a comedy and feel comfortable, and John did that right out of the gate. That was his second novel, and then he never did comedy again.

JEFF: What are some other comic novels you love?

ANDY: I think Updike's Bech books are pretty good.

There's [P. G.] Wodehouse, and I think Muriel Spark is funny. I still carry my portable Dorothy Parker from when I was eighteen. *The New Yorker* asked me to pick any story from their archive to talk about on their podcast, and I was like, "I bet you have a Dorothy Parker in there," and they did! I've also been reading a bunch of English writers—English people think it's strange I've never read them before—but like *Scoop* by Evelyn Waugh and *The Ordeal of Gilbert Pinfold*. That's such a weird book! And *Cold Comfort Farm* [by Stella Gibbons]. Why have I never read this before?! [Laughter.]

The thing about comic novels—and maybe I get to be this for some people—they're so beloved when you get a really good one. You hold them close to you in some way.

NANCY: Because they come along so rarely.

JEFF: What about travel books? I mean novels. *Less* is like a fictional travel book.

ANDY: Well, I mean, Graham Greene, I don't know if those are travel books, but I love almost every one of them. *Travels with My Aunt* is the best in that it's lighthearted, funny, laugh-out-loud, but it's super charming, it's witty, it has a happy ending—sort of. Someone has to die, of course. You can tell that he had a good old time and thought of it as a big piece of froth, but I often recommend it to people. And the travel in it is really intriguing to me.

JEFF: What about [W.] Somerset Maugham? He was a great travel writer.

ANDY: I haven't read them in a long time. But for sure. I remember a long time ago, strangely, *The Painted Veil* meant a lot to me. I remember thinking that idea of being so hurt that you're going to actually bring your spouse into danger was just chilling to me. I also remember in *The Painted Veil* that the hot guy she has an affair with is thin because he's on a no-carb diet. A no-bread diet. [Laughter.] These fads really do come and go!

NANCY: Isn't it funny what you remember from those books?

ANDY: Exactly. I don't remember character names. I don't remember what country they were set in. I remember the no-bread diet.

Some Books and Authors in Andy's Library

Alain-Fournier, *Le Grand Meaulnes*
Emily Brontë, *Wuthering Heights*
Daphne du Maurier, *Rebecca*

Ellen Gilchrist
Graham Greene, *Travels with My Aunt*
Lillian Hellman, *Maybe*
Joe Keenan, *Blue Heaven*
J. Robert Lennon, *The Funnies*
W. Somerset Maugham, *The Painted Veil*
Armistead Maupin, *Tales of the City*
Vladimir Nabokov, *Pnin*
Muriel Spark, *The Driver's Seat*
Colm Tóibín, *Brooklyn*
Jeanette Winterson, *Why Be Happy When You Could Be Normal?*
Marguerite Yourcenar, *Memoirs of Hadrian*

Madeline Miller

After spending a couple of days in the constant bustle of New York, we boarded a train at Penn Station for Philadelphia and ninety minutes later were in the comfortable suburbia where Madeline Miller lives with her husband, Nat, and their two young daughters. Their home in Narberth is just steps away from the fabled Pennsylvania Main Line, on a street so quaint and quiet it could have been transplanted straight out of the 1950s. No one would guess that behind the front door of one of the stately homes, a young mother was

writing some of the most subversive feminist fiction on the bestseller lists.

A classics major with a BA and MA from Brown University, Madeline has made creative use of her education, bringing the classics into the modern era with two brilliantly conceived novels based on the works of Homer. The Song of Achilles, which Madeline spent a decade honing while teaching classics and drama to high school students in Cambridge, Massachusetts, is told from the point of view of Achilles's childhood friend and, in Miller's subversive telling, eventual lover, Patroclus. The book was controversial but also remarkably popular for a story borrowed from Greek mythology, and it went on to win the 2012 Orange Prize for Fiction as the best novel written by a woman that year. As Joanna Trollope, chair of the judges, put it, "Homer would be proud of her." With her second novel, the equally acclaimed Circe, she once again turned to Homer for inspiration, this time using The Odyssey as the starting point to tell the story of her title character, the sorceress daughter of the god Helios.

Although steeped in and inspired by the classics, Madeline is a fan of plenty of modern literature as well. We sat down to hear about her favorites, both past and present, in a comfortable sitting room off the

*main entry as Nat and the girls retreated upstairs so
the author could talk to her guests.*

═════

NANCY: Did you grow up in a reading family?

MADELINE: I did. My mother, in particular. She was
a librarian and an English major, and there were
books all over the house. We had these huge, built-
in bookshelves, and I pretty much read my way
through them. Many of those books were wildly
inappropriate for me to read, but I didn't know. It
was all information. I was like, *Just keep reading.*
So yeah, I read everything we had in the house, and
my graduation present at the end of every year was
that we would go and have a big book binge at a
bookstore. I would get to buy a set number of books
for the summer that I would then read through in a
week. But it was very exciting, and then we'd do the
library for the rest.

JEFF: Do you remember any of the age-inappropriate
books that you read in those days?

MADELINE: A lot of them just went over my head. My
mom had worked for NOW [National Organization
for Women] for a long time, so she had *The Female
Eunuch* [by Germaine Greer] and other early feminist texts. I read a lot of those. I didn't understand

at least fifty percent of them, but even as an eight- or nine-year-old I thought it was very interesting to read.

JEFF: Was *Fear of Flying* [by Erica Jong] in there?

MADELINE: I read that at a friend of my mom's. My mom had *The Woman's Room* [by Marilyn French], and it definitely had some R-rated scenes in it. But I just read it all. I was a very undiscerning reader. And I didn't ever think about what I should or shouldn't be reading. Oftentimes I would choose a book based on how thick it was. The thicker the better.

NANCY: Do you remember any of the books that you bought that you ended up loving?

MADELINE: Oh yeah. One was *Watership Down* [by Richard Adams], which became one of the great favorites of my entire life. I love how epic it is. It's very grounded in the classics, and it has a great ending. I feel like all books should end the way *Watership Down* ends, with one hundred pages of *Ahhhhh. Are they gonna make it?* So I loved it. And I actually still have my copy.

NANCY: I see it on your bookshelves there.

MADELINE: That's actually not my comfort copy. That's a back-up copy. I have my comfort copy upstairs near my bed.

JEFF: Is that the copy you had as a child?

MADELINE: Yeah, it is. It is. I was very fetishistic about my books. I'm over this now, but I never wanted to bend the spine, and so I would read it . . . [Mimes barely opening a book as she reads.]

JEFF: I'm like that.

MADELINE: I'm mostly over it now. But—you can see that there's not a lot of bent spines on those shelves, and those that are bent are probably my husband's. Another book I remember buying as a kid is *The Hunchback of Notre-Dame* [by Victor Hugo]. That was one that my mom was kind of like, "You sure?" And I was like, "Yeah, definitely. It's really big." I got that when I was about twelve and was heading into eighth grade. And I fell in love with it. I was weeping at the end. That's another book where I feel at least fifty percent was right over my head, but the part that really spoke to me was all about injustice. It was actually one of my reading epiphanies, that you could really address stuff, seriously, in a novel, not just in nonfiction.

JEFF: When did your interest in the Greeks hit?

MADELINE: That started when I was around five or six. My mom used to read me little bits of *The Iliad* and *The Odyssey* as bedtime stories. Percy Jackson [the series of books for young teens by Rick Riordan] didn't exist, so basically you went from

D'Aulaires's illustrated *Book of Greek Myths* to Edith Hamilton's *Mythology*, and there was nothing in between. There were Mary Renault's books, but I didn't read them until much later. I read all the books about myths that I could find, but I wasn't reading novels based on the classics, because I didn't know any. *Watership Down* was the closest I could find, basically.

JEFF: What was the first classic that made an impression on you?

MADELINE: *The Odyssey.* I still have the copy that I marked up and underlined in eighth grade. That's where my novel *Circe* actually came out of, because I was really annoyed at Homer's portrait of her. At first, I was really excited: *Wow, she turns men into pigs!* But then you get there and it's this very flat, contained portrait, where she has to be tamed by the hero. I was really frustrated.

NANCY: That didn't sit well with you, what with all those feminist books you were reading?

MADELINE: I'm pretty sure I wrote something like "Ugh" in the margins.

NANCY: Was there a teacher who especially influenced you?

MADELINE: In high school I had this wonderful Latin teacher, and I was reading *The Aeneid*—this very copy [*picks up a book from the pile next to her*]—with him. I saw that in order to read Book II, you have to have a strong understanding of *The Iliad* and all the stories about Achilles and Patroclus. And so I dove into all this stuff about them. I'd been more Odysseus oriented up until that point, because he has a great wife and he's an underdog, but Achilles's grief for Patroclus was always really moving to me. He's most human in that moment of grief.

And then, because I was so obsessive about researching *The Iliad* in order to understand *The Aeneid*, my Latin teacher said, "I'll teach you Greek, and we can read *The Iliad* together." It was electrifying to be able to read *The Aeneid* and *The Iliad* in the original, and experience the poetry and mythology at once. It was just like fireworks going off for me. So that was always my way in. It was through the literature that I loved.

NANCY: And as all that was going on, what else were you reading?

MADELINE: I was reading Margaret Atwood and Lorrie Moore and Isabel Allende and Amy Tan, everything I could find of them. Mary Gaitskill, James Baldwin—I read a lot of James Baldwin—and Toni Morrison as well. I didn't know anyone else who was reading those books.

NANCY: What was it about Atwood and Moore that you loved?

MADELINE: They're just so exciting, linguistically, to read. Moore's language is so precise and wonderful. Her similes. I didn't know you could use language like that.

NANCY: I see you have my favorite collection, *Birds of America.*

MADELINE: I really like *Birds of America*, but I liked *Anagrams* and *Like Life* even more.

JEFF: *Like Life* is my favorite.

MADELINE: I've given copies of it to a lot of people.

NANCY: What about Toni Morrison?

MADELINE: Yes, definitely her language, but also because she was writing about injustice. She was having conversations in her books that a lot of people around me were not necessarily having. I mean, we read *Sula* in, I think, tenth grade, and a lot of the kids had to be dragged through it, but I was really engaged. That was frustrating, so oftentimes I would read outside of—Oh! Tennessee Williams! We read *The Glass Menagerie* in English class and I loved it. I thought, *I have to get more of this guy*, and then I read all his plays. And Shakespeare! I loved *King Lear.*

NANCY: I was going to ask you if there was a book, or an author, that made you want to be a writer, but I think you're saying that reading made you a writer.

MADELINE: Yes, yes. I mean, I always wanted to write. And I loved language so much. When I was thirteen, I wrote this time capsule to myself, for twenty-five years in the future. It said, "I want to be a writer, but don't tell anybody." And I'd forgotten I'd written it, and when I rediscovered it, I thought, *Wow, there it is.* What had moved me to write it was that my eighth-grade teacher read us a piece of *The Once and Future King* [by T. H. White], about Arthur right before the last battle, and the section she read was so inspiring and exciting that I ran home and vowed to be a writer.

JEFF: How did you feel about the sort of standard twentieth-century canon while you were busy studying all these classics?

MADELINE: In some ways, I felt that I just couldn't engage with them. I really did not engage with *The Catcher in the Rye* [by J. D. Salinger]. I'd read *The Bell Jar* [by Sylvia Plath] right before I read *Catcher*, and it really spoke to me. After that, *Catcher in the Rye* felt kind of, I don't know, like a step down. I appreciated *The Great Gatsby* [by F. Scott Fitzgerald], but I didn't love it. I did like [Nathaniel] Hawthorne more—*The Scarlet Letter*—because I appreciated the old language of it. We would get our books at the beginning of the school year, and I would read them all right away, and then I would go back and revisit them when we did them in class, because I couldn't stand going that slowly—it wrecked the book for me. I loved *Jane Eyre* [by Charlotte Brontë]. That was a favorite.

Because I'd been reading all these amazing female authors, I would get to someone like John Updike and I'd think, *These women are not really women. What are these characters? These are like—he's not even trying.* So I was very put off by a lot of the female characters in books by men. I felt they were like Circe in *The Odyssey*—like, "Well, what's happened here, Homer? You just gave up?" I was very angered by *The Witches of Eastwick* [by John Updike].

NANCY: Me too. Offended.

MADELINE: Yeah, that's how I felt. I felt very offended by it.

JEFF: Can you talk about why you felt that way?

MADELINE: I just felt that the portraits of the women were very—I felt like it was a very prurient book, that the narrative voice was interested in picking at women, but not really seeing women. When you compare the female relationships in it to those in a Margaret Atwood novel—it was so obviously written by a man. I wanted to ask Updike, "Have you ever sat and observed any women? Because it doesn't seem like you have." And the grotesqueness and the horror of women's bodies—I felt like there was a lot of that. Whatever the intellect was that was supposed to be the narrator, in the shaping of the novel there was all this emphasis on how women's bodies are disgusting.

JEFF: There's that in *King Lear* too, which you loved.

MADELINE: Yes. Yes. But that's Lear talking, not Shakespeare. That's Lear as he's going insane. Thinking about his daughters. And it's so clearly, psychologically linked to his own issues. If a character is saying it, that doesn't bother me, because then that's part of the psychological makeup of the character. But I don't want to be told that by the writer.

JEFF: Are there male writers who you think do women especially well?

MADELINE: Yes. David Mitchell does a great job with his female characters, like in *The Thousand Autumns of Jacob de Zoet*. Actually, I think James Baldwin has very strong female characters. Colson Whitehead also. I'm not one of those people who think that male authors can't write women, but I think there was a generational misogyny thing that happened. I mean, I think I read everything John

Updike ever wrote. I read my way through it because I felt like it was important for cultural literacy, but the only one of his that I really liked was *Gertrude and Claudius*, which was his prequel to *Hamlet*. But I quite liked that one.

NANCY: Do you read a lot of poetry?

MADELINE: For a couple of years I feel like I read "The Love Song of J. Alfred Prufrock" once a day. Eliot's use of language, his use of rhythm, that was really fundamental for me. I loved—who else? Sylvia Plath. Langston Hughes. I like Charles Simic, who is more recent. Robert Browning and his monologue pieces. Those are so great.

JEFF: I love "Andrea del Sarto [The Faultless Painter]," where he's talking to his wife who's about to go off with her boyfriend for the evening.

MADELINE: They're all mini plays.

JEFF: There are recordings of James Mason reading them.

MADELINE: I will definitely go look that up. That must be amazing.

JEFF: Other contemporary poets besides Simic?

MADELINE: Oh, Alice Oswald! And Carol Ann Duffy! Both English poets. I encountered Oswald's work because she wrote this long poem called "Memorial," which is all the deaths of minor characters in *The Iliad* stitched together and retold. I heard her deliver it from memory, and she was unbelievable. And then I was like, *Now I have to read everything.* So I love her work. I think it's so smart and careful and beautiful and really, really profound. Carol Ann Duffy has so much wonderful work. In her book *The World's Wife*, she takes all these stories that are familiar to us and tells them from the perspective of the women involved. Little Red Riding Hood, Shakespeare's wife. It's great.

NANCY: I see a lot of fantasy novels on your bookshelves. Are you a fan of the genre?

MADELINE: A lot of the fantasy books up here are my husband's. But there are certain fantasy novels I love. I love Ursula K. Le Guin's Earthsea series, which my husband introduced me to. They're wonderful. And one of the things I love about them is that she continued to revise her ideas about the world in each of the books. *A Wizard of Earthsea* has very few female characters in it, and then in the second book, *The Tombs of Atuan*, there's this amazing female character Tenar; in the fourth book, *Tehanu*, all the focus is on Tenar, what her life has been like, and her coming to grips with the fact that she's in this very male-dominated world, and women are not really encouraged to be magicians. You see Tenar examining all these bedrock assumptions in her world. It's wonderful to see that, to see her opening up her world and questioning those assumptions. It's such a mark of integrity for Le Guin as a writer, that she began in the *Beowulf* tradition, the hero's journey tradition, and then she was like, *Well, wait a minute. I wrote this amazing hero's journey book, but now I'm going to keep going deeper, and keep thinking deeper.* I really enjoyed Robin McKinley's *The Hero and the Crown*, and *The Blue Sword*. Those are great. And of course *Watership Down* is sort of fantasy.

NANCY: What about Robin McKinley's *Sunshine*, which is my favorite?

MADELINE: That one didn't speak to me. I don't know why. I think I just wanted more Aerin [the heroine of *The Hero and the Crown*]. Sometimes you read the next book by an author because what you really want is more of the earlier book. One thing about Robin McKinley that I really respect is that while oftentimes in fantasy books a character gets into a fight and then they're completely fine the next day, McKinley knows that if you fight a dragon, you're going to be messed up for six months, and she lays out what that physical recovery is going to be like. Doing that keeps it very grounded in the real.

Oh, and Guy Gavriel Kay. I mean, Jehane in *The Lions of Al-Rassan*!

NANCY: That's my favorite novel of his. Because Jehane is such a fabulous character.

MADELINE: Yes, and the reason you don't see it on these bookshelves is because we lent it to someone. My husband did. And I was like, "You gave the— But we have to keep it in the house!"

JEFF: Do you lend books in general?

MADELINE: Only to very, very good friends. Because I feel like, if it's something I really love, then I want it. And I am a big rereader. There's this luxury in rereading and seeing something anew.

JEFF: Plus, they might crack the spine. [Laughter.]

MADELINE: Exactly.

Some Books and Authors in Madeline's Library

Richard Adams, *Watership Down*
James Baldwin
Carol Ann Duffy, *The World's Wife*
Marilyn French, *The Woman's Room*
Mary Gaitskill
Nathaniel Hawthorne, *The Scarlet Letter*

Victor Hugo, *The Hunchback of Notre-Dame*

Erica Jong, *Fear of Flying*

Guy Gavriel Kay, *The Lions of Al-Rassan*

Ursula K. Le Guin, Earthsea Cycle (series)

Robin McKinley, *The Hero and the Crown*

David Mitchell, *The Thousand Autumns of Jacob de Zoet*

Lorrie Moore, *Like Life* and *Anagrams*

Toni Morrison, *Sula*

Mary Renault

William Shakespeare, *King Lear*

Amy Tan

John Updike, *Gertrude and Claudius*

T. H. White, *The Once and Future King*

Tennessee Williams, *The Glass Menagerie*

Michael Chabon
& Ayelet Waldman

Michael Chabon and Ayelet Waldman live in a large, comfortable, craftsman-style house in the Berkeley flats, the sort of home that seems more suited to a professor at the nearby University of California than to one of the most celebrated writers of his generation and his Harvard Law School–educated wife turned acclaimed novelist, essayist, and social media provocateur. But the

Waldman-Chabon household—which at any given time might include up to four kids from high school to grad school age and a labradoodle named Agnes—seems intent on a life of upper-middle-class normalcy rather than literary celebrity. This even as they ramp up their sideline as Hollywood producers whose slate of upcoming projects includes adaptations of Michael's Pulitzer Prize–winning novel The Amazing Adventures of Kavalier & Clay and Ayelet's nonfiction account of her experiences microdosing LSD to deal with her debilitating mood disorder, A Really Good Day.

Our interview is a reunion of sorts. Nancy first met Michael in 2003 at the offices of HarperCollins, where he mentioned how much he and Ayelet appreciated a rave review Nancy had given Ayelet's book Daughter's Keeper in Library Journal. Jeff first interviewed Michael in 1988, an assignment he barely remembers and Michael remembers not at all. "I was still trying to figure out if I should wear a tie to interviews," he says, recalling those days when he was first the toast of the literary world, thanks to his radiant debut novel The Mysteries of Pittsburgh. Twenty-five years later Jeff would dramatize Kavalier & Clay for a five-hour stage production in Seattle that Michael never got to

see—though he did read the reviews, which were,
happily, positive.

Michael and Ayelet's enthusiasm for today's subject,
their love of books, is obvious from the get-go.
Settling in over hot tea (Nancy and Jeff) and peanut
butter and banana sandwiches (Ayelet and Michael),
they traded off with bursts of excitement as they
talked about the joy of reading and their particular
areas of literary interest (some shared, some not) from
childhood to the present day.

NANCY: Ayelet, tell us about yourself as a young
reader.

AYELET: First of all, I didn't read until I was in third
grade. It turns out I was dyslexic, though I didn't
realize that until after Michael and I had our kids.
A couple of them read late, and we were sitting
in an appointment with a neuro-psych evaluator,
having our kid's diagnosis and symptoms described
to us, when I realized, "Oh my God! That's me!"

When I started to read, I went from literally
not being able to sound out words to reading *Little
House in the Big Woods* [by Laura Ingalls Wilder]
in a weekend. I dove into the rest of the series over

the next week. I was completely crazy about those books. Just passionately devoted. And after that I didn't stop. I loved book series, especially science-fiction series. There's a book called *Half Magic* that was my favorite, favorite, favorite book. I loved all the author's other books as well—remind me of his name.

MICHAEL and NANCY: Edward Eager.

AYELET: Edward Eager. All of his books. Roald Dahl. The Narnia books. [To Michael:] What's that series that I loved when I was a kid that I've told you about and now I can't remember the name of?

MICHAEL: You don't mean Roger Zelazny? You mean when you were a teenager though, right?

AYELET: Zelazny, sure.

NANCY: Was it the [Chronicles of] Amber books— *Nine Princes in Amber*?

AYELET: Amber! Yes!

MICHAEL: They're pretty adult.

AYELET: I was twelve, thirteen when I read them. When I started to read, that's all I did. I didn't have a lot of friends. We had a black-and-white TV. And anyway there wasn't anything on. So all I did, all the time, was read. I had no hobbies. [Laughter.] Didn't play any sports. I could barely ride a bike.

MICHAEL: Tell them about The Happy Hollisters [by

Jerry West, pseudonym for Andrew E. Svenson] in the library—

AYELET: Do you know the series The Happy Hollisters? I loved The Happy Hollisters. More than the Bobbsey Twins [series by many authors, writing under the name Laura Lee Hope]. More than Nancy Drew [this series also by many authors, writing under the name Carolyn Keene]. There was a girl in my class in Providence who told me about a private library that had a collection of The Happy Hollisters. My parents never had any money, but I begged them to join this library so that I could read the books. We went to the library and it was so beautiful.

NANCY: The Athenaeum?

AYELET: Exactly, the Athenaeum! My parents joined. I remember it was very, very expensive, but they joined so that I could get the books I was so desperate to read. And of course they didn't have The Happy Hollisters. I was so ashamed and unhappy when we went, even though they had this amazing children's section. But I felt like I had forced my parents to spend more money than could ever be justified. I never allowed myself to enjoy the library. Eventually I told my mother about how I felt about the Athenaeum and she said, "I don't know what you're talking about. It was like sixty bucks a year. Of course we could afford that." So I had ruined the Athenaeum for myself for nothing.

MICHAEL: All because of The Happy Hollisters.

AYELET: All because of The Happy Hollisters. After my children's series phase, I went through a very intense romance novel phase. But only gothic romances. I loved them. I would read as many as ten a week—two a day or more. If the jacket had a woman with a heaving bosom and a gown, I was all there.

MICHAEL: Didn't you read Georgette Heyer?

NANCY: Oh, Heyer is like my comfort food. I've reread my favorites over and over.

MICHAEL: They kind of carry on the Jane Austen tradition.

AYELET: I mean, that's what's amazing. There was a librarian who had been watching me gobble all these books up, and one day she said, "Hey, why don't you try this book?" It looked similar. On the cover the girl didn't have boobs, but she was wearing a pretty dress and she was standing next to a gorgeous man and it seemed good enough, so I took it home. And it was *Pride and Prejudice* [by Jane Austen]! So that was the first *quality* adult book that I read. I read a lot of quality fiction for young people, but that was the first quality adult book that I read.

NANCY: What about Judy Blume?

AYELET: Obviously, Judy Blume. When I met Judy Blume for the first time, we were at a party and I rushed up to her, managing to spill my drink all over the table. I gushed, "Oh my God!" and went on and on about how exciting it was to meet her, how her books changed my life. She was so nice. We talked for pretty much the rest of the evening, so I was there to watch one hundred and seventy-five women in their forties rush up to her gushing, "Oh my God!" etc., etc. And to each one, she was totally sweet. It was incredible. By the end of the evening I turned to her and said, "I am so sorry." [Laughter.]

So yeah, there's my quickie tour through the reading experience of my childhood and young adulthood.

JEFF: Okay, same question to you, Michael.

MICHAEL: Well, in many ways similar. Over the years, when we've talked about books, we've discovered that we've read and loved a lot of the same books. I started to read very early. I started to teach myself how to read, because my parents got in the habit of reading the Sunday comics to me before I could read, and *The Washington Post* had a great comics section. But at some point, when I was about four—it's really hard work to read comics, I think—they got sick of it and wouldn't do it anymore. So I started trying to read it to myself. When my parents saw I was trying to read it to myself, they taught me how to read.

AYELET: [Stage whispered:] He's very, very smart.

NANCY: What sorts of books did you enjoy?

MICHAEL: I never gravitated that much toward those sort of industrial series like the Hardy Boys. But there were other books that I loved pretty early on, like there was *Homer Price* [by Robert McCloskey]. And Beverly Cleary. And there are so many of them, and it was weird, because there was no internet, and depending on which library you went to, no matter how many Beverly Cleary books you thought you had read, there were more you didn't know about. And new, different series by her. And there was The Mad Scientists' Club series [by Bertrand R. Brinley]. And the Alvin Fernald books [by Clifford B. Hicks]. And The Great Brain series [by John D. Fitzgerald].

AYELET: And also whatchamacallit. The Encyclopedia Brown books [by Donald J. Sobol].

MICHAEL: Loved those so much.

JEFF: Could you solve the mysteries ahead of him?

MICHAEL: Half of them. [Laughter.] You could almost measure the books that are most important to me by the ones I introduced to our kids. Our daughter Rose loves Encyclopedia Brown—as a kid with dyslexia, just those bite-size stories. Another one like that is *Strangely Enough!* by C. B. Colby, which is this collection of unexplained mysteries, one page long, with a sort of twist ending. They were supposedly true. Anyway, for some reason that book was really, really potent for me. But once I got a little older, like nine or ten, I started to read the Sherlock Holmes books. And those were the first books I read with a love which has endured my whole life. I reread them periodically. And Edgar Allan Poe. Ray Bradbury. You know, just as I was entering my teens, I started to read John Christopher's *The White Mountains, The City of Gold and Lead*—the whole Tripods series—I read those to our kids too. I love that book *My Side of the Mountain* by Jean Craighead George. And *Julie of the Wolves*, I love that one too.

AYELET: *Island of the Blue Dolphins* [by Scott O'Dell].

MICHAEL: The Newbery winners—I remember trying to knock a lot of those off: *The Matchlock Gun* [by Walter D. Edmonds], *Adam of the Road* [by Elizabeth Janet Gray]. *Johnny Tremain* [by Esther Forbes].

AYELET: I don't think I knew there was such a thing as a Newbery award.

MICHAEL: I think at school there was a poster on the wall with the Newbery winners, or something like

that. That's how I read, just picking out a copy of—
what's it called? *The High King*? Is that the last one?

NANCY: By Lloyd Alexander? Yes, it's the last one in
The Chronicles of Prydain.

MICHAEL: And then going back and reading the other
four. Oh my God, that was so big. And then Susan
Cooper, The Dark Is Rising series. One of those won
the Newbery. That's how I discovered them. So that
Newbery thing was a big entry point for me. Because
it was pretty reliable. The more recent ones, I don't
know. I'm not sure I understand the Newbery Medal
anymore.

AYELET: [To Michael:] Did you ever read *Tales from
Shakespeare* [by Charles and Mary Lamb]? We had
a copy without a jacket, so I thought they were called
Tales from Shakespeare Lamb. And I read them
over and over again. Did you?

MICHAEL: I read it once, out of the library. I worked
in a library as a page when I was fifteen, sixteen,
seventeen. Like the last three years of high school.

AYELET: You're so good at shelving.

MICHAEL: I made a lot of discoveries that way. Like
the Georgette Heyer books.

AYELET: Did you really? That's so cute.

MICHAEL: Oh, we haven't mentioned the All-of-a-Kind
Family books [by Sydney Taylor]. Those are terrible.

AYELET: Terrible! We tried to read those to our daughter, and they're so loathsome.

MICHAEL: The kids are such suck-ups: "Oh, dearest Mommy!" [Laughter.]

NANCY: But remember the chapter when Henny dyes her dress, the one she'd borrowed—without asking—from her older sister Ella? She had to dip the dress into tea to hide the stain she'd gotten on it.

AYELET: But I loved them because they were Jewish! I mean, children's books were never about Jews.

MICHAEL: Very rarely.

JEFF: Well, Isaac Bashevis Singer wrote those Jewish children's stories.

AYELET: My parents never gave me those.

NANCY: Or Sholom Aleichem's *The Adventures of Mottel.*

AYELET: They have that whole weirdness about that *Yiddishkeit*, my parents.

MICHAEL: They love Singer.

AYELET: No, they do not.

MICHAEL: Really?

AYELET: No.

MICHAEL: They have all of his books, or they used to.

AYELET: That doesn't mean anything! They never read any of them. [Laughter.]

NANCY: What about your Mommy-Track Mysteries,

Ayelet. Did you read a lot of mysteries before you started writing them?

AYELET: Oh yeah. I read tons of murder mysteries.

MICHAEL: When I met you, you still read them.

AYELET: I would read so many. I don't have the greatest memory, so I could read the same Dick Francis book twice, and it wouldn't be until on page 312 that I would be like, *Ohhh, I remember this!*

MICHAEL: You liked Amanda Cross and P. D. James.

AYELET: I especially loved the British mysteries, and especially if they were just a tiny bit elevated. But then when I started writing murder mysteries—and by the way I'm no P. D. James—I lost my taste for it. I noticed it with Dennis Lehane. *Mystic River.* As soon as he introduced the deaf kid, I was like, *Oh yeah, that's the murderer.* That's when I realized that I was fucked; I can't read mysteries anymore. Because once you know how they're constructed, you see the murderer as soon as they appear on the page.

NANCY: Like learning the ingredients of sausages.

AYELET: So I don't read them anymore. I mean, right now I'm reading the new Kate Atkinson, but I'd read her shopping list. I'll read those, but I don't really read anybody else's. But before I started writing them, I would read Agatha Christie and Ruth Rendell and Ngaio Marsh. I read them all. I didn't know until I met Michael that there was a difference between quality fiction and shitty fiction. I didn't actually know that some fiction was considered commercial and others literary. Every month the Book of the Month Club book came into the house, my parents would read it, I would read it, and whatever it was I would enjoy it. It wasn't until I met Michael that I really started being able to make distinctions. Eventually, when I started writing, I lost my capacity to read trash. My rule became, a writer has to write better than I do for me to spend time on the book. Luckily, that means there's no shortage of books for me to read. [Laughter.]

JEFF: Michael, you wrote that great essay about starting a science-fiction club in junior high school. Was that your main—?

MICHAEL: Yes, from the age of twelve or thirteen until I was about seventeen, my primary reading diet was science fiction and fantasy. I read everything—as much as I could get my hands on. Anything that had a little atom symbol, spaceship, the planet symbol, or the unicorn, you know, I would read those.

JEFF: Who were your favorites?

MICHAEL: Ray Bradbury. I think even at a young age, what made Ray Bradbury so important to me was—and I didn't know it yet—but it was his style.

There was an immediate difference in the sentences of Ray Bradbury; certainly sentences you were not used to encountering in science fiction. The story I've talked about the most is "The Rocket Man." It's such a compressed piece of fiction, it's almost like a poem. It uses all this imagery of night and day and light and darkness, and it ends up being a story about this kid whose father, the rocket man, his ship plunges into the sun and is burned up, and so then you understand all the imagery you were getting before. And that was the first time I noticed a writer doing that kind of thing in a story.

Larry Niven is another example. In hindsight I think he was probably influenced by Raymond Chandler's style. He would tend to have first-person hard-boiled narrators who were wised-up and sarcastic. And I would respond to writers of science fiction and fantasy who had that sense of style.

Tolkien is another really important one, if you're talking about the stuff I still go back to. Every eight or nine years, I'll just reread *The Lord of the Rings*. He has a very beautiful—not fancy, but beautiful—prose style. Even though I would read almost anything, the ones who endured, the writers who were my favorites in the genre, tended to be the ones who had a very identifiable style. And then I think the transition book for me was *The World According to Garp* [by John Irving].

AYELET: I love that book.

MICHAEL: My parents read it. The other thing that really shaped me was that both my parents were big readers. My dad's gone. My mom is still around. And they read constantly. Really passionately. My dad would get the book first, he would buy it and he would read it, and then my mom would read it, and then they would talk about it. So at the dinner table, conversation was always about the latest John Updike or the latest Philip Roth or the latest Kurt Vonnegut or the latest whoever.

AYELET: That was true of my family too.

MICHAEL: So when *Garp* came out, they both really loved it. It was a bombshell of a book at the time. I don't know if there had been anything quite like it before. So I wanted to read it, and they said, "Okay, you can read it." And I remember I just stayed up. I read it over a weekend, and it just, the style, the way it's written, the way it plays games with time, and with fiction within fiction, so many interesting things that I didn't know anything about, really. But also it was about a writer, and suddenly I got really self-conscious about wanting to be a writer, and that book helped shaped my idea of what being a writer meant. And he does a good job of depicting the actual creative process, and what it's like when you're germinating the story in your mind and it hangs around for a long time, and then you sit down to write it. So it was very seductive, even though the book is so weird and the things that happen are so often unpleasant. It was just very influential.

NANCY: Did you go back and read his first three [*Setting Free the Bears, The Water-Method Man,* and *The 158-Pound Marriage*] after that? That's what I did.

MICHAEL: Yes, in fact—I think right away. And I thought, *Oh, this isn't what I want.* [*Laughter.*] But after that I started to read primarily adult fiction, mainstream literary fiction, going forward. I got curious about Jack Kerouac and the kind of things that young men, especially young men, tend to like: Henry Miller and Kurt Vonnegut. And there almost seemed to be this list of twentieth-century foreign writers that you felt you were supposed to know. Like Alberto Moravia and Heinrich Böll. It was sort of this obligation to have read certain of these European writers that were regularly cited as the "great writers" of the late twentieth century.

JEFF: Günter Grass.

MICHAEL: Yeah, I read *The Tin Drum,* and that was such an amazing book. That was like the end of high school, going into college. It's funny now, because we just don't even have that. That whole idea of European literature that you sort of have to know if you want to consider yourself a literate reader is gone, for contemporary writers.

JEFF: Maybe because of World War II, the world seemed smaller.

MICHAEL: There was a greater internationalism.

AYELET: Which reminds me: Holocaust literature. So much Holocaust literature. There were periods, probably in my mid teens, or maybe even earlier, where that's all I read. There was a whole subgenre of Holocaust literature for middle-grade readers. There's one called *Children of the Holocaust* [by Helen Epstein]. It was about kids escaping the camps, escaping the ghetto, escaping and being hidden. And I just gobbled those up. Constantly. Did you read—?

MICHAEL: This isn't really a Holocaust one, but there was that one—*Escape from Warsaw* [by Ian Serraillier]. It's not totally about Holocaust victims—

AYELET: What do you mean, they weren't Holocaust victims?

MICHAEL: They were just Polish kids. They weren't Jewish. And then there was *Summer of My German Soldier* [by Bette Greene].

AYELET: Of course. Loved that.

NANCY: That was an important book, I think, for a lot of people. And Scholastic, the Scholastic Book Club, they had really good—

AYELET: They always had a Holocaust book. I could always rely on them.

MICHAEL: I'm pretty sure I read Edgar Allan Poe for the first time in a book I got from the Scholastic Book Club.

AYELET: My parents were super snobby about the Scholastic Book Club. They would always turn their nose up, and I would just beg, beg, beg.

MICHAEL: Oh, also I forgot to mention books about mice. I loved books about, like, talking mice. *Miss Bianca* [by Margery Sharp] and *Mrs. Frisby and the Rats of NIMH* [by Robert C. O'Brien].

NANCY: Do you remember *Walter the Lazy Mouse* [by Marjorie Flack]?

MICHAEL: Yes, oh, I do. Oh my God. And we mentioned Beverly Cleary, but not *The Mouse and the Motorcycle*. Also, at the same period, *Watership Down* [by Richard Adams]—I remember feeling like, *Can I actually read this? This book is so big.* And then just loving it so much. And our two youngest, I read to them every night up until five years ago. We went out with a great series of books, and one of them was *Watership Down*, and I hadn't read it since that first time. It was just a masterpiece. I loved it even more than I did when I was a kid.

AYELET: For our younger daughter, especially, who loves to write, our daughter who's the most seriously dyslexic, just that reading with Michael every night, having him read to her, was, like, profoundly important to her. They read so many amazing books together that she never would've been able to read.

MICHAEL: The last one, the very last one, was *To Kill a Mockingbird* [by Harper Lee]. When we finished, they were like, "No, we can read our own books," so that was it.

NANCY: Has there ever been a book that one of you loved and the other just not?

AYELET: Oh, so many. I mean, he read *Finnegan's Wake* [by James Joyce] for two years, over and over again. And I was just like, "Nope!"

MICHAEL: You tried to read Proust—

AYELET: I tried to read Proust, and I can't read Proust. I can't. *How long are we going to be talking about these drapes? How many pages?!* And finally I listened to the audiobook of *Ulysses* [by James Joyce], because we were giving the *Ulysses* lecture in Dublin, and I was, like, *Dude, I've gotta finish this book.* And I didn't even make it through. And yeah, I didn't know enough to fake it. So I got on the stage and right away I was like, "Okay, people, I just have to tell you, I haven't made it through—sorry."

MICHAEL: I think the biggest difference between us as readers, more than taste, is that I'm a rereader. I like to just reread the same books periodically, and I have favorite books I like to go back to. And you—

AYELET: There's some books I will reread. Jane Austen I reread every year or two. And Ian McEwan I'll reread. But otherwise, I'd always rather read something new.

JEFF: What's your favorite Ian McEwan?

AYELET: *Atonement.*

NANCY: My favorite too. Is that the one you reread?

AYELET: No, I can't reread it. It's funny, because—I'd reread it, but it's just too painful. But the balloon one, *Enduring Love*—I reread that all the time.

NANCY: I can never reread *On Chesil Beach*—way too sad.

AYELET: Also, I wanted the rest of that book! Like, *Okay, this is the first part* [it's only 166 pages]. The first time I read that it was on a Kindle and I'm like, *I don't think I have the whole thing!* Happened with *Home* by Toni Morrison too [145 pages]. I read it on a Kindle, and I was like, *Fuck them! They didn't give me the rest of the book.* But anyway, generally, I don't reread. I mean, I love contemporary fiction. Though I've had a hard time the past couple of years. I don't know whether it's the election or whether it's, honestly, I've just been pretty seriously depressed for the past year. I'm much better now. But I would just—everything I picked up, I'd be like, *Who gives a shit?* And just toss it across the room. Over and over. People that I loved. People whose books I should've loved. And then finally, it was the new Alan Hollinghurst [*The Sparsholt Affair*], I was like, *Okay, I still love to read.* And then Rebecca Makkai's book [*The Great Believers*]. And there's something very similar about those two books. Not just the gay themes, that's not important to me, but the size of it, the scope of it—and I was like, *Okay, I'm back!*

But Michael would rather reread than read something new. I remember, when David Mitchell's book came into the house as a galley, *Cloud Atlas*, I was like, *Oh my fucking God!* And I said to him, "Read this book." He said, "Meh." I was, *"Read this book!"* And he read it and was like, *"Aaaahhhh!"*

MICHAEL: I mean, it has to be either Ayelet just ordering me that you have to read this or else enough other people that I trust. If I hear everybody saying they love it, like with Edward St. Aubyn [the Patrick

Melrose series], it's almost like I have to feel the excitement.

JEFF: How about Jewish literature? American Jewish literature in particular?

AYELET: Oh yeah. Philip Roth.

MICHAEL: Yeah, definitely. Saul Bellow.

AYELET: I loved Mordecai Richler, because my family is from Montreal. I think my dad even knew him growing up.

JEFF: For me, I grew up in a family of atheists, so I learned very little about Judaism at home. I learned more about it from reading Philip Roth than I ever learned at my home.

MICHAEL: Those writers helped give me, in large part, my sense of identity as an American Jew, no doubt.

AYELET: I think they created our parents' sense of identity as American Jews too.

MICHAEL: Well, they saw their own experience. It's like when you're watching a movie and you see someplace that's in a location near your house. Like, *Oh, I know where that is.* And then for the rest of your life you go by there and you think, *Oh, that was in that movie.* I think it's like that. The Jewish identity too. They would see the dynamic of the Jewish family represented.

JEFF: Are there particular books in the subgenre that stand out for you?

MICHAEL: Well. It took me a long time to enjoy Bellow, and I discovered that was because I was reading the wrong ones. There's sort of two Bellows. There's a really dark sort of existentialism influenced by a lot of that twentieth-century European literature—

JEFF: *Mr. Sammler's Planet?*

MICHAEL: Like that, or *The Dangling Man.* Or *Henderson the Rain King.* I kept trying to read the wrong ones, and then I read *Herzog.* Which I had always, I don't know, I had ignored it for some reason, and I loved it so much, and then I read *Humboldt's Gift,* and I loved it even more.

AYELET: And that's the one you told me to read, because I was like, "I don't like Saul Bellow."

MICHAEL: There's much more humor and there's a kind of expansiveness in those books.

JEFF: What about Roth? Are there specific Roth books?

AYELET: Oh, for sure.

MICHAEL: *The Ghost Writer.*

AYELET: *The Ghost Writer.* One hundred percent. And what's the one where he goes to Israel?

JEFF: *The Counterlife?*

MICHAEL: *Operation Shylock?*

AYELET: *Operation Shylock.* Both of them.

MICHAEL: That was my favorite period of his. That's when he wrote *Patrimony* too.

AYELET: Yeah, *Patrimony. American Pastoral* wasn't long after that.

MICHAEL: That's the one everyone loves, but I don't.

AYELET: I liked *American Pastoral.*

JEFF: What about *Sabbath's Theater?*

MICHAEL: Another one I didn't like. It's just endless talking.

AYELET: I like those. But not the later ones. It was the moment that I read a sentence that had the words "prostate" and "blowjob," that's the one that killed it for me. Wherever it was we were having blowjobs and prostates, I was just like, *Okay, I'm out. Thanks, Phil, but I'm done!* But you know, I've read every one of his books. Have you?

MICHAEL: Yeah, you—

AYELET: I'll read them. I may not like them, but I'll read them.

MICHAEL: It was after reading *Goodbye, Columbus* and then *The Great Gatsby* back to back I started writing *The Mysteries of Pittsburgh*, which is definitely influenced by them both. That was huge for me.

NANCY: Is there a book for each of you that you wish you had written?

AYELET: It's terrible to say, but if I could write a book like *The Amazing Adventures of Kavalier & Clay*, I wouldn't do anything else. I wouldn't have had kids. I wouldn't have done anything else. I would've just locked myself in a closet and done nothing but write.

MICHAEL: I mean, I guess I would say I'm envious of the idea of *Cloud Atlas*. I wish I'd had that idea. It's such a brilliant idea, and he executed it so perfectly. But that is a really amazing idea. And you know, it can never be done again.

AYELET: I mean there are definitely some writers that I read and I'm like, *How, how, how, how can you write something so beautiful?* I mean I had that feeling with—what's his name with the drapes and the fat man?

MICHAEL: Just that line? *Train* by Pete Dexter.

AYELET: There's a line. Do you remember the line?

MICHAEL: The fat man is wearing this lightweight suit and his thighs were moving around inside the legs of his pants "like children hiding in the curtains."

AYELET: And I was like, *That's everything I wish I could do.*

MICHAEL: That book is weird, though, because it starts out like the best book you've ever read for 125 pages and then you're like, *What? What did this turn into? It's not at all what it said it was going to be in the beginning, and it's awful, and I hate it.*

NANCY: Did you read *Spooner* by him? That was a wonderful book.

MICHAEL: Yes, I did. That's a great one.

JEFF: I like *The Paperboy* the best.

NANCY: *The Paperboy* has a great first line: "My brother Ward was once a famous man." I thought that was pretty much a perfect first line, because it totally invites you into the book.

MICHAEL: Absolutely. On a sentence level, he is definitely one of the best writers there are.

AYELET: We didn't mention our favorite book that we were very happy to hear is also Michael Ondaatje's favorite book: *The Queen's Gambit*.

NANCY: By Walter Tevis.

AYELET: That book was so great! I just gave it to [their daughter] Sophie and she was like, "This book is incredible!"

MICHAEL: It never fails! Every person I've ever recommended this book is like, "Oh my God! Thank you for telling me about this."

JEFF: My favorite science-fiction writer, Walter Tevis.

MICHAEL: Yeah? *The Man Who Fell to Earth* or *Mockingbird*?

JEFF: *Mockingbird.*

MICHAEL: That's a cool book. He's an amazing writer. And *The Queen's Gambit* is perfect.

JEFF: Who among your contemporaries do you most admire?

AYELET: You go first.

MICHAEL: I'm afraid to say, because I don't want to leave anyone out. So many of them are friends.

JEFF: Well, can you choose one? And then you'll have left everyone else out.

MICHAEL: Well, he's not my contemporary, he's older than me, he's still alive, however, so in that sense he's contemporary, and that's Michael Ondaatje. Some of his early books are so wonderful. The Billy the Kid book [*The Collected Works of Billy the Kid*], and *Coming Through Slaughter*, and *In the Skin of a Lion*, and *The English Patient*, and then after *The English Patient*, *Anil's Ghost*.

NANCY: And then the one on the ship.

MICHAEL: Oh yeah, *The Cat's Table*. That was so good.

AYELET: We both reread *The English Patient*. That's another one of the few books I'll reread over and over. And I reread that one to learn from—if I'm writing a novel I'll be like, *All right, let me read this.*

MICHAEL: Especially for me, I still don't understand how he did it, like in terms of his structure. It's so fragmentary, but it doesn't feel fragmentary. When I was writing *Moonglow*, I kept going back to *English Patient* to try and figure out how he was doing it.

AYELET: Zadie Smith, for sure, for me. Both her fiction and her nonfiction, but her fiction is just phenomenal. There are books of T.C. Boyle's that I love like that. Not all of them. But there are some of them that I love. *The Road to Wellville* is such fun.

MICHAEL: *Drop City.*

AYELET: *Drop City* too.

MICHAEL: If somebody asked me who your favorite contemporary writer was, I'd say Ian McEwan.

AYELET: What Ian McEwan does is he's not afraid to write plot, and so many people are, and he has these exciting, propulsive plots and then beautiful language, and they're books of ideas. [*Indicating Michael.*] He reads dead people, mostly.

MICHAEL: I get excited when Jonathan Lethem has a new book coming out.

AYELET: My favorite is the one nobody likes, the one about the red diaper baby and her mother.

JEFF: Yeah. Me too! *Dissident Gardens.*

AYELET: That's my favorite.

MICHAEL: *The Fortress of Solitude,* I felt like I was reading my life, even though I didn't grow up in New York.

AYELET: But mostly he'd rather reread something, 'cause he knows it's going to be good, and why waste the time? That's something I actually learned from him. You don't have to finish a book.

And this happened: we were in Hawaii on family vacation, and we had this book called . . . I should probably be discreet about this, but it was the fucking worst book I ever read. And on vacation, I read two, maybe three books a day. I read very fast. I was getting angry, and less pleasant, and days were going, and Michael was like, "Please, please stop reading that." And I wrote Daniel Mendelsohn an email and I'm like, "I blame you and every other reviewer, because what the fuck is this book? I can't handle this shit." And he was like, "Oh, sister." And he sends me a link to his review, which is this complete evisceration. He's like, *I got here before you did.* And I was like, *I don't have to finish this piece of shit.* And now, I'm like, *I don't have to finish anything. I'm fifty-four years old. No matter what, I'm not going to be able to read all the books I want to read, so screw it!*

MICHAEL: Life is too short for bad books.

Some Books and Authors in Michael and Ayelet's Library

Richard Adams, *Watership Down* (Michael)

Kate Atkinson (Ayelet)

Jane Austen, *Pride and Prejudice* (Ayelet)

Saul Bellow, *Herzog* and *Humboldt's Gift* (Michael)

Judy Blume (Ayelet)

T.C. Boyle, *The Road to Wellville* and *Drop City* (Ayelet)

Ray Bradbury, "The Rocket Man" (Michael)

Beverly Cleary, *The Mouse and the Motorcycle*

Susan Cooper, The Dark Is Rising Sequence (Michael)

Pete Dexter, *Train* (Ayelet)

Arthur Conan Doyle, *The Adventures of Sherlock Holmes* (Michael)

Georgette Heyer (Michael)

John Irving, *The World According to Garp*

James Joyce, *Finnegan's Wake* (Michael)

Jonathan Lethem, *Dissident Gardens* (Ayelet)
    and *The Fortress of Solitude* (Michael)
Ian McEwan, *Atonement* (Ayelet)
David Mitchell, *Cloud Atlas*
Michael Ondaatje, *The English Patient*
Philip Roth, *The Ghost Writer*
Zadie Smith (Ayelet)
Walter Tevis, *The Queen's Gambit*
J. R. R. Tolkien, *The Lord of the Rings* (Michael)
Roger Zelazny, *Nine Princes in Amber* (Ayelet)

Maaza Mengiste

We *met Ethiopian American novelist Maaza Mengiste at the Center for Fiction in Brooklyn, where an exhibit of her personal collection of archival photographs of Ethiopian women warriors was on display. Maaza told us that she'd collected these photos at flea markets and antique shops in Italy and Ethiopia, and used them for inspiration as she wrote her second novel,* The Shadow King, *which had just been published. Set in 1935, when Italy invaded Ethiopia at the very start of World War II,* The Shadow King *tells the story of Hirut, an*

orphan girl who manages to transcend her prescribed
destiny of servitude to become a warrior fighting
for her country's freedom. It was praised by Salman
Rushdie as "a brilliant novel, lyrically lifting history
towards myth. It's also compulsively readable."

Maaza was born in Addis Ababa, Ethiopia, in
1974, but by the time she was four her family had fled
the country's revolution to live in Nigeria and then
Kenya. When she was seven, the family moved to a
small town in Colorado, where she spent the rest of
her childhood. She went to college at the University
of Michigan and later got an MFA in creative writing
from New York University. Her first novel, Beneath
the Lion's Gaze, grew out of short stories she wrote at
NYU. It's about the effects of the 1974 revolution on
the members of one Ethiopian family—a family that,
unlike Maaza's, stayed behind.

Now an assistant professor of creative writing in
the MFA program at Queens College and a lecturer
at Princeton University, Maaza's fictional eye remains
focused on her homeland as she lends her unique voice
to stories that are rarely told in American fiction.

—————

JEFF: Can you tell us about your life before you came
to the US?

MAAZA: I was born in Ethiopia and lived there through the early days of the revolution. Many people were fleeing the country. My father worked for Ethiopian Airlines and requested a transfer out of the country, and that's how we were able to move to Nigeria. Because we left Addis Ababa when I was still quite young, I didn't understand what was happening in Ethiopia, because my family was really keeping me sheltered. I grew up in a large extended family, and we lived in a neighborhood with lots of kids. My life felt full, and it was happy, visits with my grandparents, birthday parties, and then all of a sudden people started being very nervous and very quiet and keeping us kids inside as soon as it got dark, not letting me open the window or even the curtains. I started trying to figure out what happened, what was going on, and I would eavesdrop on conversations that I shouldn't have been listening to. I knew things were happening and people were being jailed, but when I would ask as a child, of course, nobody would tell me anything. But there were certain moments that remained very clear in my memory and that I described in my first book [*Beneath the Lion's Gaze*], moments of running some errands with my grandparents, for example, and all of a sudden there are soldiers on every street corner. And it was such a vivid thing, going to a wedding where I was supposed to be the flower girl, and we couldn't get in because there were soldiers in front of the wedding venue, and we had to convince them we were part of the wedding, we weren't troublemakers. People suddenly disappearing from our neighborhood, or our compound, and soldiers breaking into our house.

JEFF: How old were you when you made each of your moves?

MAAZA: We moved to Nigeria when I was four; by the time I left Kenya, I was seven. And between four and seven, living in Nigeria and Kenya, and then even in America, I was still making trips back to Ethiopia, so in some ways, distance has always been connected to my experience of Ethiopia. It has always been as somebody coming back. My early experience in Ethiopia—growing up, living in the revolution, remembering some of it, having to leave and then coming back and seeing the progression of it—has been pivotal for me as a writer.

NANCY: Did books and reading play any role during that period of your childhood?

MAAZA: You know, in many ways, Ethiopia is an oral culture. I spent a lot of time listening to stories and histories told around dinner tables or in the sitting room. The stories my grandfather would tell were often about the Italo-Ethiopian wars, both the first and the second, and also life lessons. Those stories of my grandfather's really informed how I viewed history, how I viewed Ethiopia, what it meant to be Ethiopian. Those were my books, the stories that I learned. When I think back to the stories that I would hear, especially when my parents would tell stories, that cadence in which they told them, and the momentum they had while telling it, that's something I am always trying to emulate in my writing. So I count them as an influence as much as anything that I've read.

NANCY: Was there a written literary culture as well?

MAAZA: Yes, Ethiopia has one of the oldest written languages anywhere.

NANCY: I'm just interested in what you remember—

MAAZA: But I don't remember that. Most of it is biblical, liturgical texts. Scripture, with interpretations of it. The novels that were being published, I was way too young at that time to read them. And it's only when I got older that I was able to go back and look at some of the works. Some of the plays. Some of the poetry. But the poetry in Ethiopia is also mostly oral, featuring word play.

Understanding the structures of those, called *qiné*, the word plays, informed the potential I saw in a sentence or a phrase to vibrate on several different planes at once simply by using a word with multiple meanings.

NANCY: When did you learn to speak and read English?

MAAZA: I started to learn English a little bit in Nigeria. My mother sent me to school when we were there, maybe one day a week. By the time I was in Kenya I was in elementary school, and all the education was in English. Nairobi was an international city, and our friends were from everywhere; everybody spoke English as a common language.

JEFF: Do you remember the first books you read in English?

MAAZA: I think the first book I read in Kenya was about Jack and Jill. I remember that very distinctly: I got that book and I just thought, *Oh, it's fascinating. Here are these kids going down this hill.*

I didn't quite know how to read, but I was given that book. The first English word I learned how to spell was t-h-e. And my parents, my father said "the" [*thuh*] and my mother said "the" [*thee*], and I remember thinking, *I'll never learn this. I'll never learn this language. I'll never learn to read because there are so many pronunciations for things.* But I remember my father would make me spell it again and again. And then whenever we were driving through Nairobi and we would see some billboard or sign he would say, "Pick out the word." And I did.

NANCY: Were your parents readers?

MAAZA: No, no. They loved music. My mom was a big Prince fan. Boney M. Our house was always full of music. But books? My mom likes to read, but she didn't always have time to do it. My father was not so much a reader, but he was such a good storyteller. He was really good. Sometimes I think that maybe in a different world, he might have been a writer, because he did communications and PR work, and he loved that kind of work. But yeah, he wasn't much of a reader, not at that time.

JEFF: What about your reading experiences once you came to the US?

MAAZA: Well, I was in Colorado, and I didn't like the snow. I never got used to it. I remember we arrived in January, and my mom and I, we were both like, "What is this? What is this?" And somebody had said to me at some point before I got there, "Oh, there's going to be snow." I had no clue what America was like, and I had no idea of snow, and I think I started looking at books, children's books, trying to find snow. And I found a storybook that was full of igloos in Alaska, and there were these illustrations, and I said, "Oh my God, this is where I'm going!" So I was trying to prepare myself for how to live in an igloo, and I just had no clue. To me, the idea of America felt like I was going into this very backward country, and I was trying to prepare myself as best I could.

JEFF: What was your experience in school like?

MAAZA: Coming from Nairobi, I had this British accent, and kids were not very kind with that. I said words that didn't exist, or should not exist in American English, and I would say them, and I would get in trouble, and I had no idea why. For example, I raised my hand at some point because I had to go to the restroom—it was probably my first or second week in that school—and the teacher said, "Yes?" And I said, "I have to piss." That's just what we said in Nairobi at school. And the whole class turned and stared at me, and the teacher was aghast. But that was just—it was not a bad word for me.

But, you know, I keep in touch with my elementary school teachers. I've kept in touch with one of my high school teachers, who was so fundamentally instrumental in my move into English literature and eventually becoming a writer. There were some teachers who didn't know how to handle a young immigrant from Africa, and then there were other teachers who said, "We're going to try to make this as smooth as possible." And they were wonderful.

NANCY: Were there some books that you read then that were meaningful to you?

MAAZA: *The Giving Tree* [by Shel Silverstein]. Reading that book and saying, "This is how we should all be. This is how we're supposed to be." I think we find our heroes through literature. We learn how to behave through the characters that we read about, who demonstrate different kinds of loyalty, and friendships, and love. And when I read *The Giving Tree*, it just felt to me like, "Yes, this is how the world should be, giving like this." What else? I remember reading *Charlotte's Web* [by E. B. White]. We didn't have pigs in Ethiopia, but I said, "This is really cool." Those two books I still vividly remember. When I got into high school, my English teacher assigned parts of Homer to read. *The Iliad.* I remember feeling electrified by that. In a way that I just wanted to talk about it. I carried that text with me everywhere, and it's become such a big influence in how I think of writing.

NANCY: Was it the war story or the relationships?

MAAZA: The war. I still go back to the way Homer depicts the battles, and I remember sitting there glued to this and feeling my heart race, and it felt like a light bulb was going on in my head. I think what Homer was doing with that, what felt so electrifying, was he was naming every single person, and he was calling out their history and who they were, whose child, what they were good at— like describing Hector as "Breaker of Horses." I thought, *This is how we need to think of conflict,* and it brought to mind all the questions I had about the revolution in Ethiopia and the people who kept disappearing, or people I knew who were jailed and nobody wanted to talk about them or name them. But here was a text that was actually naming them, and it was pivotal for me in understanding what literature could do.

JEFF: What other books impressed you when you were in high school?

MAAZA: I read everything I could get my hands on. I was a voracious reader. What did I read then? All the Nancy Drews. All the things that kids were reading, I was reading those too. In my application to the University of Michigan, one of the questions was what book has influenced you, and

I honestly don't know why I didn't write about Homer, because it really had influenced me, but at the moment I had just finished reading—this is so stupid—a book about UFOs, and I wrote this long essay about [how] there's so much we don't know about this world, and the things we do think we can prove we can't prove, because how can we prove them? I remember that the author had already written other books, and then suddenly realized that he had been kidnapped by aliens, and here was this true story account, and I read it, and I'm like, *Oh my God. Anything is possible in this world.* I'm so surprised U of M let me in! But yeah, I was reading everything, and I was taking everything with an equal level of sincerity. Homer was no greater to me at that moment than this book about UFOs. [Laughter.]

JEFF: What about immigrant stories? My mother was an immigrant from Russia, and I remember when I first discovered Isaac Bashevis Singer and reading some of the stories that he wrote about Holocaust survivors, and how that told me something about my own background.

MAAZA: I wasn't reading much immigrant literature. I was reading every book I could find about revolutions. I was interested not in the people who left, like my family, but people who stayed. And what happened to them. I remember reading every book I could find about the Chinese Revolution, fiction or nonfiction, or the Cuban Revolution, and I continued that through high school, through college and beyond. The immigrant experience, my immigrant experience, felt less interesting to me than what my parents experienced. Or what my family experienced, and was experiencing for some of the years in Ethiopia, because the revolution was still going on when I was in the US. I was picking up those books, reading about kids growing up, like during the partition of India—reading about all of that.

NANCY: I've always felt that one of the best books about the partition of India is Salman Rushdie's *Midnight's Children*.

MAAZA: Yeah, by the time I got to college I had picked that up. Also, I was just devouring Toni Morrison's books, and Gloria Naylor's *Mama Day*. My God, it was just spellbinding. And I was finding my own stories in there, because what Toni Morrison is writing about, these black communities, and dealing with the racial structures within the US, is what I was also experiencing in Colorado and in Michigan. All those books were speaking to me. But what I looked for was anything that might help explain Ethiopia. Anything. All the literature that dealt with the Holocaust. How do people cope with violence? How do parents tell their children? What do children understand? What do you do afterwards? I was trying to find everything about that.

JEFF: Did you think you would be a writer?

MAAZA: Not at all. I never took a creative writing course in college. I just liked to read. I liked to read and I liked to analyze literature. I could sit and talk about those things for hours with classmates. But there was nothing in my framework that would have made me think that I could write. Or be a writer. I knew I could write essays about what I read, and I knew how to break things down and analyze them, but there was nothing that told me anything about short stories. It just wasn't part of my vocabulary. I became a management consultant, and I hated it. My God, it was numbing! I was working with banks. I was doing these things, and I said, "I don't know what else to do with an English degree, but this . . . There has to be something else."

Just for my own sanity, I was bartending at night—so that I could get out of my suit and go and talk to people. I was living in Detroit, and I could just hang out there and have what I felt were normal conversations with people. Most of them were factory workers, and they would cash a paycheck and then come and spend it at the bar. I remember thinking there's a world here that's so separate from this other thing, my consulting. I was trying to stay in the world of literature without ever understanding what writing was, what it meant to be a writer.

I think my first introduction to any kind of creative writing came when a friend of mine who worked in an ad agency asked if I wanted to write a few things for a new pitch they were doing. And that's really where it began. I learned about being concise but creative, and on point. Then I thought, wait, maybe I could do something creative with writing, and from working on commercials came the thought, number one, *I hate advertising, I don't want to write about cereal anymore or cakes or cars, but can I do something else with these skills?* Could I write a screenplay? And I started thinking about short films I could do, and I won a couple of grants while I lived in Michigan to do a couple of five-minute films. And from there came: *Could I write a story? Could that story be about Ethiopia? Could it be about the revolution? Could it be what I've been thinking about?* All these books I was still reading that dealt with revolutions or history in some way. Could I try to do that? And eventually I got a job in Hollywood, working in film development, thinking, *Well, this is the way I'll do it.* Maybe through screenplay, because I still had not written a short story. Then I realized, *This is not my world. I don't fit in here.*

I called an old professor of mine from Michigan and asked him what I should do. And he said, "Well, you should apply to the NYU [creative writing] program." And I said, "Oh, I'll never get in." He said, "It doesn't matter. Just apply. And apply everywhere. And then you can try again." So I did. I wrote a couple of short stories for the application. And I got in. And drove cross-country from Los Angeles to New York and NYU.

NANCY: Are there books that say New York to you?

MAAZA: When I found out that I was accepted, I tried to read every book by every professor who was teaching there. I remember Paule Marshall's work felt distinctly Brooklyn. Then I read E. L. Doctorow's *Ragtime*, which is [set in] the Bronx. Those blew me away. I thought, *Wow, if writers can do this, this is going to be amazing! To be in a commu-*

nity where I can speak to some of these writers and learn from them. Yeah.

JEFF: When you wrote the stories for the NYU application, were there writers whose short stories you admired and that you modeled your stories on?

MAAZA: No. I was reading history books, and I was reading novels. I remember reading things like *Parting the Waters* [by Taylor Branch], which won the Pulitzer when I was in college. Jon Lee Anderson's *Che Guevara*. Those kind of books. I was still reading everything I could on revolution or civil conflict, but not short stories. But it's funny you ask that, because when I went in, I thought, *Well, I don't know how to write a novel, so I'll just do a series of short stories.* I submitted this short story that I had written in Breyten Breytenbach's class. It was set during the Ethiopian revolution; it told the story of a young girl who answers the door with her grandfather and the soldiers break in. And everybody kept saying, "Where is Ethiopia? What revolution? Why are soldiers there? Wait, what's happening here? What year is this?" And I remember sitting around going, *Whoa. Nobody knows this.* And I had been so steeped in this history that I couldn't conceive that people didn't know it. I think Breyten said to me,

"This is a novel." I was like, "I don't know how to write a novel. I don't know how to do it."

So I went in to talk to another professor, Irini Spanidou, and I said, "I don't know how to do this." I felt completely lost. And Irini gave me the best advice, and I give it to all my students now, which is: Write the moments that you feel inspired to write right now, and don't worry about chronology. It turned out that that short story I submitted was actually the last chapter of [*Beneath the Lion's Gaze*]. Then I wrote backwards to get to the beginning, but it took several years, without writing in any kind of chronological order, then eventually starting to piece the parts together. Because my brain just couldn't conceive of the totality of a novel.

JEFF: While you were in your MFA program, writing *Beneath the Lion's Gaze*, what were you reading?

MAAZA: I was still really interested in how other writers depicted violent situations. How have writers grappled with both politics but also individual loyalties, allegiances, betrayals within that larger framework, and then how do they create a book that's centered in a time of conflict but isn't necessarily just about that? So I was reading as much as I could. I was reading . . . Who was I reading? I'm trying to think about way back then.

NANCY: Are there particular books that you think do that really well? That are able to capture that?

MAAZA: I think that what Jon Lee Anderson did in *Che Guevara* was eye-opening for me. He rendered Che in all of his complexities, in all the contradictions of being a freedom fighter but then killing your own people that you think are betraying you. That book was so important to me. I was reading everything on World War II. I was reading books about Vietnam. I watched, I don't know how many times, the film *The Battle of Algiers*, which I think is still one of the greatest political films ever made. It gives you a picture of a community that was completely involved in a political movement, from the little kids to the women to the men, and I understood that was also Ethiopia, because that's what was happening: little kids were getting swept up in this too.

While I was writing *The Shadow King*, I read Victor Klemperer's diaries [*I Will Bear Witness, Vol. 1: A Diary of the Nazi Years, 1933–1941*; *I Will Bear Witness, Vol. 2: A Diary of the Nazi Years, 1942–1945*; and *The Lesser Evil: The Diaries of Victor Klemperer, 1945–59*], and I remember this moment where he said, "I will make all these people known." I thought about the way that writing can become an act of defiance, and he was doing it—

just as this ordinary citizen, a professor, and he was taking incredible risks to do this. A few years ago I was telling everybody, "Why aren't you reading this? You need to be reading this. Especially now." And it still feels like an urgent text.

I remember reading *The Corpse Washer*, which was my first encounter with the work of Sinan Antoon, an Iraqi writer. I was just jolted when I read it. It's about a man during the Iraq War who helps his father in the family business of the ritual washing of bodies in order to bury them. It's such a beautiful book. The war was in the periphery: it only entered with these bodies; it was really about how does someone cope with this? And then walk out and go eat dinner and sit at home with family? There were moments of complete beauty, and also humor and some horror, and this book was profound in my understanding of how there are ways that literature can reveal things about countries that we usually only learn about from the news. And here was this introduction to a community that I had no idea about.

I realize that those are the same sort of books that I've been interested in since I was a child. It's grown, and it's developed, and hopefully gotten more complicated in the ways that I look at literature's place, not only when we talk about war but when we talk about memory. When we talk about what we do with grief and mourning and separations and the distances that memory or history force on us. But also distances that political conflict or different political ideologies create within a family.

JEFF: Are there other contemporary writers whose books you've enjoyed?

MAAZA: My friend Mona Eltahawy's *The Seven Necessary Sins for Women and Girls*, which is nonfiction, and it's a manifesto, a cry against these patriarchal systems. Reading that book was simply mindblowing. I just finished Jaquira Díaz's memoir *Ordinary Girls*, which is incredible. There's an Iranian writer who lives in Sweden [Golnaz Hashemzadeh Bonde] and wrote this book that's been translated from Swedish called *What We Owe*. I could not put it down. Laila Lalami's *The Other Americans* is a book everyone should read, so is *Kintu* by Jennifer [Nansubuga] Makumbi and everything by Aminatta Forna. Daša Drndic's *Trieste* is a masterpiece.

NANCY: What do you read when the world gets too much for you?

MAAZA: For those moments when I want to decompress, I always go to poetry. Aracelis Girmay, Natalie Diaz, Ada Limón, Zbigniew Herbert, Czesław

Miłosz, Ilya Kaminsky, Audre Lorde, Adrienne Rich. And Shakespeare. Reading *Julius Caesar* and *Hamlet.* . . . Right after the election in 2016, I was reading *Plutarch's Lives*, then I got to *Coriolanus* and I thought, *Oh my God. I'm seeing Trump. I can't read this anymore*, but I finished it and I found the end gratifying.

NANCY: What about Philip Levine? I was thinking of him when you were talking about working in the bar in Detroit.

MAAZA: His poetry is so good. Absolutely, *What Work Is*. Absolutely. And Kwame Dawes. Chris Abani. They're brilliant. They make me think more about what language can do and express.

NANCY: Who are some other Ethiopian writers you'd recommend?

MAAZA: You know, everybody should read Dinaw Mengestu. *The Beautiful Things That Heaven Bears. How to Read the Air.* He's an incredible writer. And there's a book by Aida Edemariam called *The Wife's Tale*. It's the story of her grandmother and the different moments in Ethiopian history her grandmother lived through. It's told from this very personal and intimate perspective, and the writing is absolutely beautiful. Lemn Sissay is British Ethiopian; he has a new book that is powerful and gut-wrenching and inspiring, *My Name Is Why*. I would absolutely recommend it. Sulaiman Addonia is a writer that is based in Brussels, and he has a book out called *The Consequences of Love* and also a new one, *Silence Is My Mother Tongue*. Beautiful books. Both of them dealing with the refugee experience. The writing is spectacular. And I've recently edited an anthology through Akashic called *Addis Ababa Noir*. It features fourteen Ethiopian writers, some living in Ethiopia and some in the diaspora. The stories are amazing. I would tell anyone to look for that.

JEFF: You've lived in America now for thirty-plus years. I'm wondering if you see yourself in the future writing about America and about the immigrant experience in America, or if you plan to continue writing about what you left behind?

MAAZA: I have tried over the years to write about the immigrant experience, and then I look at my bookshelf, and I look at all these writers that have done it, like Dinaw Mengestu, I think, *What am I going to add to this?* And I don't think there's anything new that I could add or say that's any better than what these writers are doing now. And then of course my inclination is to wonder not about what happens when you leave but what happens when you stay. And that, I think, has been my question right from the beginning.

Some Books in Maaza's Library

Sulaiman Addonia, *The Consequences of Love*
John Lee Anderson, *Che Guevara:*
    A Revolutionary Life
Sinan Antoon, *The Corpse Washer*
Golnaz Hashemzadeh Bonde, *What We Owe*
Taylor Branch, *Parting the Waters*
Jaquira Díaz, *Ordinary Girls*
E. L. Doctorow, *Ragtime*
Daša Drndi , *Trieste*
Aida Edemariam, *The Wife's Tale*
Mona Eltahawy, *The Seven Necessary Sins*
    for Women and Girls
Homer, *The Iliad*
Victor Klemperer, *I Will Bear Witness, Vol. 1:*
    A Diary of the Nazi Years, 1933–1941; I Will
    Bear Witness, Vol. 2: A Diary of the Nazi
    Years, 1942–1945; and *The Lesser Evil: The*
    Diaries of Victor Klemperer, 1945–59

Laila Lalami, *The Other Americans*

Jennifer Makumbi, *Kintu*

Dinaw Mengestu, *The Beautiful Things That Heaven Bears*

Gloria Naylor, *Mama Day*

William Shakespeare, *Julius Caesar* and *Hamlet*

Shel Silverstein, *The Giving Tree*

E. B. White, *Charlotte's Web*

Amor Towles

Amor Towles was forty-six years old when he published his first book, Rules of Civility, joining a relatively short list of writers who made acclaimed debuts after the age of forty. Time will tell if Towles is remembered alongside such fellow late starters as George Eliot (née Mary Ann Evans), Mark Twain, Marcel Proust, Raymond Chandler, Walker Percy, J. R. R. Tolkien, and Annie Proulx, but he is off to a promising start. He followed Rules

of Civility, *his bestselling Fitzgeraldian tale of a romantic triangle in 1930s New York, with the even more celebrated* A Gentleman in Moscow, *an enchanting novel about a Russian nobleman whose postrevolutionary sentence for the crime of frivolity is life imprisonment in the city's most luxurious hotel, with the threat of execution should he ever step outside.*

Amor was born in Boston in 1964 and went on to earn a BA from Yale and an MA from Stanford in English. He published his Stanford thesis, the short-story cycle "The Temptations of Pleasure," in The Paris Review *in 1989. At that point, he put his writing career on hold, and worked in the investment field for two decades, before returning to fiction and the kind of middle-aged career change most professional people only dream of.*

We met Amor at the elegant Victorian town house he shares with his wife and their two teenagers in Manhattan's Gramercy Park neighborhood. Our interview took place in Amor's large, book-lined home office, with floor-to-ceiling dark wood shelves on three walls, including an enviable collection of first editions behind glass. A devoted reader who seems to speak in carefully composed paragraphs,

Amor cast a spell over his interlocutors, who hardly needed to ask a question.

————————

NANCY: Were you a big reader as a kid?

AMOR: For me, reading and writing went in lockstep. I remember vividly when my first-grade teacher invited a friend of hers named David McCord—a juvenile poet of local renown—to come read to our class. He was probably in his sixties and had written a number of books of poetry. I remember thinking he was the coolest. We had the opportunity to buy his books at the end of class. I bought two, and within twenty-four hours I was writing rip-off versions of his work. They were often rhyming celebrations of everyday objects. And from that point on, for me it was: read, write, repeat.

I grew up in the '70s in a Waspy middle-class suburb outside of Boston. At the time, going to the movies or a restaurant was a big deal in our family, an unusual treat. But my father always said: "If you want a book, I'll buy it." At some point, I got the first Hardy Boys mystery, and that summer I read the entire series. I got to the point where I was reading one a day, sending my dad back to the store every afternoon, and being excited to start the next one that night. Later, I discovered the short stories of Ray Bradbury. I started with *The Illustrated Man*, and when my mother saw how much I enjoyed that book, she got me his collected stories for my birthday. That was the first time I had a sprawling body of work bound in a single volume, something I was very impressed by. Then it was Ian Fleming's James Bond novels. At each step, I was writing something. So by the time I reached high school, reading and writing were my primary passions.

NANCY: Did you read other mysteries, or sci-fi, beyond the Hardy Boys and Ray Bradbury?

AMOR: My dad was someone who always brought old paperbacks of mysteries on planes—with their yellowed pages and fragile bindings. Any time we traveled, he would have five or six of them in his briefcase: Agatha Christie's Hercule Poirot, or Erle Stanley Gardner's Perry Mason, or Rex Stout's Nero Wolfe. I read all of those series. In general, mystery and noir became a big influence, first in books and later in film.

NANCY: I'm rereading all the Nero Wolfe books now, for the nineticth time, I think. In publication order.

AMOR: I've done the same thing! During the summer, as a break, I read mystery or suspense authors, chronologically. So I did the entire Nero Wolfe series over two summers just a few years ago. I probably could have done it in one, but I *wanted* to stretch it out. Reading Stout's depiction of Wolfe over the course of his career is very interesting, because Wolfe never changes, but you get to see how New York is evolving, and how Stout adapts his narratives from the 1930s through the war and into the 1960s. The relationship between Nero Wolfe and Archie is endlessly amusing, and Archie's tone of voice is a terrific stylistic achievement.

Last summer I read the nine Smiley novels by John le Carré. As far as I'm concerned, Le Carré isn't simply one of the best suspense novelists; he's one of the best *novelists* writing in English of the postwar era. What's great about reading his Smiley books chronologically is that you're moving from relatively short and narrow books at the beginning of Le Carré's career towards *Tinker, Tailor, Soldier, Spy* and *The Honourable Schoolboy*, books which are so much more demanding, intricate, and satisfying. One thing I love about Le Carré is that he's such a deft observer of institutionalism in the modern era. He's far more interested in exploring the pig-headed behavior of bureaucrats, the inertia of institutions, and all the resulting moral dislocations than he is in representing "tradecraft."

NANCY: Do you do that outside of mystery—compulsively read writers' works in chronological order?

AMOR: When I was turning forty (I'm fifty-five now), I had just read a series of novels that were front and center in the public conversation, as it were, and I found myself . . . underwhelmed. Around the same time, I happened to read a book by Harold Bloom called *Where Shall Wisdom Be Found?* In this book, Bloom, who was in his seventies, asks himself, after his extraordinary lifetime of reading, in what books did he actually find *wisdom*? For Bloom, wisdom is gaining some command over the quandaries of being human. On the one hand, we are able to experience a sense of infinity, and yet our lives are finite. Beauty can touch us deeply, but it is generally fleeting. We have an extraordinary capacity to bond with others, and yet we are essentially alone. These are the sort of paradoxes that Bloom seeks to understand through the pursuit of wisdom. The way his book is constructed is through a series of comparisons. He looks at Plato and Homer and says: "Okay. After reading Plato and Homer throughout my life, in retrospect, from which did I gain more wisdom?" And though he's a big lover of Plato, he determines that it's Homer, the narrativist. In a similar fashion, he compares Freud and Proust—and he's a big Freudian—but ultimately, he's gained more wisdom from reading Proust than Freud.

Bloom's book had a big effect on me. I closed it thinking: *I'm turning forty. If I live to eighty and read one book a month carefully—where I underline and reflect upon what I've read and write down my thoughts—that means I've got just 480 books left!* Yet I had just spent a year reading a series of contemporary novels that didn't make a mark on me. So I decided that I had to do something different. I decided to focus on reading books that were so accomplished, so rich, you would benefit from reading them at the age of twenty and forty and sixty and eighty. I was describing this thought process to a close friend, and she said: "I'm in. However you're going to do this, I want to do it." So we reached out to two other friends—one man and one woman— and the four of us have now been reading together for sixteen years. We meet on a monthly basis to talk about a novel. We generally convene at a restaurant around seven o'clock and close the place. And we read in projects.

Project one was Proust's *Remembrance of Things Past.* It took us more than a year. But we've done many different projects since. Sometimes it's author based, and sometimes it's thematically based. One year we read Dickinson, Whitman, Emerson, and Thoreau as a preamble to reading four novels of Mark Twain and five of William Faulkner—in an exploration of the American voice. One year we read *Anna Karenina* by Tolstoy, *Madame Bovary* by Flaubert, George Eliot's *Middlemarch*, and Henry James's *Portrait of a Lady*. We called that project: Nineteenth-Century Wives Under Pressure. If you think about those books, all four were written in a twenty-five-year period. You have Tolstoy writing about Russia, Flaubert writing about France, Eliot about England, and James, an American writing about an American who goes to England and ends up in Italy. It's incredible to see how the evolution of Western society in the late nineteenth century is captured in those four books: the rise of industrialism and the middle class, the changing role of the church in society, of women in society, the shifting status of marriage—each of these sea changes are explored in the four books, despite their scattered footprint. Occasionally, we'll take a single author and read a large body of their work chronologically. We did that for Dostoevsky, Raymond Chandler, Gabriel Garcia Marquez, Edith

Wharton, Toni Morrison, and Philip Roth's Zuck-erman books. Actually, Roth and Morrison are two of the three living writers that we've read over the fifteen years, although, sadly, both passed away shortly after we read them.

At any rate, the reading that the four of us have done together has been one of the most consistent and rewarding contributors to my life as an artist.

JEFF: Aside from the bad luck of two of your three living writers dying, why have you chosen to focus on dead writers?

AMOR: As I explained earlier, our mission has been to read books that bear rereading. When we start a project, we want to have reasonable confidence that the books we're going to read are worth our attention, that they will broaden our understanding of the novel as an art form while enriching our lives. It's the pursuit of this sort of book that has sent us back in time.

In saying that, I'm not suggesting that great books are not being written right now. But from my standpoint, history—or time, or whatever you want to call it—does a terrible job of capturing all that is great in art. There are novels and symphonies and paintings of great genius that are irretrievably lost. This has happened for social reasons, political reasons, economic reasons, racial reasons—and due to plain old bad luck. But if history does a terrible job of capturing all that is great in art, it does an *excellent* job of shedding all that is mediocre. If you go back seventy-five years, or even fifty years, time has weeded out all manner of insubstantial art that was popular, au courant, or flashy, but it has retained works of great merit.

Looking back fifty years, we have the advantage as readers that the sample of great work is very diverse in terms of gender, race, ethnicity, class, and style. This is obviously less true when we go back one hundred or one hundred fifty years. But one of the reasons great works of art survive is that they don't speak from a specific corner with a specific agenda. The reason they survive is because they have a relatively open architecture, poetically speaking, where a whole array of connections can be made and conclusions can be drawn, including very subversive ones; and people of all walks of life can be touched and engaged by these works. Shakespeare, of course, is the master of writing in a rich and multilayered style, and that's why he has been read by people all over the world with great interest and illumination for hundreds of years.

NANCY: I teach this theory of why people like the

books they like, because they're looking for particular ways into a book, and all these books that have endured have multiple ways into them: they have character, the prose is great, the plot is enough.

AMOR: I agree entirely. One of the ways I think of it is that the successful novel is a machine for meaning. As you note, the novel has an array of components, such as character, plot, and prose. We can add to this list setting, voice, perspective, structure, imagery, metaphor, allusion, historical reference, dialogue, the expression of ideas and sentiments. A novel is an artistic vehicle that is drawing on all of these elements as part of its composition. The mark of a great novel is that it is engaging as a story, it feels organic in its composition, and yet the way in which all the various components interact creates an infinite number of harmonic combinations in the service of meaning. That's why different readers of great works can discover different ideas, feel different emotions, draw different conclusions, and support the validity of their impressions by pointing to various elements of the text. The best books don't mean one thing. They are machines that can be used to generate all kinds of ideas, including contrasting ones.

NANCY: Don't you think everyone reads a different version of the book? You bring your particular life experiences up to the moment of reading of each book. Which is why what you said about reading a book at age twenty, age forty, age sixty, you have a different experience each time.

AMOR: I do think we each reach a book a little differently, and that as individuals, we also read the same book differently at different times in our lives. So for a book to reach many different readers, and the same reader over time, it has to be generous in its composition. Generous in the way it's designed, so that it doesn't require you to come at it from a particular angle, and insist that you leave it with a particular perspective.

NANCY: Were there any of the books you read in your group you felt cheated or disappointed by?

AMOR: We did a project where we read the works of Nobel Prize winners who didn't write in English. In that project, we read three novels by Kenzaburō Ōe, which left us relatively cold. But in that same project, we also read the Cairo Trilogy, the three novels by Naguib Mahfouz, and those books were a revelation. We all loved them and still talk about them now, many years later. More recently, we read the four novels of the Raj Quartet by Paul Scott. I found that reading experience very reminiscent of the Mahfouz experience. Both authors seem to be drawing on the tradition of the nineteenth-century novel but with a modernist sensibility in order to examine individual lives in the context of sweeping national change in the twentieth century—one in Egypt, the other in India.

JEFF: Let's go back in time a bit in your life. You told us about your adolescent reading. I'm wondering if there's a book that crystalized for you the difference between popular fiction and literature—where you said, "This is a different, and more important, kind of work."

AMOR: I had an English teacher in high school named Dick Baker, who was a great influence. He is a serious reader with a superior intellect and an insatiable curiosity. Not surprisingly, he was also a very demanding teacher, expecting his students to have serious detail-oriented conversations in class and to communicate written thoughts with precision. So to some degree the change you're describing— where I was reading more deeply—occurred in his classroom.

But as a writer, the more precise answer would be my first reading at seventeen of Henry David Thoreau's *Walden*. As I began reading that book, I just couldn't believe that someone could write like that. It's almost like there's a tuning fork inside of us. And sometimes, something we experience or witness can set that tuning fork humming. When it happens to me, I can feel it in every fiber of my being. I feel I'm glimpsing the sublime in a way that's almost over-whelming. As a young person, I had that experience often in nature or in listening to music, but I think Thoreau was the first time I experienced it in language. I would read a paragraph and have to put the book down because I was so overcome, just hum-ming with his poetic intelligence. I still feel that way when I read him.

Having loved reading and writing since child-hood, Thoreau was the first real glimpse for me of what writing could be, and should be. I don't write like Thoreau. But through the arrangement of my words on the page, I do hope to set someone else's tuning fork humming.

NANCY: What about poetry?

AMOR: I'm not as deeply read in poetry as I am in narrative. And I'm nowhere near as knowledgeable about poetry as I am about classic rock lyrics! But I'm a great lover of the epic poets like Homer and Virgil. I'm a lover of Whitman and Dickinson. And

I must have read T. S. Eliot's "Prufrock" a hundred times. For some reason, I never tire of it. I think the first time I read "Prufrock," when I was around nineteen or so, it had that tuning fork effect on me, but in a slightly different way. While reading it, even after a few lines, I felt I knew *everything* about this person. And yet to describe all the impressions I was drawing out of a handful of lines would have taken me pages and pages to explain. Because Eliot has such a wonderful economy of language, and there is so much sentiment and nuance and conflict built into the few words he's using.

NANCY: "I have measured out my life in coffee spoons." That's a life right there.

AMOR: We could talk about that forever. As a young aspiring writer reading a line like that, I felt I was getting close to nuclear fission.

JEFF: Are there other books that have given you that same feeling, that nuclear level of excitement?

AMOR: On a grand scale, it's Melville's *Moby-Dick*. I was so struck by that book that I ended up writing my senior thesis at Yale on it. I think it's unparalleled in American English. Tolstoy's *War and Peace* and Marquez's *One Hundred Years of Solitude* would be two other novels that have reached me in that way.

On the one hand, they were totally surprising and exhilarating in their scope and inventiveness, but they were also somehow perfectly familiar to me— like they had been written in a language that I was born to read.

But as a fifty-five-year-old, I've accumulated forty years of influences. In English, I love Faulkner and Wharton and Conrad and Dickens. Among the Russians, I love Tolstoy, Dostoevsky, Chekhov, Gogol, and Solzhenitsyn. I've enjoyed reading the more "experimental" writers like Borges, Calvino, and Kundera. And then, of course, there's Bob Dylan.

NANCY: Do you ever feel you need a palate cleanser?

AMOR: That's my summer suspense and mystery reading.

NANCY: Do you read Lee Child?

AMOR: I know Lee. I had never read his books until I met him, but now I read them whenever they come out. I think some of the decisions he makes are ingenious.

JEFF: Have you read the Parker books by Donald Westlake [writing as Richard Stark]?

AMOR: I think the Parker books are an extraordinary series.

JEFF: They feel like a big influence on Reacher, right down to the name. Both Reacher and Parker have a singular focus on the task in front of them.

AMOR: But Parker is amoral. Reacher is just dangerous.

JEFF: Right. Reacher doesn't have a conventional morality, but he has his own morality. Parker will do anything he has to do to achieve his goal.

AMOR: But to your point, Westlake's staccato style with its great twists at the end of the paragraphs, and his mesmerizing central character—these attributes are clearly shared by the Reacher books.

NANCY: You're such an active and involved reader— which I think is so exciting, because that's certainly what every author wants a reader to be—do you think about how you can use what you're reading in your writing?

AMOR: Not consciously. And if I found myself doing so, I would fight the instinct. I try to read a book for what it is; I try to understand what an individual author is doing, and *how* they're doing it. But I never ask myself: *How can I use this?*

[Picks up a book and shows us copious underlining and annotations.] Whenever I'm reading, I'm underlining. I'm making marginal notes. Since I was a teenager, one of the things I've done while reading a novel is track the patterns and motifs that emerge. In the first chapter, say the author carefully describes how the main character puts a flower in his lapel before going to a party. Then in the next chapter, the hostess of the party is described dumping the flowers from a vase into a garbage can. The recurrence of the flower will make me stop. I'll wonder, *Why are there these two references to flowers here?* What sort of resonance is that creating for the reader, whether consciously or unconsciously? In what way might the reference to these accessories— accessories that seem the height of elegance at night, only to become trash in the morning—contribute to a reader's growing sense of the characters' lives and the novel's themes?

Then I'm off on the hunt. In the chapters that follow, any time something floral appears, I'll go back and cross-reference it with the original references. And that could be a reference to a petal or pollen, or to a young girl blossoming, to conversation wilting. It's sort of like pulling apart a tapestry, to understand how a certain color of thread contributes to different aspects of the overall picture.

JEFF: Do you consciously use imagery or symbols in that way in your own writing?

AMOR: No. Nor am I implying that other authors are doing so. I suspect that most recurring images, words, and themes in an effective novel are there with only the author's remotest awareness.

When a talented writer is in the groove, as it were, he or she is relying on their instincts, drawing on their subconscious, and trusting in their sense of poetry. These are the forces of inspiration. They are instilling a work with patterns that the author need not be fully aware of but which are essential to a book's composition, tone, and direction. As a result, when we identify a book's central theme, we can absolutely go back and discover scattered images, allusions, and words that have cumulatively shaped that theme.

This is why I think the mastery of elements of craft is so important for a young writer. I like to use the example of Andre Agassi. Agassi, one of the greatest tennis players of the twentieth century, did not have a great forehand. He had *hundreds* of great forehands. Over the course of his training he had to master, yes, the high topspin forehand to return a serve but also the soft forehand while he's rushing the net. He's got to master the high forehand while he's stumbling back to return a lob and another while he's crossing the court. Each one of these forehands is its own shot, and each one he has practiced thousands and thousands of times, so that when he's in the game, it's all second nature. He doesn't have to

think about how to execute his stroke under a particular set of circumstances. He already knows that.
This technical mastery frees him up to be focusing
on the bigger aspects of the game as it's unfolding.

It's the same thing for writers. The equivalent
training is the writing of hundreds of stories. Because each story is an opportunity to experiment,
and master, the elements of craft that we've already
talked about, like characterization, setting, metaphor, imagery, tone, perspective, plot, and structure.
If you've mastered these elements through repetitive
practice, then you don't need to think about them
when you're writing a new chapter. And that allows
you to get in the groove so that the more elusive unconscious artistic influences can express themselves.

JEFF: Is that what you were doing for all the years
before you published *Rules of Civility*? Were you
mastering your craft?

AMOR: Not solely . . . I was in the investment business
for twenty years. But I wrote a lot of fiction before I
got a job—between the ages of fifteen and twenty-
five; I took ten years off from writing fiction during
the early stages of my professional career, then re-
sumed writing fiction in my mid thirties, spending
seven years on a novel that I never submitted for
publication. After all that, I wrote *Rules*.

NANCY: When you were writing *Rules of Civility* and *A Gentleman in Moscow*, do you remember what you were reading? Not that they necessarily directly influenced you, but it would be interesting to know.

AMOR: I'm very careful about that. While I'm writing, I don't want to read anything that will interfere with my work, and that generally means avoiding things that come too *close* to the project, whether in setting, style, or theme. So when I was writing *A Gentleman in Moscow*, I certainly didn't want to read *Grand Hotel* [by Vicki Baum]. Similarly, Wes Anderson's *Grand Budapest Hotel* came out when I was about three-quarters of the way through writing *A Gentleman*, and I assiduously avoided watching it, or even listening to people talk about it. That said, while I'm writing, or in advance, I may read books that are very different from what I'm doing but which might inform my sensibility.

By way of example, my next book is about three eighteen-year-old boys traveling from Nebraska to New York City, and takes place over nine days in 1954. In a quasi preparation for writing this book, I read a lot of books that were written in the mid '50s, but focused on very different material. Flannery O'Connor's first collection of short stories, *A Good*

Man Is Hard to Find; *The Man in the Gray Flannel Suit* by Sloan Wilson; *The Burglar* by noirist David Goodis; and *Go Tell It on the Mountain* by James Baldwin. These were all written in the mid '50s but are radically different books in terms of style, setting, and thematic concern.

JEFF: You're steeping yourself in the era.

AMOR: I try to take it in and forget it. As a novelist, I don't pick a topic, research it, and then write a book. What I do is write books about things I have a long-standing interest in. So I didn't do any applied research for *Rules* or for *A Gentleman in Moscow*. I'm a long-standing fan of the '20s and '30s in America, and of Russian culture in general. So I had already read the novels, listened to the music, studied the paintings. Those are the foundations that I used to invent my books.

Similarly, I have a long-standing interest in the '50s in America. My parents were young adults in the '50s, and I could practically touch the decade when I was a boy. I turned ten in the early '70s, but in my house, the '50s were loud and clear, while Woodstock and Vietnam were distant realities. But I like to take that long-standing familiarity and broaden it a little further by reading or rereading some of the novels of the era. Similarly, I enjoy flipping through the work of a few painters or photographers of an era.

JEFF: Like the Walker Evans photographs that are a touchstone in *Rules of Civility*.

AMOR: Right.

JEFF: Is it fair to say F. Scott Fitzgerald was a great influence on *Rules of Civility*? The overall milieu and also Tinker's transformation seems to mirror Gatsby's.

AMOR: I know this must sound crazy, but I really didn't think too much about *Gatsby* while I was writing *Rules of Civility*. I had a notion that sprang from looking at Walker Evans's subway photos—a notion of a young man who has undergone such a transformation in his personal life over the course of a year that a photo taken of him in 1938 and a photo taken in 1939 look like two totally different people. But while writing *Rules*, what I was primarily focused on was following Katey—following her experience and tracking her point of view. I understand why people draw connections between *Rules* and *Gatsby*, but I don't think there's a female character in *Gatsby* that comes close to Katey.

JEFF: No, certainly not. *Rules* also reminded both Nancy and me of John O'Hara. You talked earlier about the way time weeds out the writers who don't deserve to last. Do you think O'Hara will be weeded out, or will he last?

AMOR: I guess I think he's at some risk, and that's a bittersweet observation for me. I'm on the board of Library of America, the nonprofit that publishes the best of American writing. LOA publishes O'Hara's work because he's such a fine writer. So when I say his longevity is at risk, it's more of a worry that readers are abandoning him. But I like his sensibility a lot. I like his point of view and his social observation. Stylistically, I think he might not stand far enough apart from his peers to hold his place in the canon. But I hope I'm wrong.

JEFF: Well, you're lucky he's not alive or he'd come over and punch you in the nose.

AMOR: I like that about him too!

Some Books in Amor's Library

Harold Bloom, *Where Shall Wisdom Be Found?*
Ray Bradbury, *The Illustrated Man*
George Eliot, *Middlemarch*
T. S. Eliot, "The Love Song of J. Alfred
    Prufrock"
Gustave Flaubert, *Madame Bovary*

Gabriel Garcia Marquez, *One Hundred Years of Solitude*

Henry James, *The Portrait of a Lady*

John le Carré, *Tinker, Tailor, Soldier, Spy* and *The Honourable Schoolboy*

Naguib Mahfouz, The Cairo Trilogy

Herman Melville, *Moby-Dick*

Paul Scott, The Raj Quartet

Henry David Thoreau, *Walden*

Leo Tolstoy, *Anna Karenina* and *War and Peace*

Louise Erdrich

We showed up early for our interview with
Louise Erdrich at Birchbark Books, allowing us an
opportunity to browse the independent store she
opened in 2001. In addition to a carefully curated
selection of Native American, general, and children's
books, the store also sells Native arts and jewelry,
carved Zuni Pueblo fetishes, birdhouses, and signed
copies of all of Louise's books. It also features
a handmade canoe hanging from the ceiling, a
confessional/forgiveness booth for "the dispensation of

random absolution," and a dozen or so dogs who come to work on various days with their people.

An enrolled member of the Turtle Mountain Chippewa, of which her maternal grandfather was tribal chairman, Louise was born in Little Falls, Minnesota, and raised in Wahpeton, North Dakota, where both her parents taught at a boarding school set up by the Bureau of Indian Affairs. The oldest of seven children, she got a nickel from her German American father for every story she wrote when she was young, the beginning of a writing career that took her east to Dartmouth College, where she was part of the school's first class to include women, and Johns Hopkins University, where she earned an MA in creative writing in 1979. By that time, she had already begun publishing her poetry and short fiction, and when she published her first novel, Love Medicine, in 1984, it won the National Book Critics Circle Award for Fiction. She has gone on to publish another fifteen novels, including the 2009 Pulitzer Prize finalist A Plague of Doves and the 2012 National Book Award winner The Round House, as well as more than a dozen other books of short fiction, nonfiction, poetry, and children's literature.

As soon as she arrives at Birchbark, she is greeted by a happy customer who was clearly hoping she'd *meet the store's celebrated owner. After a brief chat with her fan, Louise led us to the store's new basement annex, where we talked about the books that have shaped her imagination.*

———

NANCY: Were you a reader as a child?

LOUISE: Yes, but my family didn't have many books. This was small-town North Dakota. My parents were schoolteachers, but there was no bookstore or anything like that. To get books was not an easy thing. But there was a beautiful library, and it still exists. It is a stately building, one of these classical libraries, on a couple of acres of grass in the middle of Wahpeton. I would walk down there, about a mile, and just spend my time there. One of the few books at home was *Marjorie Morningstar* [by Herman Wouk]. The first problem of my book reading at home was getting it off the top shelf. My fascination was, *Why is that book way up there? Where'd it come from? And when can I get to it?* I saved Herman Wouk's obituary, because I thought, *You started me, Herman, you started me.*

JEFF: How old were you when you learned to read? How did it happen?

LOUISE: I was four when I started reading. I remember that my mother drew the word "look" with a pair of eyes in the middle, and I almost fainted, because I got it! I got it! I could extrapolate from this. So "look" with an eye in each o started me out. Humanized a word. And then the library. I would go and bring back my haul of books. My mom brought me down to the library when I was about five or six.

JEFF: Was *Marjorie Morningstar* before that?

LOUISE: *Marjorie Morningstar* was the first, but I didn't make it up the shelves until I was older. So my unattainable mystery. It was very exciting, to go from the Bobbsey Twins [by Laura Lee Hope] and Nancy Drew [by Carolyn Keene] to *Marjorie Morningstar*, when I finally got the book. It was a black hardcover with silver lettering on the cover.

NANCY: Right. Two different worlds for sure.

LOUISE: Once I was a bit older, I could wander all over town. I could go to the library all by myself. Then, of course, I wanted books like *White Fang*. I wanted to read that Jack London book very badly, so my mother had to write a special note for me. I also wanted this book called *The Nylon Pirates* [by Nicholas Monsarrat]. It had a fantastic description about divorcées on a cruise with their diamonds, and there were jewel thieves seeking to deceive. I didn't know what these fortune hunters really were, but they sounded fascinating. And living in a small North Dakota town, how do you know what a cruise is as a kid? I checked the book out again a few years ago.

NANCY: That must have been really interesting.

LOUISE: When I visit my parents—my father's in his nineties and my mom in her eighties—I still go back to the library. *The Nylon Pirates* was still there. And, of course, I'd first checked it out in the days when there was a card in the back of every book that you signed when you checked it out. Everyone could see that you'd read it.

JEFF: So your fans can come and see what books you checked out as a child?

LOUISE: If anyone had the faintest interest. Now the library's gone all digital, but yes, at the time you could see what everybody in town checked out and read. And that's pretty fine, unless you want to hide *The Nylon Pirates*, or whatever, from other people. Then I read this book called *Animal Farm* [by George Orwell], and I think I've said this before, but it was so instructive to me, because I read it and I thought, *This is the greatest pig book ever written! I can't believe how this guy knows pigs.* That was when I was eight. When I was in high school, I realized *Animal Farm* was about fascism, and I could feel my mind enlarge—I could feel thoughts zinging inside me when I realized that you could write about pigs but it would be about something else. The dawn of metaphor.

NANCY: Were your parents happy with all your reading as a child?

LOUISE: I would carry pillows around to different rooms, and I would secretly put my book under a pillow. I was the oldest, so I had a lot of chores. I'd be called on a lot, although my mother tried to shield me from much of the work. But my dad always had a job for me. So I would shove these books under pillows and then I would slip back in and read. Reading was a sneaky delight for me, and I had to have a book. I still have to have a book. I feel lost without one. It usually has to be a novel. I can dip in and out of most nonfiction, but if I don't have a novel, I feel lost.

NANCY: Did you search out women writers to read?

LOUISE: Not until I got into high school, and into college. Those were the days when everyone read Sylvia Plath.

JEFF: *The Bell Jar* or the poetry? Or both?

LOUISE: It was the poetry I liked. Later on I went to London to study Renaissance literature, and there was an incredible kind of cult around Sylvia Plath—a death cult. Oh God! There was a very dark energy around all that. But for me, they were fiery poems.

"Ariel" is fire for me. Or "Lady Lazarus": "I rise with my red hair / And eat men like air." I used to think about that line while waiting for buses, in Moorhead [Minnesota], in winter. It was very warming. My father's a great one for memorizing poems. All of my siblings know some poems by heart. He still loves to shout them now. We shout them together.

JEFF: Was Sylvia Plath the first poet you fell in love with?

LOUISE: It was probably Emily Dickinson. I loved Louise Bogan; later on, Louise Glück. The Louises. Or [John] Milton, because when you went to Dartmouth in those days, everyone had to read *Paradise Lost* your freshman year. I wasn't a very disciplined reader. I just picked up everything I could and read it.

JEFF: Was there a book that you could say changed your life?

LOUISE: I grew up with a mother who was Chippewa and a German father. There were not many books about Native experience at the time, but there were some captivity narratives. I became obsessed with John Tanner [*The Falcon: A Narrative of the Captivity and Adventures of John Tanner, During Thirty-Years Residence Among the Indians in the Interior of North America*] and eventually wrote the introduction to the Penguin edition. It completely obsessed me, because it was about what Ojibwe life was like during the fur-trade years. A young man had been transported as a captive into an Ojibwe family and was given to a strong mother, Net-no-kwa, one who was so powerful a fur trader that when she brought her boat into the fort, the guns would sound. She was an extraordinary woman, and very shrewd.

NANCY: As a children's librarian, my feeling has always been that kids should both be able to find themselves in the pages of a book and lose themselves in the pages of a book. As a Native American, was that something you lacked? Did you feel you weren't finding yourself in the books you read?

LOUISE: Perhaps that's why I was drawn to science fiction. If you don't see yourself reflected, you can travel to another world. I suppose that was probably what drew me to the captivity narrative. This idea that this was telling me something about my family.

JEFF: Do you remember the first Native writers you read?

LOUISE: Yes. James Welch's *Winter in the Blood* came out in 1972. And before that I had read historical pieces of work. My grandfather wrote a book about our tribal nation, so I knew a few things. But they weren't contemporary works. I had read Scott Momaday, but to read about your own tribe is a more intimate experience. *Winter in the Blood* blew me away. That book told me about myself and my life. The portrait of his grandmother was unforgettable. I could never forget his description of her hands. Like the claws of a tiny crow. The writing was spare, bleak, comical. My world.

Also, Leslie Marmon Silko was writing, and I read everything that she wrote. *Ceremony* was a great book. *The Jailing of Cecelia Capture* [by Janet Campbell Hale] came out around then. Joy Harjo also. I was reading midwestern and western poets, Richard Hugo, Mark Vinz, Linda Hasselstrom, Carol Bly, Robert Bly, James Wright.

NANCY: Did those books influence your poetry writing?

LOUISE: Perhaps, but I really wanted to be a French surrealist.

JEFF: Who doesn't?

LOUISE: I became obsessed with Baudelaire, Rimbaud, André Breton. Later, I found the great narcissist Anaïs Nin, read all of her profoundly self-absorbed diaries, I regret to say. But I had to do it. All the girls did. I wanted to write *Nightwood* [by Djuna Barnes]. I wanted to write anything that was surreal or experimental. I tried very hard to become a French surrealist, or an expatriate writer, even though I didn't leave the country. At last I found Flannery O'Connor. That did something huge for me. Finally a Catholic writer who had this experience of the deep, wacky belief systems of other people, their earnest ferocity. Between Flannery and Jim [Welch], there was a narrow bench. I sat down there to write.

NANCY: Were you reading as a writer when you were young? Were you thinking about how you could do this too?

LOUISE: No, no. But I always kept diaries. They were not literary diaries. They were just about . . . well, I tried to veer away from melodrama—you know, emotional melodrama—but that was very hard to do. I still read the thrashing and moaning sometimes, and feel better about getting older. It was hard to be that young woman. I didn't start reading as a writer until I was writing in college.

JEFF: So when you were younger, you weren't thinking, *I want to be a writer and I need to . . .*

LOUISE: No, I just thought, *I don't belong in this town. Because I will surely, quickly become an alcoholic.* That was exactly what I knew. It seemed impossible that there was another option. I felt very alone in whatever trajectory was mine. But my mother, listening to the radio, heard that Dartmouth College was accepting women and sent away for everything. Just last week she told me, "I still feel bad because I checked the box pretending to be you." Thank God she did it. She kept after me until I applied to colleges far away. She knew I needed to leave.

NANCY: What draws you to the novels you love? I'm kind of assuming it's not the plot that you care most about but the characters and the way it's written.

LOUISE: I have to have some plot, but it doesn't have to drive the book. I love Olga Tokarczuk's *Drive Your Plow Over the Bones of the Dead*. Language used at the behest of a compelling voice, especially a voice that's odd and funny, that draws me. *The Door* by Magda Szabó. And Clarice Lispector.

JEFF: I always wonder about books in translation. Are you getting the writer's voice or the translator's voice?

LOUISE: Both, in a good translation. Olga's sentences in *Flights* all have an idea within them. I loved the character in *Drive Your Plow*. There's times when the plot of a book sticks through like—it's like an umbrella inside out. Oh, here's that plot again. And you know, as a writer, or as an inveterate reader, as you both are, you become very aware of plot points and you feel like you got stuck by the umbrella somehow. [Laughter.]

I do like suspense, something that I want to know more about. Sometimes it's just the voice. And then other times you can see the cliffhanger coming. Elena Ferrante is like that. The language, the voice, was not as compelling as the characters. And the plot—it was as though she was playing a transparent game with you. Because they were hilariously cliffhang-y. She was giving a wink. I thought they were wonderful, but you gave up the idea that you should turn your nose up at plot. Because she let the reader in on her process.

Every summer I go through northern Minnesota, and I stop here or there, wherever I see a pile of old books. I've found books that have been transformative, like *Hope Against Hope* [by Nadezhda Mandelstam]. It's about the time before her husband, Osip, is taken by Stalin's KGB. Her account of the cat-and-mouse game before at last Osip was sent to the gulag. So brave and so closely observed. I've never read anything like it. She studies how he writes, because they're in such tight quarters. Every single moment is so meaningful, every crust of bread, encounter, bottle of wine. The search for a warm coat. They have nothing, they can't make a living, they are watched, hunted. And then what else did I find? I found Stefan Zweig's biography of

Balzac, and again, I thought, *Why worry about my life? Look at Balzac!*

JEFF: Look what Zweig had to go through! [Stefan Zweig fled the Nazi invasion of his native Austria and ended up committing suicide with his wife in Brazil in 1942.]

LOUISE: Yes, Zweig was a genius. Fascists crushed him, murdered Lorca, held Akhmatova's son hostage, sent a generation into exile. Better to have been Balzac in his magnificent squalor.

NANCY: Viet Thanh Nguyen talked to us about the blessing and the responsibility and the curse of standing for your people as a writer. Do you feel that at all?

LOUISE: I try my best to do this as a person, while reserving the right to be human, imperfect. As a writer, perhaps I stand for mixed-bloods, for embracing your confusion. It is my characters who stand for more. Yes, I'm enrolled in my tribe, and this is my community. My family is my treasure. I grew up with schoolteachers. I led a sort of, you know—we were not wealthy, we were clinging to middle class—but I led this life that was secure. Still, there's no way to stay unscathed, no matter what. As a human being and a Native American, you're scathed in a certain way. So just write about it and forget about yourself, I decided. But I am by no means representing anybody else. I have not been elected to do that, after all.

NANCY: I would think you were the first Native American writer many of your readers discovered.

LOUISE: Then, thank God, we have so many extraordinary Native writers. There's Layli Long Soldier—I love her poetry. And Natalie Diaz. My sister Heid is an amazing poet, and she's a very science-y, interesting writer, probably my favorite writer. Of course Tommy Orange's novel [*There There*], and Sherman [Alexie], Linda Hogan. Joy Harjo [US Poet Laureate] has always been one of my favorite writers. Denise Sweet. Eric Gansworth. Terese Mailhot's *Heart Berries*. Tanya Tagaq's *Split Tooth* is very good. There's so much now; the landscape is rich.

JEFF: I'm curious to know if you ever read western genre fiction?

LOUISE: Like Owen Wister [author of *The Virginian*]?

JEFF: Up to Larry McMurtry's *Lonesome Dove*.

LOUISE: I love McMurtry, but he's in a category of his own. Of course I read North Dakotan Louis L'Amour. I have some signed copies of his books that are very valuable to me personally.

JEFF: Were you affected by the way the Native people were portrayed in those books?

LOUISE: I was affected by how Native people are portrayed in the Little House on the Prairie books. They are why I wrote the Birchbark House series.

JEFF: Your recent novel *Future Home of the Living God* ventured into science-fiction territory. Do you read a lot of sci-fi?

LOUISE: I started reading sci-fi in high school, when everyone was reading Arthur C. Clarke, Andre Norton, Roger Zelazny, Isaac Asimov.

JEFF: What other authors do you like?

LOUISE: Ursula Le Guin, of course. The first book of hers I read was *The Left Hand of Darkness*. All of Octavia Butler. Ted Chiang. N. K. Jemisin. And Walter Tevis—

NANCY: Jeff and I are both Tevis fans.

LOUISE: *Mockingbird*! And I also loved *The Queen's Gambit*, but that's not speculative fiction.

JEFF: He has two other books of science fiction as well: *The Steps of the Sun* and a collection of stories called *Far from Home*.

LOUISE: I haven't read those—now I'll have to read everything. Oh, and Frank Herbert. I keep rereading the Dune [series], which is about climate catastrophe.

NANCY: What about short-story writers—who are your favorites?

LOUISE: Lorrie Moore. Alice Munro. I love George Saunders's stories. John L'Heureux—I like his stories a lot. Also I liked Carmen Machado's *Her Body and Other Parties*. Also, there's Karen Russell, Clarice Lispector, Isak Dinesen, and Penelope Fitzgerald's books *The Blue Flower* and *The Beginning of Spring*, which are short, like novellas. But again, Lorrie Moore. I think Lorrie Moore started everything for me. It's so hard to be funny—that's the hardest thing, to be funny and also heartbreaking.

JEFF: Is there a book that you just absolutely couldn't imagine not owning, whether or not you think you're ever going to go back and reread it?

LOUISE: Yes: the collected stories of Chekhov. That's what I read if I'm disturbed, depressed, or can't get back to sleep. I have Chekhov next to the bed. I would never read Flannery O'Connor for comfort. The humanity, and the clarity, and the sense of acceptance, and I wouldn't really say kindness so much as acceptance in Chekhov's work—I go back to it constantly. The books I take with me on my book tours are always the ones that are sustaining. I take Chekhov, and I often take *Middlemarch*.

JEFF: Are your books kept in any particular order?

LOUISE: My books are organized. You could ask me about any book I own and I know where it would be. But it's funny, isn't it? To have this secret library within the folds of your brain where you can go to anytime? I can close my eyes and see where my books are, and the books behind the books. The ones I've read, the ones I plan to read. I collect books about North Dakota and books about Ojibwe history and culture. Plus, I have a collection that is just books that I need, like books on farming in North Dakota. Lots of books about that and about the fur trade. Books about saints, shelves of fairy tales, guides to birds and insects, shelves of spy novels and sea novels.

NANCY: What's the best part about being a writer who owns Birchbark Books & Native Arts?

LOUISE: When you have a book you really love, you can press it into people's hands. Also, I can go in and find someone to talk to about books. Fortunately, I have a family of readers, so we also talk about books all of the time. Last winter we were all reading about Stalin and the gulags and we went on and on and on—it got terribly bleak at our house. We read Svetlana Alexievich [winner of the 2015 Nobel Prize for Literature] and then Martin Amis's book on Stalin, a host of works on what life was like during that era. We were just digging in deeper and deeper. It became unbearably sad because after all of this struggle and darkness, Putin.

We got out of it by watching a brutal comedy about the death of Stalin.

JEFF: The one with Steve Buscemi?

LOUISE: Yes. Phew.

JEFF: Haven't seen that.

LOUISE: You have to see it. It's dark, because it's true, absurd, brutal. So that got us out. Finally we said we had to leave.

JEFF: Did you watch *Doctor Zhivago* while you were doing all this?

LOUISE: No. This winter I'm going back in, reading *Zhivago*. I have to be desperate to choose the movie over the book, which tells you where we were last year. But no, we just had to get out, we had to leave Siberia. Because it was so bad *here*, you would not have believed it. You do not want to be mentally in Siberia during the Minnesota winters. It's overkill.

Some Books and Authors in Louise's Library

Sherman Alexie

Djuna Barnes, *Nightwood*

Janet Campbell Hale, *The Jailing of Cecelia Capture*

Anton Chekhov

Natalie Diaz

George Eliot, *Middlemarch*

Joy Harjo

N. K. Jemisin

Layli Long Soldier

Terese Marie Mailhot, *Heart Berries*

Nadezhda Mandelstam, *Hope Against Hope*

Leslie Marmon Silko, *Ceremony*

Lorrie Moore

Flannery O'Connor

Tommy Orange, *There There*

Magda Szabó, *The Door*

Tanya Tagaq, *Split Tooth*

John Tanner, *The Falcon*

Walter Tevis, *Mockingbird*

Olga Tokarczuk, *Drive Your Plow Over the Bones of the Dead*

James Welch, *Winter in the Blood*

Dave Eggers

We *met Dave Eggers in San Francisco, at the offices
of McSweeney's, the quarterly literary journal and
publishing company he founded in 1998, across
the street from 826 Valencia, the children's writing
nonprofit he co-founded in 2002. In between starting
those two thematically connected organizations,
Eggers published his first book, the ironically yet
accurately titled memoir* A Heartbreaking Work of
Staggering Genius, *which established him as one of his
generation's leading literary voices.*

*Born in Boston in 1970, Eggers moved with his
family to the Chicago suburb Lake Forest and attended
the University of Illinois at Urbana-Champaign. His
college education was interrupted before graduation
by the deaths of both of his parents from cancer and
his subsequent decision to focus on raising his eight-
year-old brother. They moved to Berkeley, where their
older sister was starting law school, and where Dave
worked as a graphic designer and eventually started
the satirical magazine* Might. *All of this became the
subject of* A Heartbreaking Work, *and in the two
decades since Dave has published upwards of twenty
books, including the acclaimed novels* You Shall Know
Our Velocity, A Hologram for the King, The Circle,
and Heroes of the Frontier.

*In addition to being a prolific writer, Dave is
also a prolific philanthropist: he has founded or
co-founded several nonprofits in addition to 826
Valencia, including the human rights organization
Voice of Witness and ScholarMatch, which finds
donors for students who need help with college tuition.
With everything on his plate—he is also married to
fellow author Vendela Vida, with whom he has two
children—it's amazing Dave finds time to read, but he
does, and we spent an enjoyable afternoon discussing
many of his favorite books.*

NANCY: Were you a big reader growing up?

DAVE: When I was a kid, I was not a big reader. I remember this [*holds up* Corduroy *by Don Freeman*], which I must have had my mom read to me nine hundred times. I was a repetition person. I tell parents all the time, "If your kids aren't reading a lot on their own, don't worry. Especially with the more active kids, it'll come around. You've just got to keep putting things in front of them." I was in a biggish family, and my parents didn't always have time to read to us. But I remember reading *Corduroy* a thousand times, or rather having it read to me a thousand times.

In terms of willingly picking up books and reading them myself, I was not so eager. In second grade, we had library class, where we had to check out one book a week. The idea, of course, was that our teachers wanted us to check out a different book each week. But I gamed the system. I only checked out one book, the same book, every week for a year. I just kept renewing it. It was a coffee-table book about elephants, with hundreds of photos of elephants accompanied by National Geographic–like text. And I'm absolutely sure I never read any of that text.

Mostly what I read until I was in high school

were books like this. I was an aspiring artist—I was a painter, an illustrator, and a cartoonist, and everything I read really needed a visual component for me. So I would just pore over books like this when I was in third, fourth, fifth grade. Books about gnomes, giants, *The Art of the Dark Crystal, The Flight of Dragons, 20th Century Foss*. Always these big or oversize books full of fantastical worlds.

JEFF: When did that change?

DAVE: I should say that I always read what I was assigned, and I was in a Great Books program and enjoyed that. But it wasn't until high school that I had that experience where you choose a book yourself and it rips your head off. I had a class called Advisory, in a small room that was just floor to ceiling books, and pillows, and it was deadly quiet. And you could not do anything else but read. What not everyone realizes about active kids is that you have to isolate them completely sometimes from all temptations and all distractions to get them to calm down enough to read, and I was one of those kids. So in this class, I picked up *Dune*. I didn't know anything about it except that it had a cool cover. I'd looked at science-fiction renderings, but I'd never read science fiction before. And I just read *Dune* in the first month, in that class, one hour a day. And I'd never had that kind of wholly immersive reading experience before—on my own, with unassigned reading. *Dune* was such a fully realized other world, though it had biblical and historical echoes, and the richness of that world was new to me. The next month, I read *Dune Messiah*, and I remember the exact moment I left that Advisory room having read it. I remember wandering the hallways of my high school, feeling completely apart. It felt like I'd doubled my life, as if I'd lived another full existence, and after this other, complete life—because Paul, at the end of *Dune Messiah*, is presumed dead—was dropped back into my previous life. I didn't know which world I was more in, but I felt that world of *Dune* was more three-dimensional than my high school, at least for a day or two.

NANCY: After that, were you hooked?

DAVE: After that, from sophomore year on, I was in pretty advanced English classes, and I had great teachers. I turned into one of those kids who very badly wanted to impress their teachers. We were assigned *Macbeth*, but I'd also bring in Faulkner, you know, [laughter] hoping that Mr. Criche would see it. I always had *As I Lay Dying* with me, for almost a year. But I wrote a paper about *Macbeth*, and Mr. Criche wrote at the top of it, "Sure hope you become a writer. A." Just that one sentence changed my life.

We'd never had a writer anywhere in the family. I'd never thought about the possibility of being a writer, even vaguely, until he said that. And that was sort of my touchstone, or my sort of shield, for the next ten or fifteen years.

NANCY: Did you go on to read more science fiction after the Dune books?

DAVE: I haven't read much since. I read Lethem's *Girl in Landscape*, and that might have been the next science-fiction novel I read after those two Dune books. I have no real explanation why I didn't go back to science fiction. More recently, in the last ten years, I've read a lot of Bradbury, and I loved Kim Stanley Robinson's *2312*, and I love the form. But in high school, my friends and I, because we were pretentious idiots, we were trying to get through Sartre and Camus. We were reading all the existentialists.

NANCY: Suffering internally.

DAVE: In the suburbs of Chicago. It was such a hard life. [Laughter.]

JEFF: Was that part of wanting to be a writer, the suffering and the existential nature of life in suburban Chicago?

DAVE: No, not really. I came into it from the editing and publishing side, at least in part. I had a great creative writing teacher, Mrs. Lowey, who ran the literary magazine. There was nobody else doing it, really. When I joined, they had a staff of two, so by senior year I was the editor. I edited the magazine and eventually wrote for the yearbook and had a column in the daily newspaper, and then when I went to college it was all the same stuff: editing the magazine, writing for the daily paper, working as a photographer, designer, cartoonist, all of that. I got really hooked on being involved in all the different aspects of publishing.

NANCY: Nothing's changed.

DAVE: Not much along those lines. I still love design, I love editing, I love reading a manuscript that's almost there and helping it become its best self. The joy of publishing somebody else so far exceeds publishing your own work, you know. It's really addictive. [Points to the McSweeney's back room, where the books are stored.] Because, you know, every book that we were able to bring into print was a miracle and an honor.

JEFF: It must be the same when one of your students gets published.

DAVE: Absolutely. Sally Wen Mao was a student at 826 Valencia when she was fifteen. She used to come all the way from Sunnyvale, about an hour and a half, and stay overnight at her aunt's house to take this class, and then go home. She has a new book of poems called *Oculus*, published by Greywolf [Press], that just had a three-page spread in *The New Yorker*, illustration of her, very fancy. She's awesome. Very hilarious. And then Daniel Gumbiner was a student, maybe two years older than Sally, and his book *The Boatbuilder* was longlisted for the National Book Award. We published his book at McSweeney's, actually. I loved his manuscript. I said, "This is one of my favorite books; you're going to have your pick of publishers and agents." But it didn't happen. He couldn't even get agents to take it on. So I said, "You know, Daniel, you could get paid better somewhere else, but we'll publish it, it'll be in print, it'll be a start, and then you'll have plenty of other books down the road." So we published it and it was very quiet—you know, the calm before the calm. But then the longlist comes out, and he's on the list, and it was such a vindication for all that work you put in, and it's nice that books published by small houses can get some recognition here and there.

NANCY: What are you reading now?

DAVE: I'm reading Martha Gellhorn, who was married to Hemingway for four years—

NANCY: I remember how much I enjoyed *Travels with Myself and Another*—

DAVE: That's what I'm reading.

NANCY: Isn't it good?

DAVE: It's so great.

NANCY: And the other in *Myself and Another*, Hemingway.

DAVE: I just finished the essay about China, when they travel together and she calls him the Unwilling Companion, UC for short. But I discovered her in a collection of World War II reporting, with Ernie Pyle and A. J. Liebling and a slew of others, and you know, a couple of the very best pieces in this giant 800-page collection were hers. And it was my birthday week, so Vendela got me a bunch of Gellhorn, and Gellhorn is so funny but so cranky, in a very funny way, as a traveler. But her best piece from World War II is when she accompanied the Russian Army into Berlin. It was the most joyous, hilarious, full-of-life piece you could imagine. It's the last days of World War II, and I don't know if anybody else could've written it that way. And it just occurred to me that I feel like Gellhorn got short shrift because of the Hemingway association. You know, we know that the history of literature is wildly sexist, but Gellhorn's work, to some extent, was hurt by the connection. She was a really well known war correspondent, she'd been everywhere, she'd go anywhere. And then just because she marries this guy, she's diminished. His reputation is enhanced and hers reduced. But I think she's the better journalist.

NANCY: Do you just go on these reading jags, like with Gellhorn?

DAVE: Yeah, it's just like anything, where you want that next book. Vendela reads everything. She'll read all the new books. I don't. I gravitate toward dead people, I think. I went through a Willa Cather jag after finding *O Pioneers!* somewhere. A lot of times I go to used bookstores, or used book sales at the library, and find old editions by dead people. And I'd never read this. Do you know this one by her? [Holds up Willa Cather's *Shadows on the Rock*.]

JEFF: No.

NANCY: Me either.

DAVE: Nobody on Earth has read this book, and I think it's far and away her best. *O Pioneers!* is close, but *Shadows* is the most perfect novel of hers. This is her. She really knows what she's doing with *Shadows on the Rock*, even though it's seventeenth-century French fur traders in Canada. But she knows pioneer life, and it's the most convincing period novel, and it's not tough sledding, like Fenimore Cooper, for example. *Shadows on the Rock* is almost a modern novel; the language is vivid but not too ornate or cumbersome. Not to besmirch Fenimore, but I think Cather's the more deft painter of the era.

JEFF: One of my favorite books that you published is *Samuel Johnson Is Indignant* by Lydia Davis. What a great title! And then the cover is so beautiful.

DAVE: David Byrne took the photo on the cover.

JEFF: I didn't know that.

DAVE: Yeah, we were publishing him at the same time. And I showed Lydia a bunch of pictures, and she chose that one. We always give authors first crack at a cover, which is another obsession of mine. They should have some say. Lydia's great. You think you're going to meet this severe person, because her work is so clipped and precise. But she's so friendly, so nice, really easygoing, and she was really fun to work with. We still publish her from time to time [in *Timothy McSweeney's Quarterly Concern*] whenever she sends us anything. I was in New York when I was first introduced to her work. It just sort of blew me away. I had this whole period when I moved to New York, that's when I discovered [Donald] Barthelme and other formally experimental people, like Diane Williams and Lydia Davis. But in my twenties, more than anyone else, really, the short-story writer I studied most closely was Lorrie Moore.

NANCY: We love Lorrie Moore.

DAVE: There was nobody more important when I was in college. My two favorite writers were Lorrie Moore and Joan Didion. Those people taught me how to write. Lorrie Moore was the first author who I was a completist about. In Champaign-Urbana, Illinois, where I went to college, there was only one store that had *The New Yorker*, and I went there every week to see if Moore was in it. Because that's where her stories appeared, nowhere else.

JEFF: I was like that with Denis Johnson, when the *Jesus' Son* stories were coming out in *The New Yorker* and *The Paris Review*. I know, later, McSweeney's published a lot of his stuff.

DAVE: That's a funny story, because we couldn't really pay anybody, so we'd offer to barter. And Denis said, "Well, I need a deck built in my place." In Idaho, up near the panhandle. And one of our editors, Eli Horowitz, he was a carpenter. So Eli said, "Okay, I'll go out, I'll spend the summer out there and help build the deck." Which he did, and he and Denis became really tight. And later, Denis did a bunch of plays down the street at Intersection for the Arts, for this theater company, Campo Santo, so he was around a lot for a while, and there was no sweeter guy you'd ever meet. He was this explosive genius, but he was just the friendliest, sweetest guy. It still hurts so bad that he died so young. But I think I recommend that book, *Jesus' Son*, as much as any, especially to people that are reluctant readers, in part because it's short. Don't get me started on short novels. They're so rare now, and so disrespected in this era when no book under six hundred pages is considered significant. But *Jesus' Son*—I don't know if there's a more perfect book, and it wouldn't be as perfect if it were a page longer.

JEFF: My favorite book ever.

DAVE: Really? Wow. His last story in *The New Yorker*, "The Largesse of the Sea Maiden," I loved it so much, I wrote him a note. That story just had everything in it. And he wrote a really nice note back, and then he was gone six months later.

NANCY: What about mysteries? Are you a mystery reader?

DAVE: *Motherless Brooklyn* by Lethem was the first mystery I ever read. I still haven't read too many mysteries, but for a while we lived in Brooklyn near each other, so I got to know him then. He's an encyclopedia. Nobody like him. I remember seeing him speak at panels when I was maybe thirty, and I guess he's maybe six, seven years older than me, but I'd never seen anybody with that eloquence about what he did.

NANCY: I see a lot of Saul Bellow here. I take it you're a big Saul Bellow fan.

DAVE: Whenever anyone asked me my favorite book, for about twenty years, it was always *Herzog*. I never read for plot; even now I don't really. It doesn't matter to me that much what happens. I don't turn the pages to see who did it. I'm reading for the quality of the prose, a way of seeing the world.

NANCY: I'm exactly the same way.

DAVE: And never does it matter in Bellow's books what happens. It's about the premises and the ideas, and he would sort of lasso all of the world and history and philosophy and existence and love, and put it in one page. Every page he does that. Next page he does it again. I still don't think anyone's equaled that. The density of his prose, the immensity of what he can convey in a paragraph, and the workings of a twentieth-century mind. And then he's still a working-class guy from Chicago, so there's wit there, and there's self-deprecation. *Herzog*, to me, has the most beautiful sentences in English in the twentieth century. And then put Ralph Ellison up there of course. When I was writing my first book, the memoir, *Invisible Man* was the book I kept close to me, because I don't know of any American book that ever balanced the personal and the universal so perfectly. The architecture of that book is astounding. So I had *Herzog* nearby, and *Invisible Man*; when I felt like I was writing lazy, I could just go back to that, keep me honest a little bit. People read Ellison of course, but I just can't get anyone to read Bellow. I recommend *Herzog* to everybody, even the real readers I know. But no one reads him. No one gets through *Herzog* anymore. It's baffling.

JEFF: It's not an easy book. It requires effort. And I think maybe he's just been overshadowed by Roth.

DAVE: But they're so different. I don't even think they're remotely similar writers.

JEFF: And Bellow was Roth's favorite writer.

DAVE: I know. Have you read the letters? Benjamin Taylor's collection is so great. Bellow's letters are unbelievable. Everything he writes is very gentlemanly and kind, and his sentences, in these letters, are often just as good as anything he wrote anywhere. And Roth really, you know, sees him as a father figure. Other writers did too, and he was very kind to them. I think Roth wrote to him after *Goodbye, Columbus*, and Bellow said something like, "I've been here in the workshop for many years, but I still love the sound of good metal striking iron," or something like that. Some sort of blacksmith metaphor that he used. And I thought, *Well, if anybody* *ever got that written to them by Saul Bellow, that would give them strength for decades.*

I went through a letters phase, you know, reading letters. I read all of Bellow's, Hemingway's, and then Vendela found this book of Chekhov's letters, and his are insane! He sounds like the craziest man you've ever met. "Ah, I hate you, I want to kill you, I wish you'd never lived! Love, Chekhov." It's really such a bizarre thing.

JEFF: It's a Russian thing.

DAVE: It's funny, but yeah. I don't know if there will ever be letters collections from this era.

JEFF: Yeah, right, because texts from one writer to another just don't have the same ring to them.

DAVE: After the Bellow book, I was so enthralled with those letters and how he wrote them, I decided to try to resurrect this art. I thought, *I'm going to write careful letters to people.* So I started putting real effort into letter writing, via email or regular mail, and I scared everybody. I'd meet somebody and I would write some flowery thing about how much I liked their work, and I'd never hear back from them. I think it was just considered too much. We don't do that now. We're supposed to say, "Hey," emoji.

JEFF: Thumbs-up. [Laughter.]

NANCY: I see you've got *Pale Fire* here, which is one of my all-time favorite books.

DAVE: Well, *Lolita* was a book I reread a lot throughout my twenties and thirties, and loved it for the sentences, the joy of it, the bounding lyricism, but it's hard to read it now. I don't know how we saw past it for so long, but once I was working with young people, and—you know.

JEFF: It's creepy.

DAVE: It's horrifying. I can't—I don't understand. I don't understand it now. But for so long I think we all suspended our horror because it is so beautifully written. It still is, and it's so funny, and it still reads like it was written yesterday, but I can't enjoy it now. I have a thirteen-year-old daughter, so it's not easy reading now. But anyway, *Pale Fire*—

NANCY: I think about Nabokov, what you said about Bellow, that the sentences are just—

DAVE: So he's the other guy that—

NANCY: At the sentence-level—

DAVE: And he, in a way, was writing in a second language. Well, who knows how often he was speaking English with his governess, who I guess was English, but—

NANCY: Do you know that story, where somebody asked him, somebody said, "Well, you know a lot of authors say that they don't know what their characters are going to do," and Nabokov said something like, "My characters are my galley slaves!" That he knew exactly what they would do.

DAVE: That's so funny.

NANCY: But he was not—he was a little difficult.

DAVE: Didn't seem like a guy you'd want to hang out with necessarily.

JEFF: What about memoirs? Your first big splash was a memoir.

DAVE: Yeah, I've read maybe two.

NANCY: Really?

JEFF: We were talking before we came here about two we both love: *This Boy's Life*—

DAVE: Well, [Tobias] Wolff was the one for me.

JEFF: And the other one was *Stop-Time*.

NANCY: Frank Conroy's *Stop-Time*.

DAVE: Yeah, never read it. Is it good?

NANCY: Yeah, it is good. Really, really good.

JEFF: It's great. When I read *This Boy's Life*, I thought he's obviously read *Stop-Time*, because there's a direct line there from *Stop-Time* to *This Boy's Life*.

DAVE: Wolff was huge for me.

JEFF: Yeah, what a writer!

DAVE: He was the first living writer who really gave me advice. I interviewed him, with another friend. We were doing this magazine called *Might*, and it was satirical, and my friend and I were both smart-asses. So we interviewed Wolff in the early '90s, and we made some stupid joke about the literary world being competitive, and he gave us a smackdown. "What are you talking about?" he said. "This is books. This is literature. It's not competitive." It was the first time I'd heard anybody say, "A rising tide lifts all boats." I'd never heard that expression before. I was twenty-five, and he explained the concept, and we walked away totally dazed, and I never forgot it.

When we go back and get into the history of the last thirty or forty years and the creative writing programs and everything, Wolff is going to be the most influential guy. Because he was at Syracuse and Stanford, and everyone glommed on to wherever he was—that program was the best. George Saunders worked with him and took that attitude of we're not going to compete, we're not going to go after each other, we're going to support each other. There's nothing worse than trying to do this naked, vulnerable thing, writing your pain and your fears, and then being among people trying to cut each other down. It's so sick. It's so wrong. It's so counterproductive. It can never help anybody.

Wolff and Saunders are just these big-hearted,

warm people who created radically different atmospheres from other creative writing programs. So now you see the people who direct programs all over the country who came up under the two of them, and it's so much different than it was in the '70s, when it was kind of nastier, where writers were always trying to feel like they had to one-up each other and fight in public. And that's totally gone away as far as I know, and I attribute a lot of that to Wolff, who set a different standard. He was honorable and self-secure and didn't see diminishing another writer as necessary for his own success. That's a sickness. Now, overall, I think it's so much healthier.

JEFF: It seems like you foster that with everything you do: the nonprofits and McSweeney's and everything else.

DAVE: Well, it's like Wolff said: "A rising tide lifts all boats."

Some Books and Authors in Dave's Library

Donald Barthelme
Saul Bellow, *Herzog*
Willa Cather, *Shadows on the Rock*

Anton Chekhov, *The Selected Letters of Anton Chekhov*

Lydia Davis

Joan Didion

Ralph Ellison, *Invisible Man*

Don Freeman, *Corduroy*

Martha Gellhorn, *Travels with Myself and Another*

Daniel Gumbiner, *The Boatbuilder*

Frank Herbert, *Dune*

Denis Johnson, *Jesus' Son*

Sally Wen Mao, *Oculus*

Lorrie Moore

Vladimir Nabokov, *Pale Fire*

Diane Williams

Tobias Wolff, *This Boy's Life*

Laurie Frankel

*L*aurie Frankel lives in a comfortable hillside house in *Seattle's Queen Anne neighborhood with her husband, Paul, and their preteen daughter. As Laurie has written in her occasional nonfiction, her daughter is adopted. As Laurie has also written, her daughter used to be a son. The challenges of raising a transgender child are front and center in Laurie's life, so it's not surprising they became front and center in her latest novel,* This Is How It Always Is. *A New York* Times *bestseller, it looks at the challenges of raising a*

transgender child in the twenty-first century—though, as Laurie is quick to point out, the multichild family in her novel is nothing like her own single-child family.

Laurie's talent for combining an absorbing plot with sympathetic characters and smart, frequently humorous prose, is also evident in her first two novels. Her first, The Atlas of Love, *is about another unconventional family, with three graduate students co-parenting a child. Her second,* Goodbye for Now, *is about love, death, and whether a brilliant computer scientist's algorithm can allow us to communicate with the dead.*

A college literature professor before she became a full-time writer, Laurie has books shelved all over her house, including a prized first edition of The Great Gatsby, *as well as numerous copies of the literary work that she returns to most often, Shakespeare's* Hamlet. *After a brief introduction to her husband and a quick scan of the books in her living room, we sat down at her dining room table and talked about—what else?— books.*

―――――――

NANCY: How did your love of reading come to be?

LAURIE: My parents read to me every night before I went to bed until I was in middle school. I remember getting made fun of by other kids for this. I don't know how they knew, but it was definitely after other parents' kids had stopped reading to them. I was taken to the library regularly, and I was given books as gifts, so it's probably due to a combination of all those things. I was allowed to read whatever I wanted, set loose in the library to do as I would. And I was not discouraged from rereading things, so when I became obsessed with the Beezus and Ramona books [by Beverly Cleary] nobody ever told me to stop reading them and find something new. And my parents are both big readers, so there were books around the house. And I was allowed to read those too.

JEFF: Were there characters that you really identified with when you were a kid?

LAURIE: It's interesting because I always identified more with Ramona than Beezus despite the fact that I'm the older sister and frankly was a pretty well-behaved child. I was really afraid of not being well-behaved and still I aspired to be Ramona, the badly behaving sister. I wanted to be Pippi Long-stocking, because she was so cool. And again, such a risk taker, and I wasn't. So I think it was less that I identified with than I wished I were like these girls that were risk takers and adventurers. I spent a long time thinking how I could make my life like Meg's in *A Wrinkle in Time* [by Madeleine L'Engle].

JEFF: What about when you got older? When you were in high school, college? What was your reading experience like?

LAURIE: In high school we were assigned the canon, more or less, and everyone else felt grumbly about it, like, "Oh, this is really boring and I don't want to read this." And I had the opposite reaction, where I was like, "Where has this been? This is amazing!" Because I had been reading YA books, and they were good, and they were interesting, and they were age appropriate, but then I was given *The Great Gatsby*, and it blew my mind how good the writing was and how amazing these characters were.

I have very clear memories of reading the beginning of *Hamlet* the first time, waiting for it to get boring. And it never got boring. And here I am, all of these years later, and that's still how I feel about it. The books I read and the books I write are very character driven, and yet at first what I loved was at the level of the sentence. And at the construction level. How this particular thing is raised in chapter one, and then I'd forgotten about it, but oh, look, it's motif, and it's going to come back, and I wasn't even paying attention, and there it is again. That stuff rocked my world.

NANCY: Are you enjoying sharing books you loved with your daughter?

LAURIE: Yes, absolutely. She and I have read all of those books I loved as a child. Not only do we get to read them together but we can talk about them. We have this shared language and it's like we have friends in common, these people who we know together, these experiences we do together, and that's great too.

JEFF: Has your attitude toward the canon changed as the political environment in the country has changed? Have you found that there were books that you loved that you can no longer love?

LAURIE: I read much more critically than I did when I was fifteen, of course. But I also think I am more understanding than I was then, of different times, different values, different sensibilities. A different sense of what it means to read critically. And therefore, more forgiving, I guess. I also think I have come to value some stories themselves apart from the authors—which is heightened for me by becoming one. You learn the difference between the necessity of one's public persona versus who you actually are as a human being.

NANCY: Does reading equal pleasure for you, or is there that line through the equals sign?

LAURIE: It's like that wavy equal sign. What does that wavy equal sign mean? Sort of? Approximately? The answer is yes, and also never. All reading is pleasurable. I love reading. It's all pleasurable for me and yet I'm never not working. Everything I read, I am reading critically, with an eye toward *How is this helping me?* Or *How can I use this?* Or *How can I avoid this?* Or *What are they doing?* Looking at how it's put together, and how it works, and why this sentence is great, and how this book began, and why they've chosen to narrate from this point of view and . . . All of those things I never turn off. I don't remember a time when that was not true. It doesn't bother me to have to be doing that. Once my cousin and I were on vacation, and I'm sitting on the beach reading whatever I was reading with my pen in my hand making notes in the margins. And she was like, "Do you always do that?" And I said, "What?" I didn't even know what she was talking about. She's a big reader too, but she said it would make her miserable to always have to be working while she was reading for pleasure and always have to be reading like she was studying for an English exam. And I said that doesn't make me miserable at all. That is part of reading—part of reading is the words, your eyes reading these words on the page, and they go in your brain, and then you write stuff in the margins. For me that is part of the reading process. I wouldn't give it up.

NANCY: So you underline in your books.

LAURIE: Lots of underlining. It's nice to have a record. Sometimes when I reread I actually change pen colors so I can see what I thought the first time versus the second time or reading it for myself versus teaching it. You never know when you pick up a book what it is that is going to ring true for you, in what part of your life. For instance, Mark Haddon's *A Spot of Bother* changed my life. I like his other books as well, but they're not necessarily in my top five. But I love that particular book. It isn't so much that I think, *Wow, this is the greatest thing ever written,* as much as I think, *Oh, look, here's how this is done. Here's how this goes together.* And why this is so enjoyable, and why you get to the end and it's revelatory and makes you feel and think and learn, and that is life-changing in a really interesting way, I think. How a book changes my life is often a surprise to me, so I write in them and about them. Like, maybe a book has nothing to do with my writing, but it's changing my attitude towards parenting or whatever. Or, you know, I would never write this kind of book, it's not my kind of book, it has nothing to do with me, but look at this sentence! So then I underline in it, and I put it on a bookshelf, and I forget where it is, but then I'll think of it again, I'll remember there's something remarkable in that book about a third of the way through on a left-hand page, and after tearing up the house for an hour and a half, I find the book and I flip through it, and there's my note and this record of my awe at the time!

JEFF: How do you choose what to read at any given time?

LAURIE: That's such a good question. It varies widely depending on any number of things. Right now I am in what I hope are late-stage revisions of the novel I am currently working on, which is written in three alternating first-person voices. I'm disinclined to write in the first person; therefore, I'm trying to limit myself to only reading things that are written in the first person. So I was going back through my recent-ish list of books to read, but looking only for books that are written in the first person, which actually turned out to be a relatively small number, at least on my list, at least at the moment. I was surprised, because it's one of those things I would've guessed was about fifty-fifty and in fact was not. So I chose *The Mars Room* by Rachel Kushner, which is killing me at the moment. It's beautiful, but it's brutal. It's really hard. It takes place in a woman's prison and is the kind of project I would come up with and then immediately throw out, because the amount of research you'd have to do is staggering. She does that research so well and then crafts this amazing novel with it.

JEFF: So typically do you seek out books that are in the third person?

LAURIE: No. What I read really depends on what I'm currently working on. A while back I was reading only books with multiple narrators, whether or not it was written in the first person. Before that I was looking at books about big families, because there's one in this new novel of mine. At the moment I'm also reading lots of things to blurb, so I've not necessarily chosen them, which is a problem I am really lucky to have. So really, sometimes I'm reading something because someone asked me to nicely; sometimes I'm reading something because I've put it on reserve at the library and it's become available; and sometimes I'm reading what I'm reading because I've gone up to Queen Anne Books [in Seattle] to buy a birthday present for a party that my kid is going to and while

I'm there accidentally bought three other books, and I'm reading those.

JEFF: Are there writers whose books you'd never miss reading?

LAURIE: I have to read Ruth Ozeki and Karen Joy Fowler the first day their new books come out. Richard Russo as well. Kate Atkinson. Recently I've become a complete evangelist for Naomi Alderman. I'm going to say this on tape: I honestly think her book *The Power* is the best book I've read this decade. I read it when I was on book tour—I read it on an airplane, crying and crying, not because it was sad but because I couldn't believe how good it was, and how she was pulling this thing off! The woman in the seat next to me was like, "Oh my God, are you okay?" and I was like, "Oh, it's this book," and she was like, "Oh, I don't like to read sad books," and I was like, "It's not sad," *sobbing, sobbing*. So amazing. So then I went and read her three earlier books. They are all really good and they are all wildly, wildly different from one another. But *The Power* blew me away. I couldn't believe it. And another novel that I loved for the same reason—playing an idea out to the very end—is Omar El Akkad's *American War*. What an achievement that is, especially for a first novel.

NANCY: What about rereading?

LAURIE: I'm a big proponent of rereading. Sometimes I feel bad about rereading because there's so much to read and I'm never going to get through all of it, and here I am reading something I already read and already love. Whereas if I pick up something new, I might love it, but then again I might not love it, and then I'm just irritated. Which isn't good. But also, it happens not infrequently that I loved something the first time and I don't love it the second time. But if I go back and read David Mitchell, I know I'm going to love it, because I love it every time, because I've already loved it. Because I love his first-person-ness, and in fact everything he does. I'm reading *Black Swan Green* again and *Slade House*. And *Slade House* is useful for me at the moment because it's all first person, but each chapter is narrated by a different narrator. It's such an excellent lesson in voice.

Another thing I do that's weird is I read while writing—literally *while* writing, with my laptop in my lap and the book on my desk. Or the other way around. Because it's useful to me to have something that both reminds me how to write but is also inspirational.

NANCY: Are you a short-story reader?

LAURIE: When I was teaching, I read a lot of them,

and now not nearly as much as I did then. I write novels, and short stories are such a different game. But when novelists I love come out with collections, I have to read them. Or when novelists I love turn out to have written collections that I haven't read yet— after I finished *The Great Believers*, I went back and read Rebecca Makkai's gorgeous short-story collection. Or someone reaches out—I just read Polly Rosenwaike's *Look How Happy I'm Making You* because a mutual friend put us in touch, and it was my favorite short-story collection of the year. But for the most part, because I am preoccupied with long form, I am not usually seeking out short stories.

JEFF: Is there one book you love to reread above all others? That you go back to time and time again?

LAURIE: Yeah, I mean, this is so embarrassing, but *Hamlet*. [Laughter.]

JEFF: That's not embarrassing. It's great.

LAURIE: Well, I feel like—it should at least be a book. But *Hamlet* is—this also sounds so stupid, but it's nonetheless true: when I get stuck and don't know what's going to happen next in a novel I'm writing, the answer is often *Hamlet*. It's also a play I have read hundreds of time and seen probably fifty times, and every time, *every* time, I hear things, I notice things, that I just did not before. As I said earlier,

David Mitchell is someone I read over and over again. And also Richard Russo, because they're big and dense and character-y.

NANCY: Which Richard Russo do you go back to?

LAURIE: Lots of them, actually. I've read all of them at least twice. *Straight Man* I've read many times, partly because it's a very funny book.

JEFF: *Hamlet* aside, do you like to read plays?

LAURIE: Plays are really interesting to read because they're so short, so I can read one in one sitting. I read a lot, but I'm not a fast reader, and it takes me a long time to read a novel. Plays are easy. They're very quick, in a way that I don't even find short stories to be. With stories I read a paragraph and then I have to read it again, and then I finish the story and then I have to read the next story, and then I think, *Oh, that reminds me of something in the story before*, and I have to go back, and then I'm lost. But I find this isn't true of plays. They're self-contained. And they're relatively quick to read because they're not long and it's all mostly dialogue.

So I've read *Angels in America* [by Tony Kushner] many, many times. It must stimulate different parts of my brain. You know the thing where the machines are connected to your brain and you can see what parts light up when you're doing different things—reading plays must be a different part for me than reading books, because I'm also thinking about different options for staging it. Like, what if you give this character this accent instead of that accent, what changes? That's how I read plays. And then you see them, and they're completely different than what you were imagining, and that always fascinates me. Another play I come back to again and again is *The History Boys* [by Alan Bennett].

JEFF: When you're talking about the books you love, I notice a pretty even split between male and female writers. Do you see a distinction there? As a reader?

LAURIE: Yeah. I mean, that's so interesting: the extent to which books by women are marketed exclusively to women, whereas books by men, whether they're about men or women, are marketed to everyone (but frankly, mostly represented by, edited by, purchased by and read by women) is an enormous, enormous topic. And a strange and difficult one. I do find that without trying I read almost fifty-fifty. Sometimes I decide to only read women because I can't deal with men's fiction anymore. It's usually because I've read Philip Roth and I'm like, *No more men. I'm off men! I'm off male authors for the next six months.* But all things being equal, left to my own devices, I do end up reading more or less fifty-fifty.

I know a lot of people who read less than I do, who in fact, without trying, read almost exclusively female authors or almost exclusively male authors, which I also think is very interesting. Much has been said about the extent to which, when men write about relationships and men write about families, that is considered high art, whereas women do the same and that's considered women's fiction or domestic fiction. I also think that there is an extent to which male authors are allowed to and even encouraged to embody characters who are not like themselves, and female authors are not, and, in fact, get in trouble when they try to do so.

JEFF: Can you talk a bit more about that?

LAURIE: For instance, when men write female characters, often the first thing that one reads in a review is what an impressive job the author's done channeling this female human, as if female humans are fundamentally different and alien. There's a lot of discussion in my own circles about the question of writing outside of one's race, which is the conversation of the moment. It's an important one: writing outside of one's anything, however you want to fill in that blank. And the problem with that is that soon enough the job of imagining someone you aren't, and making windows into worlds that are not your own, becomes male. Because they're the ones who don't get shit for imagining lives that are not their own, whereas I know many women who feel really reticent about doing so, not because they don't think they can pull it off but because they think that they're going to get shit for it. And I think that that fear is legitimate.

NANCY: Does that fear of criticism affect your writing?

LAURIE: Well, by way of example, I have just written this book that is about a family with a transgender child, and I am a member of a family with a transgender child. But the book is completely made up, the characters are completely made up, the plot is completely made up. The mother in the book has so little in common with me that in fact the great challenge of the book was researching it, because she's a doctor and I am basically the opposite of a doctor. And so many readers have been very kind and generous and wonderful and enthusiastic, and I do not want to suggest otherwise, and I am incredibly grateful for it, really incredibly grateful for people reading and loving it. However! There is the extent to which some people have said, "She's too close to this. She couldn't write this because she was too close to this. It was too personal." And then the opposite has also happened, which is, people saying,

"She didn't go far enough because she wasn't imagining anything. It wasn't fiction. No feat of imagination has happened here; this is just her writing down what happened in her day-to-day life." I don't remotely want to sound bitter, nor has either been the overwhelming response. But it is just interesting to me that those things are opposite things! And they are both considered problematic!

The book that I'm writing now is about a number of things, but among them, two of the three protagonists have disabilities, or what some would consider disabilities, and though I have much in common with all three, their disabilities aren't ones that I have myself. And I have put more energy into making sure that I am getting all of that right, and not appropriating, and not taking anybody else's story, and all of that is wonderful—but at the same time, of course, that's my job! That's why we read fiction!

Some Books in Laurie's Library

Naomi Alderman, *The Power*
Alan Bennett, *The History Boys*
Beverly Cleary, *Beezus and Ramona*
Omar El Akkad, *American War*

Mark Haddon, *A Spot of Bother*

Rachel Kushner, *The Mars Room*

Tony Kushner, *Angels in America*

Rebecca Makkai, *The Great Believers*
and *Music in Wartime*

David Mitchell, *Black Swan Green*

Polly Rosenwaike, *Look How Happy I'm
Making You*

Richard Russo, *Straight Man*

William Shakespeare, *Hamlet*

Viet Thanh Nguyen

Time will tell, but Viet Thanh Nguyen's The Sympathizer *may be remembered as the most acclaimed debut novel of its era. Not only did it win the 2016 Pulitzer Prize for Fiction, it also won the Andrew Carnegie Medal for Excellence in Fiction from the American Library Association, the Center for Fiction First Novel Prize, the Dayton Literary Peace Prize, the Asian/Pacific American Award for Literature in Fiction, and even the Edgar Award for Best First Novel from the Mystery Writers of America.*

It also earned him a MacArthur Fellowship—the so-called Genius Grant—and a Guggenheim Fellowship. Heady stuff for a writer and college professor whose only previous book, Race and Resistance: Literature and Politics in Asian America, *was published in 2002 by Oxford University Press.*

Viet was born in Vietnam in 1971 and fled with his family to the United States after the fall of Saigon in 1975. He grew up in San Jose, California, earned both a BA and a PhD in English from the University of California, Berkeley, and shortly thereafter began his academic career at the University of Southern California, where he is an associate professor in both the English and American Studies and Ethnicity departments.

Since winning the Pulitzer, Viet has gone on to publish another book of nonfiction, Nothing Ever Dies: Vietnam and the Memory of War, *and a collection of short stories,* The Refugees. *He has also edited* The Displaced, *which features seventeen essays on writers' refugee experiences, and co-written, with his six-year-old son, Ellison, the children's book* Chicken of the Sea, *which was illustrated by Caldecott Honor winner Thi Bui and her thirteen-year-old son, Hien Bui-Stafford.*

Viet lives on a perfectly tended street in an

*idyllic section of Pasadena that might be featured
in a chamber of commerce brochure. After briefly
meeting his wife, Lan Duong (an associate professor
of cinema and media studies at USC), and Ellison, we
go downstairs to Viet's study, where we talk about the
books that have informed his worldview and shaped
his writing life.*

NANCY: When you were a child, did you do a lot of
   reading? Do you remember the first books you
   loved?

VIET: That's hard. In 1975 or so we arrived as refugees in Pennsylvania, and I learned how to read
   in school. I remember bookmobiles and the Har-
   risburg public library. I remember a book I didn't
   like, which even then I knew I should like: *Where
   the Wild Things Are* [by Maurice Sendak]. I think
   it was just literally too dark for me. I was living
   in a dark house under the shadow of the refugee
   experience. Now I look back and think: this is the
   story about a boy who runs away from home on a
   boat to a wild land. It was too close to me. But I
   remember *Curious George* was an early example of
   a book that I loved a lot. When I was a little older, I
   was really into war stories. The library had a series

of books by a man named C. B. Colby. They were boys' adventure stories, like picture books about war. So I learned all about the Marine Corps, for example, the leathernecks. That's what I was into. And I was totally fascinated by that kind of stuff, unfortunately.

JEFF: It doesn't seem to have had any lasting impact on your personality.

VIET: But it's had a huge impact in terms of my obsession with war stories.

JEFF: What do you think of the classic American Vietnam War fiction, books like *The Things They Carried* [by Tim O'Brien]?

NANCY: Or Michael Herr's *Dispatches*. Do they speak to you at all?

VIET: Of course. I certainly respond to them as art. I just taught *The Things They Carried* this semester in my Vietnam War class. I think it's very smart. My hesitation about it is probably about whether it's sentimental, whether or not it holds back. I'm not saying that O'Brien himself holds back, but I'm questioning whether the book itself is as dangerous a book as something like [Larry] Heinemann's *Close Quarters* or *Paco's Story*. I read *Close Quarters* when I was about twelve. Much too young. It's a scarring book. Michael Herr's *Dispatches* is a great work of literature as well. I think that part of the appeal of *The Things They Carried* is precisely because it's highly teachable, it's highly polished, because it's not too dark, and it's not as critical of the United States as the others. If you go into Heinemann's work or *Dispatches*, they're much darker, much more pointed, without any sentimentality. I hated *Close Quarters* when I read it as a kid because of its depiction of the Vietnamese and the atrocities that were being done to them. I don't know which book is going to survive the test of time, but it's interesting that *The Things They Carried* is the book that's chosen as a staple of high school English classes.

NANCY: Maybe it's because of that sentimentality, or the happy ending you could read into it.

VIET: When I reread O'Brien, Heinemann, and a bunch of other books in preparation for writing *The Sympathizer*, I thought, *Oh, Heinemann did the right thing*, because he didn't refrain from showing the depths of American psychology and atrocities, and I realized that I had to do some of the same things for myself. In other words, what I'm trying to say is that I understand that my place in relationship to these books as a Vietnamese person is very ambivalent, because I see the racism, for example, or sexism that's in there. Sometimes it's done artfully and self-consciously, and sometimes it's not. But the best works are still powerful works of literature. And I think it's an important relationship for me to have with them.

It's the same kind of relationship that Chinua Achebe had with *Heart of Darkness*, with Conrad. It's something I think about a lot. Like Achebe, I try not to say that something shouldn't be read simply because it's deeply racist, or that the racism invalidates the art. Instead, I try to respond. I want to incorporate these works into my own as things I can refer to or satirize. For me, it's more dangerous to say I'm not going to deal with Heinemann, or I'm not going to deal with [Francis Ford] Coppola (who directed the Vietnam movie *Apocalypse Now*), simply because I'm offended in some way. I think it's more powerful to have the dialogue. To respond rather than just ignore.

NANCY: What about *The Lotus Eaters* by Tatjana Soli? I found that novel very powerful and moving.

VIET: I read it too. It's one of those books I read in preparation [for *The Sympathizer*]. It opens with the fall of Saigon, and I thought, *That's not a bad rendition—she set a high standard and I have to do better.* Also, very interestingly for an American novel about the war in Vietnam, it incorporates

Cambodia. I thought that was a very important gesture.

The best part of reading these works—especially when writing *The Sympathizer*—I need to know what other writers have written so I can do just as well, or do better, or do it differently. Especially since I wasn't there, right? What's on my mind is, *How can I write a novel about the Vietnam War when I wasn't there?* All these veterans have a moral claim to authority, but I didn't have their experience, so I thought a lot about, you know, Stephen Crane. *The Red Badge of Courage*: supposedly the greatest novel about the Civil War, by a guy who was never there.

JEFF: Were there other war books from other wars that particularly influenced you?

VIET: Of course. Antonio Lobo Antunes's *The Land at the End of the World*, which almost no American has ever heard of or read, was my touchstone for writing *The Sympathizer*. It's an autobiographical novel about a Portuguese medic who is drafted and sent to fight in Portugal's war in Angola, which was their colony. It was basically their own version of the war in Vietnam. It's a deeply poetic, deeply scabrous novel, and I was hungry for that. *Catch-22* [by Joseph Heller] is another one. *Journey to the End of* *the Night* by Louis-Ferdinand Céline, which begins with World War I, and in the first ninety pages goes from the cafés of Paris to the trenches of World War I to a French colony in Africa, then to Detroit. How do you do this?! It was exactly this kind of fantastical journey that I wanted to incorporate into my work as well.

JEFF: I see you have James Jones's *From Here to Eternity* on your shelf.

VIET: Unfortunately, a novel I have not read. The big World War II novel that I read when I was a kid was *The Naked and the Dead* [by Norman Mailer]. For me, that was very impressive.

NANCY: My parents had a copy of *The Naked and the Dead*. And if you're looking for something to read when you're twelve years old, how could you see that title and not pick it up? What shocked me most about it at the time was that Mailer didn't use any quotation marks around the dialogue—I found it unreadable!

VIET: What I remember about it was that I was impressed by what I thought was an intellectual feat.

JEFF: How old were you?

VIET: Probably somewhere in my teens; certainly before college. And, you know, I knew that Mailer was young when he wrote it [he was twenty-five when it was published in 1948], so I was awed by that. But the one thing I was perplexed by in the book was, I guess he couldn't use four-letter words, so instead he wrote "fug." It was very interesting.

NANCY: It's fascinating, the things we each remember about it. I wonder, was there a book you encountered as a teenager where you said, "This is what I want to do; I want to be a writer"?

VIET: Good question. Back then the writers that I felt most passionately about, the ones whose work totally blew me away, were people like Robert Heinlein, Isaac Asimov, J. R. R. Tolkien, Anne McCaffrey—the science-fiction/fantasy writers that were considered classic during the '80s. As for literary writers, I remember *The Color Purple*, but I didn't think I would be a writer like Alice Walker. It wasn't until I got to college that I encountered writers that I thought I wanted to write something in their general neighborhood: Toni Morrison or Ralph Ellison or the Asian American writers like Maxine Hong Kingston, who were my teachers as well.

I think high school was less of a period for thinking about who I could become as a writer and more just about loving literature and narrative and being swept up in the idea of being a writer, without really knowing what it meant. I remember the fantasy was wrapped up in a figure like [F. Scott] Fitzgerald, because he got published when he was twenty-three, and I had read his first novel when I was young. It wasn't *The Great Gatsby*—I think we probably read *The Great Gatsby* in high school—but it was *This Side of Paradise*, and I thought, *Okay, this is my target*. And I remember telling my freshman college roommate, when I was seventeen or eighteen, "I'm going to graduate and become a novelist, and I'll be published by twenty-five." [Laughter.] That was the idea.

NANCY: Do you still read science fiction? Do you ever think about writing that?

VIET: I don't know if I could actually write a science-fiction novel. And science fiction is the genre, along with detective and spy novels, that I avoid reading, because every time I pick one up it's guaranteed I'll stay up until six a.m. to finish it. The last one that I read was Ben Winter's novel *Underground Airlines*. And *Red Mars* by Kim Stanley Robinson was also great.

NANCY: What about Neal Stephenson—have you read him?

VIET: Yes. I thought *Snow Crash* was fantastic.

NANCY: When you read what we call literary fiction, do you miss that sense of forward movement you get with a fast-moving plot? I find that with most genre fiction it's the plot that propels you through the book.

VIET: I don't like the distinction between so-called genre fiction and literary fiction. Or if we have to say genre fiction, we have to say literary fiction is a genre as well that pretends not to be. But yes, in genre novels, plot is fundamental, and for me plot *is* fundamental. My beef with a lot of literary fiction is that there's no plot. Which is okay, I guess, if we're talking about modernist masterpieces that have stood the test of time and therefore I've got to read them. But your average contemporary American literary fiction that is plotless and is also lacking a lot of other things that might make it compelling to me, I find totally boring. But one problem with so-called genre fiction, for example, like Jo Nesbø—I love his books, but I cannot tell you what I've read by him—I literally cannot remember one book from the next. But that's part of their pleasure, right? They're very disposable.

JEFF: Would you say genre fiction has been important to you in your writing?

VIET: What I used from those novels are the importance of plot, and the politics. A lot of detective and crime fiction is very political. And they'll go directly into contemporary political controversies in an un-embarrassed way. Contemporary American literary fiction sort of backs off from both plot and politics. So I wanted to take these elements from so-called genre fiction and bring it together with the more so-called literary elements of what we would think of as high literature.

NANCY: Graham Greene divided his own writings into literary fiction and what he called entertainments.

VIET: I was actually a fan of Graham Greene in high school. I remember reading *The Power and the Glory* and *Our Man in Havana*, and they worked for me as thrillers, with very serious stuff going on. I didn't read *The Quiet American* until I got to college, because in college I became more interested in the Vietnam War. I read quite a bit and wrote a couple of papers on literature related to Vietnam. And one of them was on *The Quiet American*. I'd also read Edward Said's *Orientalism* shortly before that, and the thesis was just purely an application of *Orientalism* to *The Quiet American*.

JEFF: That sounds fascinating.

VIET: It was a very good exercise for me to go through. And it laid the foundation for what would eventually become *The Sympathizer*. There's a small and very deliberate reference to Graham Greene in that novel, one sentence meant to be a rebuttal to *The Quiet American*. I also teach it in my Vietnam War class, and to me it's still a fundamental text. It still holds up well. Even with the Orientalist elements.

NANCY: Then there's Ward Just's *The Dangerous Friend*.

VIET: I haven't read that yet.

NANCY: Oh, you have to read that, because it's *The Quiet American* a generation later.

VIET: I read an article recently in LitHub that called Ward Just one of our unappreciated American masters.

NANCY: I think he definitely is. It's a good choice for book groups too, because what begs to be discussed is just who the dangerous friend is.

VIET: In the same vein, have you read Bob Shacochis's *The Woman Who Lost Her Soul?*

NANCY: Yes. I loved it. Sometimes I read a novel and think, *What on earth can that writer possibly do next?* Because it seems like he put everything he had into that book, and it's brilliant. What did you think?

VIET: I loved it too. I read it partly because it was short-listed for the Pulitzer. What an incredibly ambitious novel—a very deliberate attempt to confront all of America, but from this leftist, radical vein instead of, let's say, *Underworld* by Don De-Lillo. It was so historically grounded, and very explicit about its political intent in this confrontation with some centers of American power that I rarely see in American literature. Still a very readable novel as well.

NANCY: And it was a love story. I remember that right from the beginning I couldn't stop reading it. That first chapter was amazing, and then it just got even better. What a powerful book.

JEFF: Are there Vietnamese classics that you wish would be translated for American readers?

VIET: Well, there's the classic of Vietnamese literature: *The Song of Kieu*, which is usually translated as *The Tale of Kieu.* Up till now, there's only been one major interpretation by Yale University Press by a Vietnamese translator, and now we have a new one coming out from Penguin Classics. So at least Vietnamese people will be able to say, "This is the core, this is our Shakespeare."

JEFF: What about contemporary Vietnamese fiction in translation? Do you have favorites?

VIET: A lot of it's not getting translated. When I read some of the translated stuff, I sometimes wonder if it's the translation that's faulty or the original prose that's faulty, because the prose often seems pretty flat. What's usually been translated is stuff that deals with the war, because it's what Americans care about. Now some of the classics are being brought out because American veterans are doing their best to get Vietnamese literature out there. But the contemporary writers that get translated are usually the ones that were publishing in the '80s and '90s, the older generation, and the younger ones—the completely postwar generation who are just writing about urban ills and things like this—have not been able to find translators yet.

A contemporary Korean writer that is hot right now is Han Kang, and apparently part of her popularity is due to the freewheeling translation of her books. I'm fine with that. Maybe we need more of that in Vietnamese literature because maybe the translations have been too literal. I listened to one of her books—not *The Vegetarian*, but *Human Acts*, which I thought was a very powerful novel about Korea, the Gwangju uprising of 1980, the dictatorships, violence, oppression.

JEFF: Who among your contemporaries particularly speaks to you today?

VIET: Paul Beatty. Big fan of *The Sellout*. It's my kind of book—it's a book I wish I was capable of writing. Such wild energy. Edward Jones. *Lost in the*

City was a big deal for me. When I was writing *The Refugees*, I was modeling it on *Lost in the City* as a short-story collection. Of all the collections that I read, that was the one I really wanted to try and emulate.

JEFF: That leads into my next question: short stories versus novels. Do you think about them differently as you're reading them?

NANCY: Or writing them?

VIET: For me, writing short stories was such an agonizing experience. It took so long. Like seventeen years to write *The Refugees* and another three years to publish it, and then each individual story was painful. There was no story that was easy to write; it was either painful or extremely painful to write them. So that even now the very thought of writing short stories fills me with dread. I don't know if I'll ever go back to it. And part of the dread is that I can't articulate for you how to write a short story. I can explain, I think, almost everything I did in *The Sympathizer*, and give you a rationale for every aesthetic decision. But with my short stories it was such an intuitive experience. Trial and error. That's why it took so long. And to this day I find it very hard to articulate why the stories are constructed the way they are.

But that doesn't reduce my pleasure in reading short stories, and I think there's something very magical about the ones that work for me. I find them to be a form that's even more appealing than poetry. I can read poetry for a different purpose. Novels for a different purpose. But short stories are something that to me are perfect because they have sort of the grace and insight of a poem and the narrative of a novel but, you know, much shorter, so you can have your fix in twenty or thirty minutes with a great short story.

And I think the reason why I like *Lost in the City* so much is because I felt the whole book worked for me collectively. The stories added up to a greater whole, and most short-story collections don't do that. Story collections are like albums—there are usually two or three good ones in there and the rest you can take or leave. That's why sometimes it's more fun to read the Best American collections or a book like *The Best American Short Stories of the Century.* That's another reason why short stories were very scary for me, because I wanted to write a book in which all the stories work, but I'm not sure I did. It's perfectly possible to write a finely crafted song, but it may not be magical. There's something in a short story that's magical in that way, and if you can do eight or ten in one book, it's an amazing feat.

JEFF: Are there other collections like Jones's that come to mind?

VIET: [James Joyce's] *Dubliners* worked for me. When I reread it, it still seemed as original to me as it did when I first read it. I think any of Tobias Wolff's collections would work for me. And Tom [T.C.] Boyle's stories as well.

JEFF: Speaking of short-story collections, what about one of my favorite books ever, Denis Johnson's *Jesus' Son*, and also his Vietnam novel, *Tree of Smoke*? Any thoughts about those books?

VIET: Well, I loved *Jesus' Son*. Loved the movie. Love the book. So I fall into the camp of Denis Johnson admirers. When *Tree of Smoke* came out, I was very excited about it. I think he knew some of the pitfalls of writing about Vietnam. I think it was very important in that book that there was a Vietnamese character right from the beginning, so he was already doing a lot more, I thought, than other American writers of the Vietnam War. I think it probably had to do with the fact that he had some distance from the war, someone who didn't go, someone who was younger.

NANCY: Did you read Karl Marlantes's *Matterhorn*?

VIET: Yeah, I liked that quite a bit. That's, you know, the Vietnam War's *The Naked and the Dead*: the big war book. I thought he did a great job of capturing a very particular kind of war experience that was unique even in the case of the Vietnam War. And also that it was a book that was about race, in terms of black and white race relations among American soldiers. He focused on the internal dynamics of the American soldiers, which is what Americans really want to hear about, in that they can hear about it without worrying about the racism of Americans directed against Vietnamese. But I thought it was really powerful. I thought his nonfiction book [*What It Is Like to Go to War*] was good too. There he's trying to deal with the effects of being in the war.

NANCY: What are you reading now?

VIET: Right now, on Audible, I'm listening to *Blood in the Water*, the history of the Attica uprising by Heather Ann Thompson that won the Pulitzer a year or two ago. I just finished reading on my Kindle Jess Row's book of essays called *White Flights*, which is his take on whiteness in American literature, and of course he's white, so it's an important angle to take. And before that I read David Mura's *A Stranger's Journey*, which is his book on race, narrative, and writing. And I'm about to start reading Susan

Straight's new memoir *In the Country of Women* that's about to be published. We're friends, and I'll probably do a blurb for it.

NANCY: Susan Straight. I remember how much I enjoyed *I Been in Sorrow's Kitchen and Licked Out All the Pots*, which was, I think, her first novel. Plus that simply stunning title—I don't think I've ever encountered a better title.

JEFF: You mentioned listening to books and using a Kindle. Are there differences for you between reading a book on audio or on an e-reader versus reading a traditional book?

VIET: I find that it's really hard for me to listen to literary fiction, so I have to try each book before I can tell whether I can listen to it or not. The last audio book that I listened to was Jesmyn Ward's *Salvage the Bones*. That worked for me, but I also recently tried Virginia Woolf's *Mrs. Dalloway*, because, oddly, I hadn't read it, but it was too much to follow it in the car. So there's certain books that work for me and certain books that don't.

NANCY: Do you think it was the reader of *Mrs. Dalloway* or do you think it was the style?

VIET: I think it was the style. Annette Bening's narration was great, but the free-association narrative that's happening from the very beginning of the book made it challenging, whereas *Salvage the Bones* is straightforward realism, and the narrative's very clear. *Invisible Man* on Audible was terrific. It was read by Joe Morton, and he gets into all the different kinds of dialects and voices; this was a case where I thought the audio version lent a whole new dimension to the novel that I hadn't really intellectually understood. Hearing it, you could totally get that Ellison is also exploring the varieties of African American and African diasporic culture in that book through the language, through the voices.

NANCY: And e-readers?

VIET: I often use the Kindle for pragmatic purposes. Like if I'm reading intellectual stuff that I need to highlight, then it's very useful for me, because I can highlight and save the notes for my research purposes. And sometimes I just need my Kindle to trick myself. I read *1Q84* [Haruki Murakami's 900-plus-page novel] on the Kindle, for example, and carried that around, which of course would have been much harder if it'd been the actual book. But otherwise, yes, I prefer books. For example, I recently read Michael Ondaatje's *Warlight* because he was coming to USC. I make it a policy, if I'm meeting a famous writer, I'm getting them to sign first editions for me. So I bought it and read it. And it was a qualitatively different experience, the physical experience of holding an artifact like that. Plus the beauty of the language made a big, big impression on me.

JEFF: With old books, it's especially important to me to read the actual book. Because if it's on an e-reader, it doesn't feel old.

VIET: It's like listening to a song on vinyl as opposed to hearing it on a CD or an MP3 player. It just does something to our perception of it.

Some Books and Authors in Viet's Library

Antonio Lobo Antunes, *The Land at the End of the World*
Paul Beatty, *The Sellout*
Louis-Ferdinand Céline, *Journey to the End of the Night*
Ralph Ellison
Denis Johnson, *Jesus' Son* and *Tree of Smoke*
Edward Jones, *Lost in the City*
James Joyce, *Dubliners*
Han Kang, *Human Acts*
Maxine Hong Kingston

Norman Mailer, *The Naked and the Dead*
Karl Marlantes, *Matterhorn*
Toni Morrison
Michael Ondaatje, *Warlight*
Edward Said, *Orientalism*
Bob Shacochis, *The Woman Who Lost Her Soul*
Kim Stanley Robinson, *Red Mars*
Alice Walker, *The Color Purple*
Ben Winter, *Underground Airlines*

Jane Hirshfield

*J*ane Hirshfield lives in a hillside retreat above Mill Valley, California, the sort of place that is paradise for either a gardener or a poet—intersecting vocations of which Jane can claim both. Her poetry is infused with allusions to the plants and fruit trees that surround her house and the bookshelf-lined shed where she does her writing.

Jane was born in Manhattan in 1953 and raised on the city's Lower East Side. She first declared her *intention of becoming a writer at age six. The first book she herself bought, at age nine, was a collection of haiku. By the time she reached Princeton, she was already an accomplished poet and while there won* The Nation *magazine's undergraduate poetry contest. But rather than immediately pursue a career as a poet, she decided to study Zen Buddhism, spending eight years learning at the San Francisco Zen Center, including three years at their isolated Tassajara Zen Mountain Center retreat south of Carmel. In 1979, she was ordained as a monk, and in 1982, she published her first book of poems,* Alaya.

Since then, she has published ten more collections of poetry as well as the acclaimed essay collections Nine Gates: Entering the Mind of Poetry *and* Ten Windows: How Great Poems Transform the World. *Her work has earned praise from the Nobel Prize–winning Czech poet Czesław Miłosz for her "profound empathy for the suffering of all living beings . . . In its highly sensuous detail, her poetry illuminates the Buddhist virtue of mindfulness."*

We spoke to Jane in her bright living room overlooking the garden that serves as inspiration for much of her work.

NANCY: Were you a big reader as a child?

JANE: I spent my childhood reading, often late into the night, far past my bedtime. I'd go to the public library every week, take out my full allotment of five books, read them all, and the next week do it again.

NANCY: Are there particular books you remember?

JANE: I'm a person of poor memory, and most of the titles into which those childhood hours were poured have vanished. I can say I devoured pretty much everything on offer—classics like *Black Beauty* [by Anna Sewell] but also the Nancy Drew mysteries [by Carolyn Keene]. I do remember that I was undone by *Charlotte's Web* [by E. B. White], read aloud to me by my mother. I was inconsolable when Charlotte died; I just kept weeping. When I reread it as an adult, I realized this response was not the intended effect. E. B. White surely meant to instruct, to show loss as a survivable part of life, to demonstrate that the world goes on . . . But I didn't see or feel that at all. There was only the shock of disappearance.

I also remember the first book I couldn't finish. I was ten years old, reading Dickens's *David Copperfield* in my summer camp's infirmary, and I just couldn't keep going. That was a trauma. I was so sure I could read any book, just like the grown-ups, and I felt defeated. As it turns out, even as an adult, I haven't finished most of the Dickens I've started. The one exception is *A Tale of Two Cities.* The final one I tried was *Bleak House.* For the first 400 pages, I was delighted, sure I'd finally gotten the hang of enjoying Dickens, then one day I set it down and simply never picked it up again. So it may be that *David Copperfield* didn't defeat me because I was ten. Perhaps even then I just wasn't a Dickens reader. Tolstoy, yes. *Moby-Dick,* yes. *The Tale of Genji,* yes. It wasn't a matter of length. Just: Dickens, no.

JEFF: What was the first grown-up book that you read and fell in love with?

JANE: Would an early poem do? I fell entirely in love with Walter de la Mare's "The Listeners."

NANCY: I'm still haunted by that poem.

JANE: It threw open a door. It showed there can be other worlds, worlds that can be pointed toward, even when you can't see them. It showed me that the experience of mystery is in itself a pleasure, and that what exists past words' perimeter can still be entered through them. The poem's music is gorgeous. And much of its meaning is held in what isn't said and what doesn't happen. It leaves everything open, to continue inside the reader.

JEFF: How old were you? Do you remember?

JANE: Nine, maybe ten. It was included in the poetry anthology we were given that year in school, *The Magic Lantern*. I still have my copy. On the page with "The Listeners," I underlined the phrase "the forest's ferny floor." Next to it, in my round child's cursive, is the word "alliteration."

NANCY: Was poetry your primary love as a child?

JANE: I was one of those children who would read the cereal box if nothing else were at hand—but poetry was what I wrote for myself, not stories.

The first book I bought as a child, with my own allowance money, was a collection of haiku, one of those Peter Pauper Press editions you'd find on circular wire display racks at the front of stores. I was seven or eight. I can't know now what I took from those poems. I grew up on New York's Lower East Side, and my glimpses of the natural world—haiku's basic image vocabulary—were almost non-existent. Perhaps what I recognized was how much I was missing? But those brief poems, into which so much is folded in the way a large sheet of paper is folded into a small origami bird, caught me for life. Again—as with the De la Mare poem—they showed me that there was *more*. It's the experience of the keyhole. I could look through and see that more life, more beings, more worlds were out there, beyond the edges of my own knowing, and they showed me, again, that much of what is being said is being said past the literal words and the literal image. That recognition must have given me some early sense that the world is, as the English poet Louis Mac-Neice wrote in "Snow": "crazier and more of it than we think, / incorrigibly plural."

Another poem comes to mind, one that for me was life changing. In 1985, I was working with Mariko Aratani on co-translating Japan's two great classical-era women poets, Ono no Komachi and Izumi Shikibu, for what became the book *The Ink Dark Moon*. Mariko sight-translated this, one of many thousand-year-old poems by Izumi Shikibu, and I knew right away it was one I would want to include, but even after I'd written down the word by word literal version, with the Romaji and each word's potential meanings, and took it away to work on, I couldn't find its meaning. I had the grammar, the English word order, the nouns and verbs and conjunctions; I knew something important was in it, but not yet what that was. Then suddenly, the poem became clear. Here's the English translation:

Although the wind
blows terribly here,
the moonlight also leaks
between the roof planks
of this ruined house.

What I understood was this: if the house of your life is walled so tightly that no cold winds can enter, the moonlight will also be barred. Buddhist enlightenment, awakening, the fullness of existence . . . if you close yourself off to the unwanted experience of cold winds, you'll lose everything wanted as well. But become a person willing to have a leaky roof, cracked windows, permeable walls, and the fullness of a human life will spill in. The capacity for knowing moonlight is not separable from the capacity for suffering.

JEFF: I wonder if another Buddhist—Leonard Cohen—read that poem before writing "There's a crack in everything. That's how the light gets in."

JANE: That's a perfect connection. I'd guess, though, that it's simply a case of a single discoverable understanding being found and given to us by two great artists, both atypical Buddhist practitioners, a millennium apart.

NANCY: The poem also has some of the same mystery "The Listeners" does.

JANE: Yes, it does, doesn't it? I've never written an essay directly about mystery in poems, but there are essays in *Ten Windows*—my most recent prose book—describing things in mystery's neighborhood: hiddenness, uncertainty, paradox, surprise. Mystery is awake inside each of these things. You can recognize mystery but can't ever know it completely. A mystery solved isn't one anymore; it's reducible knowledge: the butler did it. Yet it may be that we love the reminding of mystery in detective stories or spy tales not for their solutions but because they repeat the experience of our human lives as a whole. A life can never be known completely, not one's own, not anyone else's. We read those stories for their complexities and perplexities, not for their solutions. Poe throws away the "discoveries" in his stories. That isn't their point. The purloined letter is lying out in the open. It's the searching and what it brings out about us that's the point.

The letter might be on the tabletop, but there's always something more, something hidden. Poems are instruments of perception seeking just that, the way microscopes, telescopes, X-rays, and CAT scans are instruments of perception. A poem extends our capacity to see and know beyond the perimeter, to glimpse, for a radiant moment, the radiant moment.

They teach that if one thing can be hidden, then shown, more will surely be hidden beyond it. And so, in turning toward mystery, we begin to feel ourselves part of infinitude and immensity.

NANCY: What poets do you read and reread?

JANE: I do have a set of poets I find medicinal for certain conditions. It's a fairly big shelf. [Murasaki] Shikibu and [Galway] Kinnell are among them. Two other such poets, throughout my adult life, have been the two Polish Nobel Laureates, Czesław Miłosz and Wisława Szymborska. At different points in a life, a writer's work brings you different news. Miłosz is especially interesting to me now, for instance, as I begin to cross into a different stage of life, because so much of his work comes from the later decades of a very long life. I find myself deeply encouraged by the strength of the poems he wrote into his early nineties; they show that a continuing evolution, both as a poet and as a person, is possible. Not guaranteed. But possible.

NANCY: Did you know him?

JANE: Yes. We met by the accident of geography and mutual friends. He lived for many decades in exile, in Berkeley, and we met at a large picnic party on Angel Island. Not long after, he read my 1988 book of poems and also *The Ink Dark Moon*, within two weeks of when they came out. He and his wife, Carol, invited me to dinner, and the friendship began. It's hard to fathom that a great poet might be lonely for conversation, but it seems people were so in awe of him they didn't want to intrude. Knowing Czesław was one of the great pieces of luck in my life.

The central question for Miłosz was the question of suffering . . . Did a poem, a choice, a culture, an idea, increase suffering or lead to its lessening? A moment free of suffering was for him a rare gift. And he knew himself as a person complicit in our species' many failures. His poems hold what I think is the only viable stance for poems of political critique: to admit that you yourself are not without blame.

NANCY: How much do you think your practice of Buddhism influences the kind of poetry that you read?

JANE: Most of the poetry I read isn't "Buddhist," except for what comes into poems that are good because good poets are persons of close attention, who notice they live amid time and transience, permeable to and in intimate connection with others. "Nothing human is alien to me," the Roman playwright Terence's famous assertion, comes to mind. Gerard Manley Hopkins, Zbigniew Herbert, Emily Dickinson, [Constantine P.] Cavafy, the contemporary poets whose work I love have—with one or two exceptions—no intentionally Buddhist elements in their work. They simply understand our human lives. I'm not—even as a practitioner of Zen—interested in doctrine. I'm interested in this life I've found myself part of, and in shared fate. I'm interested in agreeing to reality, to whatever arrives on its hooves and fins and wings, and I'm interested in increasing what ranges of being can be increased. I'm interested in attending to the difficult as best I can. Both poetry and Buddhist practice are, for me, useful ways of entering these things. But you know, poems of grief are poems of grief, in every culture. An aphorism from ancient Sumeria can still ring true today. The poets and mystics of every tradition would, I have always believed, understand one another perfectly. Their words remain relevant and wanted exactly because they speak of fundamental things in ways that are not oversimplified, in language both awake and unexpected.

JEFF: Are there books or writers who bring back your childhood in New York for you, who evoke that?

JANE: Some things are . . . warmly familiar. The restaurants in Isaac Bashevis Singer's stories, or the depiction of New York life in a recent novel by Kate Walbert [*The Sunken Cathedral*], or a newsstand in a Frank O'Hara poem. Susan Cheever's description, in *Home Before Dark*, of her father working in their apartment building's basement storage bin, going down there each morning in the elevator with the other fathers in suit and tie—I know those men. I know those basements.

NANCY: Sometimes I'll begin a book—usually a novel—and I'll know from the first paragraph, the first sentence, that this is a book for me. Do you ever have that experience?

JANE: Last fall, I read Toni Morrison's *Song of Solomon* for the first time. And from the first paragraph I knew I was in the hands of a master: of sentences, imagination, perception, life depiction, story, investigation. I continued to feel, throughout that provocative, precise, wild book, that I could give myself over to it completely, surrender to the experience I was being given, and know I would come away from it altered, informed, transformed. I know from her interviews that Toni Morrison would not call me the person that book was written for. I have to hope she wouldn't mind that, asked your question, it is her book that springs forward.

NANCY: What led you to read it at that particular time?

JANE: I was working at the MacDowell Colony, in New Hampshire, finishing my next book of poems. Toni Morrison had received the [Edward] MacDowell

Medal, which means her books are displayed prominently, on the medalist shelf in the library. I saw them and thought, *Song of Solomon! How can I have missed it before?* When you're in an artist colony, there's time to do your work and time to read. Having enough time, and then more, is the gift of such places.

MacDowell had just renamed their on-site library after James Baldwin, a three-time fellow, and so I also reread *The Fire Next Time.* I'd read that first when I was seventeen and decided to get myself up to speed in what we then called Black Literature. I read Ralph Ellison's *Invisible Man*, Eldridge Cleaver's *Soul on Ice*, Malcolm X's autobiography. I read Baldwin. Morrison hadn't yet begun publishing. Returning to *The Fire Next Time*, I was so grateful for Baldwin's grandeur of language and insight, for his enormous, forgiving heart coupled to an absolutely unflinching perception and naming. In 2018, as in 1970, the book felt indispensable, needed, and in itself, by its very existence, restorative. I was told by Florence Ladd, who knew Baldwin until the end of his life, that he died, in France, thinking his work had been forgotten. That is heartbreaking to ponder.

JEFF: What else were you reading in your high school and college years?

JANE: I was lucky. At my high school, we were introduced to a broad range of English and American writers. Of the poets, I was wildly in love with Whitman, and quoted him [from "Song of Myself"] on my high school yearbook page:

> Missing me one place search another,
> I stop somewhere waiting for you.

I reveled in Shakespeare, Wordsworth, [John] Keats, [John] Donne. By twelfth grade we were reading [T. S.] Eliot, [Ezra] Pound, William Carlos Williams. On one test, I came across [W. H.] Auden's "Musée des Beaux Arts." I'd never read the poem before, and I fell into it, and forgot I was taking a test. I'm still in awe of that poem, what it holds, how it holds it. It's one of the poems that never wear themselves out.

NANCY: It's one of my favorites too.

JANE: I felt its greatness before I understood the subtext, how much it addresses the coming of the Second World War. Poems do let you feel what they address without needing to spell it out, just as you can hear and be moved by their music without being able to name it as iamb, trochee, assonance, slant rhyme, parallel structure, villanelle. I went to college in the last moments of New Criticism, which proposed that a poem should stand on its own, free of its biographical circumstances and backstory. I still feel that way of reading is valid. Not the only way, but valid. "Musée des Beaux Arts" is one of the world's great poems whether or not the reader knows it was written by a person who was gay and lived in Berlin in the '30s.

NANCY: You and I went to college around the same time, and I remember that I ran across a collection of poetry that didn't include the authors and titles of poems: a perfect example of New Criticism.

JANE: Oh, I love that. Or I should say: leaving off the authors, I love that. Titles are too often part of a poem's meaning to be quite so casually lopped off. But we'd know a Gwendolyn Brooks or Gerard Manley Hopkins poem as extraordinary without Gwendolyn Brooks's or Gerard Manley Hopkins's biography attached to it. And, you know, every writer begins as a person effectively anonymous. Some end their lives still anonymous. Dickinson's life and its still unfathomed course fascinate now, but it's the poems that made people want to know more. Our current ways of reading are the opposite of New Criticism, but I'd still love to see an anthology like the one you describe come out today. It would counter the whole celebrity-is-what's-interesting tilt of our culture.

JEFF: How did your reading evolve during your college years?

JANE: I'd had a pretty good high school education, and so, with the hubris of the very young, I thought I didn't really need to keep reading in English. I designed my own major, which let me take courses reading world literature in translation—Greek tragedy in translation, Russian novels in translation, Japanese and Chinese literature in translation. That was how I first discovered the two foremost Japanese classical-era women poets, Izumi Shikibu and Ono no Komachi. A half dozen or so of their poems were in a Donald Keene–edited anthology. Later I took a course reading N plays, and several of those are about Komachi, a legendary and rather proto-feminist figure. I thought someone would surely translate more of these poems; it was an obvious idea. Eighteen years later, no one had, and so I ended up working with Mariko on *The Ink Dark Moon* collection.

Komachi and Shikibu both wrote tanka, a five-line, thirty-one-syllable form a thousand years older than the three-line, seventeen-syllable haiku. The fourteen extra syllables allow for a completely different kind of poem than haiku, one which works much in the way a sonnet does, with what's called a "turn" in it. Something happens over the poem's course, something changes. There's usually just enough information that you can intuit a narrative backstory, which is rarely possible with haiku. My own sense of the lyric poem has been built upon the music of transformation and discovery that's shared by the sonnet and the tanka, and on their flash of added perception. I also loved, and still love, the Greek tragedies. Reading the ancient works of multiple cultures, you begin to learn what's foundational in human lives. The dilemmas of these works remain our dilemmas, their emotions remain our emotions, their epiphanies, however provisional, awaken our epiphanies.

JEFF: Are there particular poems or poets that you love to teach?

JANE: Yes. I believe in the lastingness of art, and in the cross-cultural relevance of art. World literature is the world's inheritance. Borges's poems, Sappho's poems, second-century love poems written in Sanskrit, Miroslav Holub, Su Tung-Po . . .

I tend to teach poems rather than poets, but certain poets' work is especially good for teaching certain things. When I teach, it's usually in a creative writing context, not literature study, and so the task is to convey some specific craft point. For example, there's a James Baldwin poem I love, "Untitled." I teach it because, first, I'm smitten, and then also because it's a great example of a poem of intimate, direct, second-person speech, in this case a prayer. Poems of direct speech interest me. I use Philip Levine's poems for this frequently, because he had a particular genius in using a shifting second-person pronoun. The pronoun "you" has something like seven or nine possible understandings. A poem not handling that with care will utterly confuse the reader. But Levine, in poem after poem, changes from one "you" to another and then another over the course, and the reader is never lost. It's a rhetorical device of enormous power. A poem says "you," and you can't help but sit up. A poem changes its "you," and you—the reader—find yourself moved. Neruda changes an ode from third person to second person and the poem's world grows intimate. As a young writer, most of my poems began with the interior, murmured "you"—the "you" that means "I" but also, equally, "anyone."

NANCY: Any particular poem of Levine's?

JANE: "The Simple Truth." If you look at the pronouns in it, you will see a master magician's sleight of hand work. I don't know if Levine did this consciously or deliberately, but he seemed to know how to move that second-person pronoun the way a gymnast knows where to put her elbows when she does an aerial cartwheel. Another speech-including poem I love is a not-much-mentioned one by William Carlos Williams, "The Act." It says:

> There were the roses, in the rain.
> Don't cut them, I pleaded.
> They won't last, she said.
> But they're so beautiful
> where they are.
> Agh, we were all beautiful once, she said,
> and cut them and gave them to me
> in my hand.

JEFF: That's wonderful.

JANE: A beautiful, revelatory portrait and philosophical debate, all done through dialogue. There's also a Jack Gilbert poem in which the speaker is filleting a fish and talking to God, and a Robert Hass poem in which he's talking with a raccoon, who doesn't respond. The poems by Komachi and Shikibu are also filled with acts of direct speech.

In teaching, I like to find poems that show the same task undertaken by different people, from different time periods, in different ways. And I never teach a poem I don't love. Because why would one waste one's time and one's students' attention when there are so many poems you do love and admire? I could go on . . . Adrienne Rich's "Dedication" is another poem I teach.

NANCY: I've never forgotten the end of her poem "Living in Sin," where she talks about "daylight coming / like a relentless milkman up the stairs." So wonderful.

JANE: Yes. That's a not-quite-twin of Philip Larkin's "Aubade." When I look at "Aubade" and "High Windows," these poems open into a sliver of something close to the sense of mystical possibility. They glimpse reprieve. I realize mine is the minority view here, and that I'm likely putting my own psyche's fingerprints on this famously bleak poet. I'm not blind to Larkin's bleakness. He was famously misanthropic and also misogynist. If you ask poets for the most misanthropic poem they can name, a majority will offer Larkin's "This Be the Verse." That's the one that opens "They fuck you up, your mum and dad. / They may not mean to, but they do," and ends by advocating having no children. But—and I know this is a liberty-taking; I'm not saying the poem warrants this reading—I can see the poem as a kind of Theravadan Buddhist longing for liberation from the wheel of suffering. "Man hands on misery to man. / It deepens like a coastal shelf." That sounds a reasonable—and beautiful—account of karma to me. Not having children is, in this poem, a choice to not pass on suffering.

NANCY: You talked about reading *Song of Solomon*. Do you read much fiction?

JANE: For twenty years I've been part of a reading group made up primarily of research scientists. I wanted to read books with people from outside the realm of working writers. Our next book is George Saunders's *Lincoln in the Bardo*. Our last book was Stendhal's *The Red and the Black*. We do a lot of classics, which always makes me happy. It's given me reason to reread Homer's epics, Joyce's *Ulysses*, and *Moby-Dick*; we also read Melville's *Billy Budd*, "Bartleby, the Scrivener," and "The Confidence-Man." Our first book was Conrad's *Lord Jim*. Our second, at my suggestion, was Ron Hansen's *Mariette in Ecstasy*. I think that's one of the most beautiful books ever written; it was not popular with the scientists. We read several of Virginia Woolf's novels in the early days, and also a lot of Faulkner. We read Colson Whitehead's first book, *The Intuitionist*. We did a run of short stories—Alice Munro, Raymond Carver, Chekhov, Borges. I may try advocating next for Ted Chiang.

We're a bit haphazard in how we choose what to read. Shortly after the 2016 election, we chose *The Plague* [by Albert Camus], and more recently, Svetlana Alexievich's *Voices from Chernobyl*—the only nonfiction book we've ever chosen, though we read a play, usually Shakespeare, aloud every year for the holidays and have read a handful of poets: [Walt] Whitman, [Elizabeth] Bishop, [Tomas] Tranströmer, [Emily] Dickinson, [W. H.] Auden . . .

Since the November 2016 election, I've wanted to read only work by people who have lived through dire times. I want to know, how did they live, how did they write and live through what they had to live through? (Or, as with Osip Mandelstam, did not live through.) And I've been reminded that during the early years of the Russian Revolution, Marina Tsvetaeva lost a child to starvation, fell in love, and wrote a poem of high-spirited resistance: forbidden to use horses to clear snow from their street, people hired camels. Matisse painted landscapes in the south of France during the years of the war. We know that through the most harrowing times, the full range of human existence continues. That is the description of Auden's "Musée des Beaux Arts": ". . . how it takes place / While someone else is eating or opening a window or just walking dully along." Matisse understood himself to be an example, preserving the spirit of France by carrying on.

Another book our group read was José Saramago's *Blindness*. At the same time, I was reading Ilya Kaminsky's astounding book-length poem, *Deaf Republic*. The two books have much to say to one another: each is a parable of loss and chaos, each shows the imagination grappling with a time of almost incomprehensible and still unknown-of-outcome outer events.

Of course every event's outcome is still unfinished.

That is the thing: it's hard to know anything with real sureness. Literature, other people's stories and words, helps us abide this impossible suspension of knowing. Here we now are, watching what might well be an environmental catastrophe that erases the world we grew up in, the world we can't help but believe we're still living in now. Here we are, possibly watching the end of this country's experiment with democratic governance. It could happen. And yet, you know, here we are. The morning is beautiful, the garden is blooming, there's food in the grocery store. It's harder to see what isn't than to see what is.

NANCY: That also goes back to Auden's poem, doesn't it, when Icarus is falling from the sky but nobody sees him falling. Everyone's gaze is turned elsewhere. Or William Stafford's poem "A Ritual to Read to Each Other" with the line about how "it is important that awake people be awake."

JANE: These poems are as sustaining and necessary as any meal. We need the reminder that somebody has thought this, spoken this, lived this, before. I think of another Auden poem, "September 1st, 1939," which circulated so widely after September 11th. Auden seems to become only ever more relevant, doesn't he? Most poems fade from the vocabulary of reference after a certain amount of time. Auden's are strengthening.

NANCY: I've always felt that your poems were explaining the world to yourself. That you were using your poems to work out where you were in the world.

JANE: Yes. I write to remake my own relationship to existence.

It does seem likely that others will share my dilemmas. For example, it's pretty hard for a person to believe they are actually going to die. We know we will die, but most of the time we can't take it in, can't hold it in mind or believe it. The knowledge of death is hardly news; you have to unbury it, each time, to see it. Mortality is always a fresh discovery. If a person were continually aware of their own imminent departure—and death is always imminent, a life always too short—they might, inside their sadness or futility or anger, lose the appetite to keep going, lose the capacity to sleep or to dawdle, to desire this radiant and suffering world. Optimism in this matter is built into us by evolution.

Poems, though, say over and over again, "You're going to die, all those you love are going to die." The psyche boggles before it: "The world is—I am—transient? How can that be?" But then, because a poem is in some way beautiful and because its passageways, doors, and windows open to the mysterious, this basic truth becomes for a moment not only visible but a thing we can agree to. The shock of grief and the ecstatic joy of this life become an alloy, one that lets us, for its duration, understand the incomprehensible and not be blinded by seeing it.

That's close to the heart of how art works in a life, at least for me. It brings a person into those rare moments when the colors of the painting are suddenly, implausibly, brighter or deeper or larger than your eyes have been, until then, able to bear to see.

And now, through art's power of the keyhole, you can see.

Some Books, Poems, and Authors in Jane's Library

Anna Akhmatova
Svetlana Alexievich, *Voices from Chernobyl*
W. H. Auden, "Musée des Beaux Arts"
James Baldwin, *The Fire Next Time*
Walter de la Mare, "The Listeners"
Ron Hansen, *Mariette in Ecstasy*
Ilya Kaminsky, *Deaf Republic*
Philip Levine, "The Simple Truth"
Czesław Miłosz
Toni Morrison, *Song of Solomon*
Izumi Shikibu
Wisława Szymborska
Marina Tsvetaeva
Kate Walbert, *The Sunken Cathedral*
E. B. White, *Charlotte's Web*
Walt Whitman
William Carlos Williams, "The Act"

Richard Ford

*R*ichard Ford's home, in the town of East Boothbay, Maine, is in the far reaches of the northeast corner of the country, a spot we were happy to visit both for its natural beauty and to talk to a writer whose work we admire so deeply. Jeff fell in love with Ford's work in the mid '80s, when he first encountered the novel The Sportswriter and the short-story collection Rock Springs, two touchstones of the era. Nancy not only shares Jeff's appreciation for Ford's work, she also headed the jury that awarded him the American

*Library Association's Andrew Carnegie Medal for
Excellence in Fiction in 2013 for his novel* Canada.

*Richard met us on a beautiful July day on his
woodsy property, where he was puttering in an
outbuilding. Also on hand was his wife of fifty-odd
years, Kristina, a city planner whose assignments
around the country helped facilitate the peripatetic
wanderings of Ford's fiction, including the 1995
Pulitzer Prize winner* Independence Day.

*After brief introductions, Richard led us to his
comfortable waterfront writing studio, where he
assumed his natural role as southern gentleman,
insightful analyst of modern fiction, and often
hilarious raconteur who spoke enthusiastically about
the books he loves and regaled us with stories of
his decades of fellowship with many of the greatest
writers of the last half century.*

―――――――

NANCY: Did you grow up in a reading family?

RICHARD: My mother read books. My father did not.
The closest to literary I came while growing up was
going to the Jackson Public Library, which seemed
important to my mother. She was for all intents and
purposes a single parent; my father was mostly traveling for his job. My father hired someone to keep

the house. So she could read. She'd learned to read in high school, by which I mean she learned to like reading. I, however, am dyslexic, which nobody knew. I didn't, therefore, have much interest in books. Like most kids who have a learning difference, I found other (in my case) transgressive things to do, rather than develop the patience to read books, which I didn't do until I was almost twenty.

NANCY: How did that happen?

RICHARD: I was shamed into it, I suppose. My teachers always said to me that I wasn't stupid but that I just didn't "apply" myself. But after the vicissitude of my father's dying and my mother being marooned with me in Jackson, I needed to get my act together, since my act had been not together at all: troubles with the police, troubles with stealing, troubles with fighting. My mother sent me to my grandparents, who were not literate people either, but they had a station of life that was higher than my parents had had. I began to understand, from them and others, that there was such a thing as a future, and that I didn't want to be constantly a failure. So all of the kinds of laying on that people do to children to get them to do better, be better, finally worked on me. The guy I was running with, my partner in crime, actually got sent to the state prison. I really didn't want that—largely because I thought it would just destroy my mother.

JEFF: Do you remember the first book you really loved when you started reading?

RICHARD: Yes, I do. The first serious novel I ever read was *Absalom, Absalom!* By William Faulkner—one of the more difficult books in American literature. It made a big impression on me, because of course I didn't understand it at all, but I thought, because I felt I should, that I should finish it, so I did. But what I figured out from reading it was a number of things. One, it was very engrossing even though I didn't understand much. I thus understood that it was *okay* not to understand completely what you're reading. I also felt it was about a world, Mississippi in the South and race and history, that I knew something about. So I thought it was relevant. I felt that my life was a kind of dreary life. I was at a point where I thought I was probably going to be just a conventional joe. But here was this enormous, wonderful, magical, incomprehensible book written by a guy right up the road from me, and it kind of made me think that life was maybe worth more than I thought, because life could be the subject of this great book. Reading that novel created what I call an extra beat. If life is dreary, literature gives it an extra beat, consequence—by making life its subject. I credit Faulkner with showing me that. With making me understand that literature was worth the trouble, because it brought you back to life with something you didn't have before.

NANCY: Did it make you want to write as well?

RICHARD: Not directly. I went on to read the sort of standard things people were reading then: Fitzgerald, Flannery O'Connor, Hemingway, Ford Madox Ford. Just a diverse assemblage of readings. And I think when I understood the effect books were having on me, I realized that it would be attractive to do something that would have the same effect on someone else. I didn't have any greater aspiration. I was kind of a natural doodler with words. You get very close to language when you're dyslexic. The cognitive part of language doesn't enter your brain and find a residence there very easily. And so I was very much aware of words, how they looked, how they sounded, how many syllables they had, what happened when I said them one way, what happened when I said them another way. There was a certain kind of suppleness to language which I was attracted to.

NANCY: Did your teachers recognize your dyslexia or was it not diagnosed until later?

RICHARD: Not diagnosed until I was in my forties. I'm not intensely dyslexic. If I were, I don't think I'd be able to write. Kids who are very seriously dyslexic usually don't write novels. I did *not* have attention deficit, however. I was just frustrated by not being able to read fast when everybody else could. But when you're slow like I was, what you read imprints certain things in your mind in a way that, were you a faster reader, they might not. Even at my age now I'm still a ponderously slow reader. A ponderously slow editor. I write with a pencil or a pen. At one time I wanted to be a lawyer and went to law school, but I found the reading to be so onerous that ultimately I just quit. I thought, *I'm putting forth this gigantic effort and I'm not really liking it very much, and probably I'm going to be putting forth this gigantic effort and not really liking it very much all my life.* So I figured, well, better to try something else I do like. Because I liked to read; I just wasn't very proficient at it.

JEFF: As a southerner, do you feel a special affinity for southern fiction?

RICHARD: I feel the opposite. I had to turn my back on it after *The Ultimate Good Luck,* and, really, I should have done it after *A Piece of My Heart.* I realized that most everything I thought about the South, as a setting, as a residence for characters, as an event landscape, as a subject—it was all Faulknerian. Everything I knew about the South, I had read in Faulkner (or Welty or O'Connor or Styron . . . you name them). I was, therefore, never going to be able to write anything truly original if I wrote about the South. And I also thought that the audience for those books were all going to be southerners. And I didn't want to write just for southerners. I didn't even like southerners. [Laughter.] I like a few now. But I wanted to write for the whole world.

I had to find a way to get away from the South. But I also made Frank [Bascombe] a character who was born in Mississippi, just in case I wanted to reach back there and grab something, a little flare from the South I could install in the book. I also found when I was writing *Rock Springs* that a lot of vernacular, a lot of southern humor, southern language, southern attitudes, transferred easily to Montana. Which was freeing to me, because I didn't feel like I had to *completely* cut myself off from everything I'd grown up knowing. The country—America—which is what I try to write about, allows those kinds of these transferences. So what I thought was, *I'm going to be from the South, which definitely is a region, but I'm going to write like an American.*

NANCY: Do you have a preference as a reader between stories and novels? Or do you read both regularly?

RICHARD: I just read what comes over the transom. For better or worse, I'm a soft touch. So when people send me their novels, people I don't know, out of the blue, I'll always open them and read in a ways. Often I don't finish them, because why should there be a lot of really good novels in the world? There aren't. But I always give almost every book that comes anonymously or from friends a try.

JEFF: The first book of yours I fell in love with was *Rock Springs*, which is still one of my all-time favorite books of short stories. Who are the short-story writers you most admire?

RICHARD: Frank O'Connor said short stories were the native American form. They aren't, but there are people who are good at it. Deborah Eisenberg. Dick [Richard] Bausch. Ann Beattie, although she's a novelist as well. As is Dick Bausch. Let's see, those are the first three names. You know, Bob [Robert] Stone was a wonderful short-story writer. Tim O'Brien only wrote one great book of short stories [*The Things They Carried*], but it was really a life-changing book. Oh, and Toby [Tobias] Wolff, for God's sake. Toby Wolff is a great, great, great story writer. Mary Robison. Lorrie Moore. Yeah, you see,

I've grown up with these people. And Raymond Carver, one of my dearest friends, hardly contemporary now because he's been dead thirty-one years, but yeah. It's because of my contemporaries that I think I started writing short stories, because they were so good at it. I kind of felt left out. Plus, they had places they could go and read them aloud. And I was, at the time, writing novels, and it was hard to think I could ever read a piece of a novel aloud at a reading someplace. So I started writing stories to have something to read in public and so I could do things with my pals.

JEFF: *Rock Springs* came out right after *The Sportswriter*, didn't it?

RICHARD: They were written at the same time. When I was writing *The Sportswriter*, which was largely in Missoula—I started it in Princeton and then wrote it mostly in Missoula and finished it in Mississippi. When I would write that for six or seven weeks and kind of hit a flat spot, I'd write a story, and that's how those stories got written. They were being written at the same time. *The Sportswriter* got published in '86, and *Rock Springs* in '87.

JEFF: That's interesting. It seems like that was the moment when your career really took off.

RICHARD: Well, I don't look at things in that way. No

doubt *The Sportswriter* and *Rock Springs* both had a critical reception which was very different from the first two books I wrote, and the processes of writing particularly *The Sportswriter* were very different from the process of writing the previous two books. After *The Ultimate Good Luck*, I had to kind of bump up my game and get better. I had to work harder, and I had to develop ways to get everything I knew onto the page. Before that, I wasn't getting everything in. I was hitting parts of things, but not everything.

JEFF: Were there particular books that influenced your writing when you were working on *The Sportswriter*?

RICHARD: Walker Percy's *The Moviegoer*, of course. I tried to steal as much as I could from that. Fred [Frederick] Exley's book *A Fan's Notes*, which was wonderful. *Something Happened* by Joe [Joseph] Heller. Those were the three that got me able to write *The Sportswriter*.

JEFF: Can you talk a bit about what each of those books meant to you?

RICHARD: Well, Walker—and this is one of the things I realized I wasn't doing in my previous books—Walker, in *The Moviegoer*, was able to actualize Henry James's little dictum, at the beginning of his preface to *What Maisie Knew*, where he says "No themes are so human as those that reflect for us, out of the confusion of life, the close connection of bliss and bale, of the things that help with the things that hurt." *The Moviegoer* could be for me amazingly funny, and yet it was amazingly serious. And I thought that was something I needed to do. Exley did it. And Joe Heller did it too, particularly in *Something Happened*.

The first-person, present-tense verbs were, for me, also crucial. You know the line of Wittgenstein, "He who lives in the present lives in eternity"? I wanted my books to have that sense of the eternal. So present-tense verbs were important for me. All three of those writers could use those pronouns and tenses to their advantage.

Finally, I thought that all three of these books were at times extremely smart. By which I mean that the speaker of the books would say things that were indelible, or that became indelible. I wanted to try to write smart things, because I thought it would make me a better novelist. It would make me be as smart as I could be, maybe even smarter than I was. Books should make you smarter than you are.

NANCY: I loved *The Moviegoer* when I read it, when I was about eighteen.

RICHARD: [Surprised:] You liked it when you were eighteen?

NANCY: Because I totally identified with Kate.

RICHARD: Not with Binx?

NANCY: No, not with Binx, but I felt like I was Kate. Or I wanted to be Kate.

RICHARD: Dabbling in drugs a little bit. Disenchanted—

NANCY: Disenchanted, and depressed. I mean, in her own way, as depressed as Binx was depressed. And then I tried to read it again a few years ago, and I didn't identify with her at all. I felt impatient with her. You know, *Come on, Kate, you have a lot there going on for you!*

RICHARD: And you're not mentally ill.

NANCY: Right, right. Totally. But at that time being mentally ill was attractive to me, and here was this person to whom it was attractive as well. So that was an interesting rereading experience for me.

RICHARD: I'll tell you why I was shocked at you liking *The Moviegoer* when you were eighteen. When I was about twenty-nine, I taught a class on southern literature to PhD students at the University of Michigan, and one of my charges was to teach *The Moviegoer.* These were all high-strung, high-performing Michigan PhDs in literature, and they just said, "We don't understand. We don't know why this is a good book." And they were, many of them, that age of Binx Bolling in the novel. And they couldn't get it. Which may say something about my teaching skills.

NANCY: That's interesting, because I assigned it to a class I taught at the Information School at the University of Washington. I'd assign one book that the whole class would discuss, and *The Moviegoer* was the book I chose one year. And it was the only book in all the years that I taught that class that universally people said, "I don't understand why you chose this book." Like, what? Come on. I mean, exactly the same.

RICHARD: I liked it partly because of New Orleans. Everything I'd read about the South up until the time I read *The Moviegoer* had preoccupations of history and race and, you know, mixed blood and the Civil War. And here was Walker coming along fairly immune to that stuff. He was just writing about contemporary life—in New Orleans, amongst the grandee. I thought, *God, this is so fresh.* It made me think that I could at some point even write about the South myself.

The Percy family asked me to write an introduction to *The Moviegoer* a couple of years ago. So I boned up. I read the biographies. And as I said I had known Walker, was fond of him. He was apparently fond of me. Though he was also quite *erect*, not hail-fellow-well-met. He was a guy who treated you at some remove. So to write the introduction I read *The Moviegoer* again, having read it many times. And I found things in it that I didn't want to have to argue for. It wasn't Walker's fault. History had simply, not really passed it by . . . But with all of this complete cultural lunacy going on in America now, the novel's attitudes about race, about sexuality and relationships between women and men, seem dated—and to some would seem offensive. And I thought, *No, I am not going to subject this wonderful book to this.* Because if I didn't properly disclaim all of the things I would've needed to disclaim—and didn't want to disclaim—some "cultural critic" is going to weasel into that book and make light of it. And I couldn't provide an opportunity for that. And so I ended up sending the money back and declining to write the introduction.

NANCY: Do you read poetry?

RICHARD: I read poetry a lot, because my teachers were all poets when I was in graduate school at Michigan. James McMichael. Donald Hall.

NANCY: Oh my.

RICHARD: And Galway Kinnell. They were my teachers. So I was led to read poetry a lot, particularly by Donald Hall. He used to bring poets in every week—James Wright, Tomas Tranströmer. Galway. Seamus Heaney. Just one week after the next after the next. And Robert Lowell. Philip Larkin. They were just right in front of you, like a banquet. So I went to poetry readings every week for five years.

NANCY: Do you read poetry differently than you read prose?

RICHARD: No, I try to read it *as* prose. Consequently I like those long prosey Whitmanesque lines, where you read through the line breaks and basically read the lines as sentences. I try not to read poems the way I was taught in high school. I try not to pay much attention to the meter. I just try to read it conversationally. Like Eliot said, poetry should be at least as good as prose. So I try to read it somewhat as prose. For me it's another form of sentence writing, of sentence reading.

Charlie [C. K.] Williams. There's my main man. He has a wonderful poem called "My Mother's Lips." It's just about how, when he was talking to his mother as a child, his mother used to say his words silently as he was talking to her. That was just such a galvanizing poem. Again, he wrote these long Whitmanesque lines.

JEFF: What did you think of Carver's poetry?

RICHARD: Oh, I always told him that his poems were just the things that fell out of his stories onto the floor and he picked them up and made poems out of them. But he took offense at that, a kind of amused offense. Though I also really meant it. Ray thought of himself principally as a poet. That was his first love—to write poems. And I think he wrote poems easily. But I loved the stories, so the poems were for me a second order of literary achievement. I mean, there are poems of his that I—you know, when he was dying, a poem called "What the Doctor Said." Have you read that poem? He could do it.

JEFF: Yes.

RICHARD: And you know, at the end of that poem, he's been told that he has two weeks to live, and he jumps up and shakes the doctor's hand and, "I may have even thanked him habit being so strong."

JEFF: What a great line. That book was so powerful for me.

RICHARD: Yeah, it was for me too.

JEFF: Carver's favorite writer was Chekhov, and you edited a wonderful collection of Chekhov's stories that really encapsulates his genius.

RICHARD: Well, it covers the whole arc of his career, from the early stories in the 1870s, when they were funny and absurd and comic, on into the end of the '90s and beyond, when the great work was done.

NANCY: Were you a fan of Chekhov before you were asked to—?

RICHARD: Not very much, because when I was first made to read it, I didn't know what the hell was going on. I mean, I shamefacedly said I was a fan of Chekhov, because I was *supposed* to be a fan of Chekhov. But when this project came along, I thought, *Here's an opportunity for me to make good on what I've been lying about all these years.* So I had to kind of devise and invent an ethic for why Chekhov was worth reading. As I said in the introduction, Chekhov is not for young people. I was young when I first read him; but I was no longer young when I figured out why he was so great.

Reading "The Lady with the Pet Dog" over the years was, for me, a very important experience. When I first read it, in the '60s, here was a story that everybody said was a great story. So I went into it expecting all the guns to go off, but the guns don't really go off in that story—not for me. I kept saying, "What makes this a great story? Ultimately, I figured out that the story acquainted me with what human beings do when they're alone together in rooms. Those things might not be appreciable if you were looking through the window; but when you're looking through the artistic and narrative window of a piece of fiction, more becomes apparent. That's what Chekhov does.

JEFF: I wanted to ask you about Harold Brodkey. I was surprised that you read one of his stories for *The New Yorker* fiction podcast, because he's not someone I would necessarily associate with you.

RICHARD: That first book of stories of his, *First Love and Other Sorrows*, that's a book up my alley. Harold wrote those stories when he was at Harvard. He was in his late teens, early twenties. I was really impressed by that. But the later books that he wrote, and the novel [*The Runaway Soul*], I don't think I even finished it.

JEFF: The reviews for *The Runaway Soul* were just savage.

RICHARD: Probably that was unfair. He had made such a personal and celebrated literary spectacle of himself, he probably couldn't have gotten a fair shake in those days. But, you know, those young stories, those stories of those young boys living in St. Louis, those are deeply affecting to me.

JEFF: Yeah, I love those stories too. Another book of

stories from that era that I always associate with Brodkey's book is *Eleven Kinds of Loneliness* by Richard Yates.

RICHARD: Perfectly reasonable comparison, although I think that Yates was a fundamentally better writer, because he exerted a great deal more control over what he was doing than Harold ever really wanted to. He probably wasn't as raw-talented or as brainy as Harold. Wasn't as nascently gifted. He was like me—not a natural. A little more workmanlike. I wrote Yates a fan letter in the last year of his life, and he was so grateful to get a fan letter from a younger writer. He was living over in Alabama, and I was living in New Orleans, and he was, you know, carrying this oxygen bottle around with him everywhere he went, and schlepping up his stairs to a poor little apartment; teaching at the University of Alabama. Not the end he ever imagined.

JEFF: You know, we talked a bit about Chekhov. But who might—who's going to last from our lifetime?

RICHARD: I don't care. I don't care about my own books lasting. I do not care. Present mirth is present laughter to me. You know, we'll be lucky if anybody reads anything in twenty-five years. Read 'em now—that's all I care about. Legacy, all these made-up sentiments, I don't care about them at all. But that the books that I have written, that they get read now is to me a complete miracle. A complete miracle, because I—I teach at Columbia, and nobody ever talks to me about Carver anymore. I mean, think about Melville, think about Kafka, not appreciated in their lifetimes. So—

JEFF: It shocks me that people aren't reading Carver, though.

RICHARD: They may be reading him, but I don't think that my graduate students—though I don't teach writing, I teach literature, so I don't really see their work, don't see influences get borne out. But nobody's asking me about Carver. And now, you know, men read men, women read women, blacks read blacks, Bengalis read Bengalis, queers read queers. There's not much crossover, you know. When I give readings, I don't see any black faces out there, and I think to myself, *Couldn't I just have a couple of black readers, please?* Because I, you know, I read black writers—I read everybody. I write black characters. I think that the nature of identity politics has bled into literary outcomes. The whole worth of literature is that it's trying to show us we're less distinct from each other than we thought we were.

NANCY: Who from your generation, or the generation before yours, do you wish had written more?

RICHARD: I mostly wish people had written less. I myself haven't written all that much, and that's good. It's probably better for that being so.

NANCY: I knew you were going to say that. I knew that. [Laughter.] Because that's what I would've said too.

RICHARD: Who do I wish had written more? I wish Carver had had the chance to write more. Maybe Jim [James] Salter, who lived into his nineties. I wish Joan Didion had written more novels.

NANCY: I've always thought *Run, River* was one of her best books. Or *Play It As It Lays*.

JEFF: Was Carver planning to write a novel?

RICHARD: He didn't really want to. It was too hard. He saw me slaving away on *The Sportswriter*. I think he sort of thought, *I don't want to be doing that*.

JEFF: What about Philip Roth? Are there Roth books that particularly speak to you?

RICHARD: Yes, many of them. *American Pastoral*, of course. The early books. The funny books. *Goodbye, Columbus*. The stories, the first stories. Let's see—what else? *Sabbath's Theater* I kind of liked, although it was published the year I won the Pulitzer Prize, so I had a slightly unseemly attitude toward it. I liked the memoir about his father [*Patrimony*]. But I wasn't one of those guys who needed to read every book. So, for instance, all of the related books—

JEFF: The Zuckerman books?

RICHARD: I didn't read all of those. I just found I couldn't read all of them. They seemed to me, as a little white Protestant boy, a little more Jewish than I could understand. I mean, my great mentor was Stanley Elkin, but that was Jewishness I *could* understand. That was traveling-salesman Jewish. I really got that.

NANCY: Elkin was so funny! But nobody even mentions his books anymore.

RICHARD: When I was in law school at Washington University, he was teaching across the hall from where I was taking Real Property, and I would slip out after my Real Property class and go and sit in on his classes. As much as anything that made it possible for me to think that there was life after the law. And he became a great friend of mine. Thank God. My life would be a much less good life had it not been for Stanley.

NANCY: You've talked about so many other writers who are your friends. Do you think part of that is because you are a reader?

RICHARD: It might be. But I never wanted to meet writers of books that I admired. I always felt that it was probably going to be underwhelming. That they wouldn't live up to my feelings for the book. That it was the work that mattered most. I feel that way about myself. For instance, I read *Herzog* in Chicago, and when I met Bellow I couldn't quite match how I felt about *Herzog* with Bellow himself.

But I meet people because I'm friendly. It's as simple as that. I'm just a naturally friendly person. It could be my friendliness is an inch thick. It could be completely a false front. You know, my grandfather ran a big hotel. And my father was a traveling salesman. They *had* to be polite to all of their guests and customers. It's how I grew up. Shaking hands with people, looking them in the face, trying to say something to make them happy.

NANCY: What about a fellow Jacksonian, Eudora Welty? You were friends with her.

RICHARD: Well, she was my main person, you know? I didn't know Eudora until 1986, but we grew up in the same neighborhood, more or less. If you lived in Jackson you would not say we grew up in the same neighborhood, because there was a big street between her neighborhood and my neighborhood, North State Street. I lived on the slightly lesser side, and she lived in the slightly upper crust side. But she came to a book signing of mine—in a bookstore in Jackson, when I was signing *The Sportswriter*—and I was just shocked. I just thought to myself, *Have I lived so long to see Eudora Welty waiting in line for me to sign a book?* So after that we became friends, and for a little while I was her literary executor—in fact, right up until the time she died. But what a talent! What a vivid, munificent, mirthful, deep-going talent. My God!

NANCY: Those short stories—

RICHARD: "No Place for You, My Love"—oh my God!

NANCY: What about another Mississippian, Willie Morris?

RICHARD: Sure, I knew Willie Morris. In the late '60s, early '70s, when he was briefly the editor at *Harper's*, I was a young writer, and I sent every story I was writing to him. Because I had a professor at Irvine who knew him, had been at the University of Texas with him. All my stories came bouncing back, bouncing back. "Not for us." "Not for us." "Close but no cigar." Eventually, Willie got fired, and many, many years later, he was living in Oxford, and I knew him a little bit and liked him. So Kristina and I asked him to come over to our house in Clarksdale to have dinner. And I got out all my rejection slips and laid them out on the table around his plate. So when we sat down for dinner, there were all my rejection slips, and he was so great! He read them all aloud. And he said, "Oh, 'Not for us.' Oh! A mistake of a lifetime." Or he said, "Oh Lord, no wonder I got fired!" And he would read another one: "Oh, look at this, what a fool I was!" [Laughter.] You live long enough, everything happens.

Some Books and Authors in Richard's Library

Saul Bellow, *Herzog*
Harold Brodkey, *First Love and Other Sorrows*
Raymond Carver, story collections and "What the Doctor Said"
Anton Chekhov
Joan Didion
Frederick Exley, *A Fan's Notes*
William Faulkner; *Absalom, Absalom!*
Joseph Heller, *Something Happened*
Lorrie Moore
Tim O'Brien, *The Things They Carried*
Walker Percy, *The Moviegoer*

Mary Robison
James Salter
Eudora Welty, "No Place for You, My Love"
C. K. Williams
Tobias Wolff, *Our Story Begins: New and
Selected Stories*
Richard Yates

Siri Hustvedt

Everything about Siri Hustvedt—from her name, to her blond hair and ice-blue eyes, to the polished, uncluttered surfaces of her Brooklyn town house— bespeaks her Scandinavian heritage. It was, perhaps, a heritage she was eager to escape when she left Minnesota for the noisy, cluttered confines of New York City in 1978, shortly after getting her BA in history from Saint Olaf College, where her father was chairman of the Norwegian Department.

She published her first book, a slender volume of

poetry entitled Reading to You, *in 1982. In 1986, she got her PhD in English from Columbia (her dissertation was on Charles Dickens's novel* Our Mutual Friend*), then shifted her focus to writing fiction. She published her first novel,* The Blindfold, *in 1992. Since then, she has written six more novels, including the 2015 Los Angeles Times Book Prize–winner* The Blazing World, *and six books of nonfiction focusing on art, literature, psychology, feminism, and her own seizure disorder.*

Married to fellow novelist Paul Auster and the mother of singer-songwriter Sophie Auster, she is also a lecturer in psychiatry at the Weill Cornell Medical College of Cornell University. Our interview took place at the end of the book tour for her latest novel, Memories of the Future, *and in between her seemingly endless schedule of international lectures.*

———

NANCY: Did your parents read to you when you were a child?

SIRI: Yes, my mother read to me and my three sisters, but we quickly took over our own reading. I read to my daughter for years, but I had one child, not four. I remember reading the Nancy Drew books in the second grade with tremendous avidity, followed by

Beverly Cleary in the third. I loved *Ellen Tebbits*. Its heroine nicely matched my child self.

NANCY: That's my favorite Cleary book as well.

SIRI: Ellen wants to be so good and cooperative, but the effort is also a strain. I was the oldest child, and I rarely lived up to my fantasy of who I imagined I should be.

NANCY: And her best friend's mother is a terrible seamstress, so when Ellen and Austine want to dress as twins—

SIRI: And Austine shows up in this wreck of a dress. The plan to be twins is dashed, and the painful episode hurts the friendship. I ordered *Ellen Tebbits* in school, from the Scholastic Book Club. I could get three or four books for a dollar. I chose them with great care, waited impatiently for them to arrive, and then read them in a state of drunken pleasure. Some of my earliest reading memories take place at the Carnegie Public Library in my hometown, Northfield [Minnesota], when I was still learning to read. It had a summer reading program for children. I loved the quiet, the smell, the books wrapped in plastic, the cards slipped in and out of the back pocket. I found The Lonely Doll books [by Dare Wright] in that library.

NANCY: Oh, those books are bizarre!

SIRI: Bizarre, if not perverse. I found them compelling and disturbing. They were illustrated with black-and-white photographs of the doll, Edith, and her stuffed bear companions. I felt those toys had secret lives, that there was more than what I read on the page. My own work is full of dolls. I am hardly alone in my fascination. Think of Daedalus and Pygmalion. Dolls are like characters breathed to life by their authors, but also corpse-like, empty of life. *Alice's Adventures in Wonderland* [by Lewis Carroll] had a similarly powerful effect on me. I remember puzzling over some of the hard words. The book still haunts me. Great children's literature has shadows.

I was seized by bibliomania or what I call "lexiphilia" early on. I read all the Tom Swift books I found on a shelf in a cabin in northern Minnesota my parents had borrowed from friends. I was eight or nine. I vividly remember lying on the dock, finishing one and picking up the next one. As an older person, I have come to think reading insulated me from an overactive nervous system, allowed me to retreat from the world and its pounding stimuli.

NANCY: I think many readers these days are using books to distance themselves from what's happening in the world.

SIRI: Well, I have mirror-touch synesthesia. When I see someone touched, jostled, or hit, I have a mirroring sensation in my own body. I have also had migraine with aura from an early age, although it wasn't diagnosed until much later. But when I turned twelve, my reading exploded. I was able to read little print. Of course it had nothing to do with the size of the print, but my comprehension of what I was reading. Before then, I had had the pretension and desire to read "hard" books but couldn't penetrate them.

In the fifth grade, I became interested in the abolitionists, no doubt because of the civil rights movement, which I witnessed only on television, although I didn't consciously connect the two. Along with a wonderful biography of Harriet Tubman by Ann Petry for children, I slogged my way through Booker T. Washington's *Up from Slavery*. I missed a lot of it, but I pursued it doggedly nevertheless. I recorded these efforts in *Memories of the Future*. The relentless pursuit of difficult texts remains part of my life. I have been reading Kierkegaard since I was a teenager, slowly incorporating his thought and layers of irony into my own thinking. Edmund Husserl is another writer I've been reading for years with increasing comprehension but many blanks remain. I'm relaxed about it now. I've come to realize that material goes in even when I can't articulate exactly what meanings I've imbibed.

JEFF: Was *Up from Slavery* the first adult book you read?

SIRI: I read *Uncle Tom's Cabin* [by Harriet Beecher Stowe] the same year. The nineteenth-century language was a struggle, but the book's terrible scenes stayed with me. I can still see the library shelf where I found those books—*Uncle Tom's Cabin, Up from Slavery,* and the Silhouette biographies for children.

JEFF: Why do you think you were so fascinated with slavery and the black experience? Minnesota must have been a very white place in those days.

SIRI: It was all white. I didn't know any black people. I suspect I was smitten by a noble cause, but I also had feelings of being different, marginal, that may have spurred my identification, however unjustified. What did I know about racism? I think I was seven before I saw a black person. My great-uncle David took me and my sister, Liv, to Chicago when my mother was giving birth to our younger sister. We couldn't have been away for more than a week or ten days, but I missed my mother desperately. David lived in a white working-class suburb, Highwood, but when my mother came to get us, she took us to the Loop in the city, and I saw "Negro" girls my age with amazing hairdos—barrettes, braids, and ribbons. My hair was plain, blond, and straight cut. My mother was not interested in arranging four heads of hair, but when we returned from the trip, I talked my paternal grandmother into giving me lots of braids to mimic the look I had envied in Chicago. Naïve appropriation.

My parents sympathized with the civil rights movement, although they were hardly activists. They shielded us from comics (a vulgar form), coloring books (not creative enough), and "inappropriate" movies, but not from the news. My father had known James Reeb, the minister and civil rights activist, when they were in college together at Saint Olaf. White bigots murdered Reeb in 1965 just after Bloody Sunday. The white hospital refused to take a white man in league with blacks, and he died of his wounds in a Negro hospital. My father learned about the murder on the news. I will never forget how he responded, as if he had received a physical blow. That second-hand experience was as close as I got to a personal memory of the movement, but it made a deep impression on me.

What interests me now is the degree to which my reading was directed by what was happening far away from me. At fourteen, I became a passionate opponent of the Vietnam War and spent a lot of time reading about French colonial history in the Saint Olaf Library. I had access to it because my father was a professor there. I also became caught up in the women's liberation movement. I read Germaine Greer, Kate Millett, Simone de Beauvoir, and every essay in Robin Morgan's *Sisterhood Is Powerful* several times.

NANCY: You mentioned that you got books from your school library. Do you remember the librarian?

SIRI: Yes, it was a man, Mr. Edwards.

NANCY: A man. That was unusual at that time.

SIRI: He had a tremor. I remember asking my fifth-grade teacher, Mr. Lindner, another man in a sea of women teachers, about our librarian's shaking. He said, "I think he has a touch of the palsy." The sentence never left me. I call sentences like that "brain tattoos." Years later I would have my own shaking episodes and write a book about them: *The Shaking Woman or a History of My Nerves.*

I was in Bergen, Norway, at a Rudolf Steiner School in the seventh grade when I truly began understanding books for adults. My father had a sabbatical year. I had teachers who took a genuine interest in my reading. The school was so different from my public school in Minnesota, where the authorities were obsessed with discipline and keeping order. I felt free in school for the first time. In hindsight, I am grateful for the fact that at a crucial moment of my development I was encouraged, not shut down.

NANCY: Do you distinguish now between reading for pleasure and reading for work?

SIRI: Yes, I do a lot of research for the scholarly half of my life, preparing scientific and other academic lectures and papers. As a respite from turgid texts, I read poems. Emily Dickinson is my first choice. When I travel, I have novels as well as science and philosophy on my iPad. I have the complete Henry James. I'll reread one of his novels on a plane or train.

NANCY: And Edith Wharton?

SIRI: I reread *The House of Mirth* not long ago with great pleasure. The ironies are terrible. Lily's bid for autonomy in her world is both misguided and ruinous. My mother, now ninety-six, was a great reader before her memory began to dim. Not long after my father died, when she was still in her eighties, my mother gave me an excerpt from either Wharton's diary or a letter she had written to her lover. My mother said, "I think this is the most erotic thing I've ever read." After I had read it, I had to agree. It wasn't explicit, but it was charged with sexual desire.

My Norwegian mother, who studied English at the University of Oslo, orchestrated my reading when I was young. She recommended [Jane] Austen, the Brontës, [Mark] Twain, [Alexandre] Dumas [père], and [Charles] Dickens. Years later, I wrote my dissertation on Dickens at Columbia.

JEFF: Your first book was a collection of your poetry, wasn't it?

SIRI: It was. In 1982.

JEFF: You should bring it back into print. It's impossible to find.

SIRI: No doubt. Five hundred copies were printed. I wrote hundreds of poems, pared the book down to thirty-two pages, and I still stand by the work I published.

JEFF: Who were the poets who inspired you back then?

SIRI: My mother gave me Dickinson and Blake when I was eleven. I loved those poems. As a teenager, I read the canonical English poets and the modernists—[Ezra] Pound, [T. S.] Eliot, [Wallace] Stevens, [William Carlos] Williams, and the dreadful poet Archibald MacLeish, whom I thought I should like but didn't, but also Sylvia Plath, Lawrence Ferlinghetti, Diane Wakoski, Adrienne Rich, Allen Ginsberg, and Audre Lorde. After I moved to New York, I became enthralled with the New York School poets. I took Kenneth Koch's undergraduate course in poetic form when I was a graduate student. I was his graduate assistant for a year, and we became friends.

NANCY: Do you read poetry in other languages?

SIRI: I read a lot of French, German, and Scandinavian poetry too. Baudelaire and Rimbaud, but also Ingeborg Bachmann and Inger Christensen—the latter two remain deeply important to me. I loved the Russian poets [Anna] Akhmatova and [Marina] Tsvetaeva, although I read them in translation. Now I teach a seminar at Weill Cornell Medical College where I am a lecturer in psychiatry and often teach poems.

NANCY: My husband also used poetry when he taught psychology courses—quite different from a psych textbook.

SIRI: When I began the seminar, I assigned longer texts: Kafka's "A Country Doctor" and a long excerpt from Charlotte Perkins Gilman's "The Yellow Wallpaper," but also a philosophical text related to psychiatry. Louis Sass and Josef Parnas's "Schizophrenia, Consciousness, and the Self" was one. I learned fast that the doctors are too tired to read anything lengthy for a class that is not required. Now I assign a poem or a short passage from a longer work.

JEFF: Which novels would you give them pieces of?

SIRI: Last year I gave them a passage from *Finnegan's Wake* [by James Joyce] and a verbatim extract from one of Emil Kraepelin's psychotic patients (dementia praecox, 1896)—a rich study in counterpoint. I also gave them a small piece of *The Bell Jar* [by Sylvia Plath], Esther's first meeting with her psychiatrist, Dr. Gordon, which worked well. It opened up questions of power, empathy, and vulnerability. Despite the fact that doctors have more power than their patients, psychiatrists are vulnerable too. They have to maintain a balance between authority and empathy. Too much empathy in a doctor can interfere with good practice.

NANCY: Were they already familiar with Sylvia Plath?

SIRI: Yes, they knew Plath. Other writers I've taught—Theodore Roethke—not a clue.

JEFF: Do you have favorite books that involve psychiatry?

SIRI: I have a fairly extensive collection of mental illness memoirs, all published in the late nineteenth and early twentieth centuries, including Tolstoy's *A Confession*, Daniel Schreber's *Memoirs of My Nervous Illness*, and Clifford Beers's *A Mind That Found Itself*. It's become a popular genre. I may be alone in not liking [William] Styron's *Darkness Visible*. He fell for a fashionable neurochemical explanation for depression, and it mars the book. Very little is known about the biology of depression. Novels? *Zeno's Conscience* [by Italo Svevo] with a nasty preface about his patient by Zeno's analyst.

There's *Tender Is the Night*. Zelda's illness led to [F. Scott] Fitzgerald's immersion in psychoanalysis. I used an excerpt from the novel in class. The psychiatrists were pretty hard on Fitzgerald's hero.

NANCY: Dick Diver.

SIRI: Dick Diver, what a name!

JEFF: What about [Philip Roth's] *Portnoy's Complaint*?

SIRI: There's no dialogue in *Portnoy's Complaint*. It's a tirade that ends with a joke.

JEFF: "Now vee may perhaps to begin?" [Laughter.]

NANCY: Was there a novel that you read and afterwards said, "I want to write a novel."

SIRI: *David Copperfield* [by Charles Dickens]. I was thirteen. My family spent the summer of 1968 in Iceland. My father was studying the sagas. It never got dark in Iceland, and I couldn't sleep, so I lay awake and read and read and read. David's story entranced me—his suffering from Mr. Murdstone's sadism, Peggotty's goodness to him, his humiliation in the warehouse. I was David. I remember putting the book down after a particularly moving scene, walking to the window, looking out at Reykjavik, and thinking, *If this is what books can do, I want to do it too*. I announced my ambition. I'm sure people thought I was a pretentious twit. I began writing terrible stories and poems.

JEFF: Did *David Copperfield* inspire any of your fiction?

SIRI: Genuine influence becomes unconscious, but I have alluded to Dickens in a number of books. *Memories of the Future* is dense with nods to Dickens's prose and humor. *Don Quixote* [by Miguel de Cervantes] and *Tristram Shandy* [by Laurence Sterne] pop up throughout. Charlotte Lennox's *The Female Quixote* makes an appearance. My older narrator addresses the reader directly—an eighteenth-century convention. It's in part a novel about reading, about being transformed by what you read, and being both blinded and . . .

NANCY: Awakened.

SIRI: Yes, awakened to new realities and possibilities. I quote Simone Weil in the book: "Imagination and fiction make up more than three-quarters of our real life." Weil did not approve of this truth, but I have a more optimistic view. It's hard to occupy a place in the real world you haven't imagined. Reading fiction can move us into new places and provide new perspectives on the world. It can create an expansion of consciousness and serve as an intimate form of knowledge. This has been forgotten in our culture because the imaginary is regarded as soft, feminine, and unserious. Science is hard and masculine. Real men don't read fiction, right? This prejudicial, frankly absurd, hierarchy keeps boys away from novels, shrinks overall knowledge, and impoverishes our culture.

For four years, I was a volunteer writing teacher at the Payne Whitney Psychiatric Clinic in New York. I came to understand that writing does have therapeutic benefits. I saw it in the patients. I would bring in a short literary text, and they would respond in writing. Empirical studies by [James W.] Pennebaker have shown that twenty minutes of emotionally driven writing a day improves immune and liver function and overall mood in patients and non-patients alike.

JEFF: Like meditation.

SIRI: Meditation has similarly good effects, but for different reasons. Writing moves the inside outside. Meditation doesn't. It's purely internal.

NANCY: Do you think then that reading takes the outside and puts it inside?

SIRI: Reading means being inhabited by the voice of another person that originates outside you, a form of possession, which is not purely passive. As you read, you generate images; your whole body participates even though you aren't moving. Vittorio Gallese, the neuroscientist who's also a friend, calls it "embodied simulation."

NANCY: Brain stuff. You're creating. Paul [Auster] has an essay where he talks about the writer collaborating with the reader.

SIRI: Paul is right. Reading is a collaborative act between reader and text. In one of my essays, "On Reading," I argue that the reader reinvents the text through her own embodied reality, for better and for worse. Any writer who has ever been reviewed knows how different readings of the same book can be.

JEFF: When you were still in Minnesota, were there particular books that influenced your view of New York? Is that part of what brought you here?

SIRI: I had read a lot by the time I left college and moved to New York, but I was naïve. I thought I was emotionally mature . . .

NANCY: Don't we all?

SIRI: I had a fantasy of a teeming metropolis. I had seen movies—the skyline, Central Park, the bridges. I imagined a place of freedom. After I arrived, my imaginary city mingled with the real city. I wasn't looking for happiness. I wanted adventure. The city of the novel is an idea as much as a place, and it goes by different names: New York, London, Paris, Saint Petersburg. Like so many heroes and heroines in books, I wanted out of the provinces.

JEFF: Were there books, though, that informed that view?

SIRI: I had read about many New Yorks—[Edith] Wharton's novels set in the city, [Herman] Melville's "Bartleby," [Henry] James's *Washington Square*, [Henry] Roth's *Call It Sleep*, [Ralph] Ellison's *Invisible Man*, [J. D.] Salinger's *The Catcher in the Rye*, [Mary] McCarthy's *The Group*. I already mentioned [Sylvia Plath's] *The Bell Jar*, [James] Baldwin's *Go Tell It on the Mountain*. Erica Jong's narrator in *Fear of Flying* is from the Upper West Side. But if you think about it, these books don't create a unified image of the city. Baldwin was important to me as a teenager. I've been rereading him recently. His ruthless intellectual honesty, his embrace of ambiguities, his luminous classical prose, continue to impress me. Then he represented an urbane, black, gay, passionate intellectual, and writer, an ideal. I was drawn to the so-called New York intellectuals of the *Partisan Review*. Baldwin was associated with them. I studied with Steven Marcus at Columbia, who was a protégé of Lionel Trilling.

NANCY: Were there other women writers that were important to you?

SIRI: Continuing a theme, the philosopher Hannah Arendt. I have recently returned to her work and her concept of "natality." I loved [Grace Paley's] *The Little Disturbances of Man*. I read it after I had moved to New York. And Flannery O'Connor's novel *Wise Blood* and her stories had a strong impact on me. There are other writers who were powerful. I've read *Middlemarch* [by George Eliot] four times. [Jane] Austen's wit, irony, and rhetorical genius continue to amaze me. [Virginia] Woolf's *To the Lighthouse* is an astonishing work. I reread it after years of being immersed in the French philosopher [Maurice] Merleau-Ponty and felt multiple echoes between them. Gertrude Stein's rhythms were important. I discovered Margaret Cavendish's fiction and natural philosophy not long ago, a profound thinker Woolf insulted. I forgive VW. I have read *Wuthering Heights* [by Emily Brontë] four times too. What a diabolical structure. It explodes all conventional borders, between human and animal, reason and emotion, waking and dreaming, male and female. There are countless interpretations of that book, all coherent. I think the form emerged from Emily Brontë's highly literate unconscious. She was only twenty-eight when she started it. And I've read all of [Jean] Rhys's books. Those diamond-like sentences gleaming with clarity. But they are depressing.

NANCY: Yes, indeed.

SIRI: When my daughter, Sophie, was eleven, she begged me to read *Wuthering Heights* to her because she had loved *Jane Eyre* [by Charlotte Brontë]. I was dubious. It's an amoral book. We read it anyway. When we had finished it, Sophie said, "You know what, Mom? Great books can be really, really sad, but they're never depressing." She's right. This truth may be what Aristotle meant by catharsis—a shattering art experience that's nevertheless liberating.

NANCY: And are there contemporary novelists you run out and—

SIRI: I admired Anna Burns's *Milkman* and Katja Petrowskaya's *Maybe Esther*. I'm a great fan of the Israeli writer Zeruya Shalev, hugely famous in her own country and in Europe but she's been badly published here so far. *Pain* is her new book, published by Other Press. Shalev's psychological acumen is nothing short of breathtaking. I loved Julie Otsuka's *The Buddha in the Attic*, told in the first-person plural in elegant rhythmic prose. Kate Zambreno's harrowing *Book of Mutter* impressed me. Katie Kitamura is another writer I follow.

NANCY: What about genre fiction? Did you ever go through a phase where you read, say, Agatha Christie?

SIRI: During the year of little print, I discovered my aunt had all of Agatha Christie in her house outside of Bergen. I would read two in an afternoon. The plots keep you hopping. Suspense involves expectation, prediction, and surprise. It's also essential to narrative. Many years ago, Paul and I were in Sweden at a literary festival. Paul was on TV with Mickey Spillane, who uttered a sentence we have been quoting ever since: "Nobody reads a book to get to the middle."

JEFF: So true.

SIRI: Novels often sag under their own weight halfway through. At the same time, not all good novels are plot driven. Don DeLillo, a friend and writer I admire, doesn't write books with narrative push. I read his books for his tightly sprung, musical sentences, his humor and ironies, and his gift for describing phenomenological reality—a fully sensual world. There is nothing "natural" about Don's dialogue, but it's wonderful. Every book of his has a highly developed inner logic.

[Robert] Musil's *The Man Without Qualities* is an immense, unfinished novel, attenuated by brilliant essays. It's deeply absorbing, and yet I read many hundreds of pages twice and never finished it. Djuna Barnes's *Nightwood*, a beloved book of mine, does not rely on suspense but has an intensity that crushed me. I read it not long after I moved to New

York and wrote about it for a seminar with Carolyn Heilbrun. When I reread it years later, I worried it wouldn't hold up, but it's tremendous—a dense excursion into what was then called "sexual inversion," a startling, lavishly written text about blurring borders—the feminine, masculine, and in-between.

JEFF: Who do you think writing today is most likely to outlast our own time?

SIRI: We can't know. Writers celebrated in their time often vanish. Think of Booth Tarkington. What looked brilliant then seems mediocre now. American literary consensus has often tended toward the middling. Women disappear because they are women. Some have been revived. Eliza Heywood is now in the eighteenth-century English canon. Sexual prejudice and race prejudice have frequently been routes to oblivion. Zora Neale Hurston, famous in her time, fell into obscurity but is now deservedly canonized. When the *New York Times* published a hundred years of its reviews, they couldn't find a decent review of Faulkner. The review of Dostoevsky was an embarrassment marked by British-style snobbery about Russian "emotionality." Nothing has changed.

We don't know what the future of literary culture will be. Fictional stories aren't leaving us. The hunger for narrative is immense. Symbols aren't going away. We are symbolic creatures. As a writer, I have discovered that literary culture varies enormously from country to country—different histories and traditions—much longer than ours in the United States. Alarmist scenarios about the end of the book and reading have created the curious idea that reading in itself is good. Not true. It is what you read that matters and that you read not to shore up your own smug beliefs but to press yourself beyond them. Books become us. They are literally embedded in our nervous systems in memories. Those memories shift over time, but they form us nevertheless. Newer forms of delivering stories are far more visual than poetry and the novel. Virtual and interactive fictions are growing, and this may alter human beings in unknown ways. But reading fiction is already a virtual reality the reader creates, and I hope long prose fiction will survive, because when it's good, it changes our minds.

Some Books and Authors in Siri's Library

James Baldwin, *Go Tell It on the Mountain*
Djuna Barnes, *Nightwood*

Emily Brontë, *Wuthering Heights*

Anna Burns, *Milkman*

Margaret Cavendish

Charles Dickens, *David Copperfield*

George Eliot, *Middlemarch*

Zora Neale Hurston

Erica Jong

Mary McCarthy

Flannery O'Connor, *Wise Blood*

Julie Otsuka, *The Buddha in the Attic*

Katja Petrowskaya, *Maybe Esther*

Ann Petry

Jean Rhys

Zeruya Shalev, *Pain*

Edith Wharton, *The House of Mirth*

Virginia Woolf, *To the Lighthouse*

Kate Zambreno, *Book of Mutter*

Charles Johnson

When Charles Johnson was fourteen, in 1962, he told his father he wanted to be a cartoonist. "They don't let black people do that" was his father's reply. Chuck, as he's been known all his life, wasn't discouraged. He got a second opinion from cartoonist and teacher Lawrence Lariar, with whom he ended up studying, and under whose tutelage he became a professional cartoonist before he was old enough to vote. In 1970, he created a television show for PBS, Charlie's Pad, in which he taught cartooning.

At the same time, the Chicago-area native went to Southern Illinois University, where he earned a BA in journalism and an MA in philosophy, and also began to develop his literary craft, studying with author and legendary creative writing teacher John Gardner. With Gardner as his mentor, he wrote six unpublished apprentice novels before finally publishing his seventh, Faith and the Good Thing, *in 1974. It was praised by the* New York Times Book Review *as "an ebullient, philosophical novel . . . a many splendored and ennobling weaving together of thought, suffering, humor, and magic." He earned a PhD in philosophy from State University of New York, Stony Brook, and joined the faculty of the University of Washington in 1976, eventually heading up the school's creative writing program before retiring in 2009.*

*Along the way, Chuck has published three more novels (*Oxherding Tale; *the National Book Award– winning* Middle Passage, *and* Dreamer*), four collections of short stories, works on philosophy and Buddhism, and several children's books. In* Being and Race: Black Writing Since 1970, *he called for black writers to create "a fiction of increasing artistic and intellectual growth, one that enables us as a people—as a culture—to move from narrow*

*complaint to broad celebration"—which is exactly
what he himself has done.*

*Our interview took place at the home of his friend
and fellow writer Sharyn Skeeter, and touched on the
wide variety of interests that inform Chuck's reading
life.*

NANCY: What are you reading now?

CHARLES: Almost everything I'm reading now is related to what I'm working on. So I'm reading lots
of science articles, because my daughter and I are
writing a children's book series about the adventures
in science of a little boy named Emery Jones. It's
a series devoted to trying to get kids interested in
STEM [science, technology, engineering, and math-
ematics], particularly kids of color, because there is
a tremendous dearth of children's books with kids
of color in them, or by authors or illustrators who
are of color. So I'm reading as much science as I can
that's written for non-scientists.

JEFF: What inspired your love of reading?

CHARLES: My mother always wanted to be a teacher
but couldn't become one because she had severe
asthma. I was an only child and so she more or less
made me her student. She belonged to three book

clubs and kept the house full of books. I could easily pull down any title from the shelves. She had books on yoga, costume design, and home repair manuals. The way I learned about meditation was from the book my mother had on yoga. When I was fourteen, I discovered what a wonderful thing it is to meditate for half an hour. She had another book that was a pictorial history of the American theater. I remember that it was really fascinating, all those photos of different productions. After she passed away, I brought her library back to my house.

But you have to understand I was passionate about drawing as a teenager, rather than reading. My orientation was always toward the visual arts. I did the illustrations for the catalog of a magic company in Chicago from 1965 all the way through high school and won two second place awards from Columbia University for high school cartoonists. I was accepted at an art school, but in the spring of 1966, just before graduation, my high school art teacher, who was very direct and probably kind of demoralized, said to me, "You know, Chuck, if you're going to be an artist, you're going to have a hard life. Art school is a big gamble." So I ran upstairs to my adviser's office and asked her what schools were still accepting students that late in the spring, which is how I ended up at Southern Illinois University. She pointed out that I could major in journalism and still be able to draw. For four years I drew for *The Daily Egyptian*, the college paper, and then for *The Southern Illinoisan*, the town paper, where I also worked briefly as a reporter before going on to get a master's degree in philosophy there. So that's sort of my genesis story: it starts out with the visual arts, but I always read because the visual arts—as any cartoonist will tell you—draw upon literature for ideas.

NANCY: When you were a kid, were you conscious of the lack of people of color in the books that you read?

CHARLES: Well, yeah. The very first book I ever found by a black writer was in my mother's library. It was Richard Wright's *Black Boy*. I remember looking at it thinking, *What is this?* Because my teachers in middle school and high school never mentioned any black authors. They weren't part of the curriculum in the '50s and '60s.

JEFF: What about books like *Huckleberry Finn* and *Uncle Tom's Cabin*? Were those books you read in school? And how did you feel about the way they depicted black characters?

CHARLES: I didn't read *Uncle Tom's Cabin* until I was asked to write an introduction to it for the Oxford

World's Classics edition. I remember telling August Wilson that I was doing this introduction, and it turned out that he hadn't read it either. We decided we'd both read it at the same time. You know, that's a very well written novel, with all the virtues of good entertainment. But Stowe's problem was that she believed, like Abraham Lincoln and others, that while slavery was a horrendous and evil thing, particularly after the Fugitive Slave Act—where those who made it to freedom could be dragged back into slavery in the South, which is when the novel came out—despite knowing that this is evil, they believed black people should be recolonized somewhere else. Which is why Liberia was created. They still saw America as a white man's country.

There's one black character in *Uncle Tom's Cabin*, I remember, who's going to do something like go back to Africa. And the whole idea is that if the races were separate, black people would do okay, they would thrive on their own, right? So when I read those books you're talking about I obviously could not identify with the characters in them. For one thing, I didn't grow up in the South, I grew up in Illinois, in the Midwest, and the complexity and diversity of black people that I knew was not represented in anybody's book, whether it's Faulkner or Hemingway or any of the major modernists. It just wasn't the case that you saw that complexity or depth of character, which is probably one of the reasons why I and many other black writers started writing stories and novels.

JEFF: You mentioned Richard Wright. Who were the other black writers who influenced you?

CHARLES: Wright was one of my heroes. He's rightly called the father of modern black fiction, because he just kind of left his imprint on the genre—and I think we can call black literature a genre. It has certain conventions that have to be followed, and he actually started that. If you look at his work, you see the elements of what makes the genre: relentless depictions of black victimization and a rather grim portrait of black American life. That wasn't true during the Harlem Renaissance. You look at those writers, and you see a whole lot more diversity. But Wright just kind of nailed it down. So that Sartre, who was Wright's friend, can say in *What Is Literature*, if you are a black writer, as soon as you pick up the pen you know what your subject is: segregation, Jim Crow, victimization. And I've always thought about that statement, because I don't believe that.

I mean, I was eighteen in 1966, the civil rights movement was basically over. I lived through some things in the '50s involving segregation, because I ran into it here and there, but not a whole lot in the Evanston, Illinois, suburbs I grew up in. I saw it in the South when my family would go down there and visit relatives. But to me, it was something that was in the past. I grew up with a much more optimistic and positive vision of the possibilities of black life and my own life.

JEFF: Who were some of your other early favorites as a reader?

CHARLES: I read everything. Everybody I could find who was a good storyteller. That's really all I cared about. Some of them were probably people who today would be regarded as racist. For example, Jack London. And then any writer who was imaginative. In high school I read a lot of sci-fi; I was in a science-fiction book club in high school. I got sci-fi books every month that I paid for with my paper route. I had an original copy of Philip K. Dick's *The Man in the High Castle*, the classic novel in terms of alternate universes. Then in high school we read Shakespeare and *1984*. *All the King's Men*.

NANCY: The racism in *All the King's Men* is pretty horrifying. Not that Robert Penn Warren was a racist, but the picture of the period in US history that he was writing about.

CHARLES: Well, yeah, if you go to any white author prior to 1960, there's probably going to be something in the text that we would deem today to be racist. Why is that? Because segregation forced people to be separate and so they could never get to know each other. On the white side you had people who were very progressive and wanted to know more, like Sinclair Lewis, who wrote *Kingsblood Royal* by talking to a lot of black people. What happens is that this white character comes back from World War II, and discovers he has black ancestors. And in America he's living in an all-white world. When he tries to tell people he's part black, they say, "Don't tell me, don't tell anybody." So he goes over to the black part of town and starts meeting people, all kinds of people, black people who are exemplary human beings, and some who are not exemplary human beings. I mean, it's this continuum, right? But nevertheless, at the end of the novel, he winds up barricaded in his home with black people and fighting for black folks.

JEFF: What about when you were developing your craft as a writer? What books influenced you then?

CHARLES: In the early '80s, when I was developing my own sense of craft, I deeply appreciated the series of lectures the critic Northrup Frye had delivered on

Canadian radio in the 1960s, which appeared as the book *The Educated Imagination*. I recommended that text to my students for thirty-three years. I also valued back then, and also today, Jean-Paul Sartre's phenomenological description of the experience of writing and reading in his chapters "What Is Writing?" and "Why Write?" in *Literature and Existentialism*. And an important text a colleague at UW gave me during my first year of teaching was *What Is the Short Story?* by Eugene Current-Garcia and Walton R. Patrick. For many years I had my students read all the essays from Washington Irving to Joyce Carol Oates, because they provide a clear picture of the evolution of the modern short story.

NANCY: Tell us about John Gardner—I know you were his student. I really appreciated his book *On Moral Fiction*.

CHARLES: You like that book? Why?

NANCY: I do. Because I think that in addition to everything that fiction does to entertain and enlighten us, it needs to make us better people, give us insights into, or at least empathy for, other people.

CHARLES: I agree that there should be something like what you're talking about in our experience of literature—we should come out of it not as clean as we went in; it should clarify things for us. If it has a moral vision, that's all the better. I actually wrote a piece called "A Phenomenology of Moral Fiction," where I look at what John's doing philosophically in that manifesto. His book was controversial because he attacked everybody in the world of literature. I mean, he found fault with everybody, and his publisher didn't want to publish it because they also published many of those writers. When the book came out, other writers would look at the index to see if they were mentioned.

Gardner was a medievalist and got me interested in medieval literature. Who else would get me to read Chaucer or *Sir Gawain and the Green Knight*? And there were enough similarities between him and me that I thought, *I can work with this guy.* Because I think before you take an art class with somebody you should look at their art to see a couple of things. One is, can I get along with this person if he or she's my teacher? But also, what can this person teach me? I'd read *Grendel* before and thought Gardner was interesting. I knew he liked philosophy, because the whole book is a send-up of Sartre. Okay, Gardner's saying, if you believe Sartre's philosophy, you will become a monster like Grendel. Gardner said to me that he told the story to himself over and over again, for years, and then he just sat down and wrote it in six months. So he was philosophical, he was learned.

You know, John was my mentor; he brought me into the book world. He got me my agent, who was his agent. He was brought into the agency by Stanley Elkin, and much later I brought my student, David Guterson, into the same agency. But John once wrote a letter to our agent when he was first being represented by him where he said, "I'm the best writer of my generation." That's what he thought. But he truly was the best creative writing teacher of all time as far as I'm concerned.

NANCY: Getting back to *On Moral Fiction*, I'm wondering what books you feel reflect Gardner's beliefs? For example, *Middle Passage* exemplifies exactly what he's saying, right?

CHARLES: Yeah, I wouldn't write and publish something that wouldn't give you some vision of hope. That's one reason I'm not writing a novel right now, when everything's so bad. We don't need another novel telling us everything's falling apart. I mean, I don't want to, I don't need to write that book.

But when you talk about books that have a clear moral vision, I think of Hermann Hesse. What fascinated me about Hesse was the way he was trying to arc in his thinking toward the East. He does that in *Siddhartha* and does it pretty well for a German in the 1920s, because he grew up in a household that had all kinds of quote unquote Orientalist texts that he absorbed. And he gets it. I had to respond to that. I wrote *Oxherding Tale* because I just had to respond to that from an African American perspective, using a slave narrative as the form. One of the things I found interesting about Hesse was his use of forms. For example, he uses a literary form popular in Germany in the eighteenth and early nineteenth centuries called *Bundesroman*, translated as "the league novel," in *Journey to the East*. He takes it from its pulp beginnings and adds a kind of spiritual component to it that elevates the pop form to art.

One of the things John used to say is that an awful lot of American literature actually starts out with trash, and we find a way to elevate it; you know, whether it's music or whatever, you take the form and you open it up to greater questions. And then the platform is more expansive in this reinterpretation. So I looked at a lot of Hesse for that reason. Some of the forms he was working with I found to be very interesting.

When I get into a writer, I read everything. I did with Hesse, and when I was introduced to D. H. Lawrence, I did the same thing: the stories, the novels, his letters, his poetry, until I hit an essay he did for an American publication in the '20s and it was racist, and that really disappointed me. But again, he was a creature of his time. And nobody could describe the landscape better than Lawrence. I mean, there's things I could learn from this guy. If you read all of a writer, you know what the value of that is? You're not just reading them at their best, the classic work that is adored, you're reading when they're trying to get to that work. Where they're failing, right? So you see them in their underwear.

Take Melville. You can see him building up to writing *Moby-Dick*. In some of the earlier writings, he's looking for *Moby-Dick*. And the critics are saying, "Well, give us another one about being a sailor who's lost at sea." But he's searching for *Moby-Dick*. Then finally it's all there. He writes it! And nobody understands it. He goes off into obscurity and becomes a New York customs agent.

JEFF: What about voice and rhythm? Were there particular writers who influenced those elements of your style?

CHARLES: Well, yes, I've always preferred writers we call prose stylists because their writing is poetic, musical. A book that pops into my head every now and then is by Samuel Delany, the science-fiction writer, *Babel-17*. This guy can write. I mean, you have to die for sentences like his, you know, they're just beautiful.

To me, if you don't have that kind of elegant prose, then I'm going to be disappointed. If it's just utilitarian like journalism? Okay, that's fine. You know, you get the job done. But I can read that kind of prose in the newspaper. I want something that elevates the language, that shows me the possibilities of expression in the English tongue. That's what I want. And then I'll go right to my writer's notebook and jot down how this writer achieved that. You look at Richard Wright. I hate to say it, but there isn't a sentence in Richard Wright that I consider to be stylish or poetic. He's very utilitarian, coming out of the Marxist philosophy. Then you get Ralph Ellison, and he ups the ante on the language. It's gorgeous. He obviously worked consciously at that. What are we talking about here? There's different forms of art. This is literary art—it's about the performance of language. Movies are about something else; paintings are about something else. This is about language, so it should change our perception.

JEFF: What about the three giants of your youth: Faulkner, Hemingway, and Fitzgerald. How do you feel about them?

CHARLES: If Richard Wright is the father of black

American literature, then Hemingway created a style of writing and everybody adopted it. Whether it's literary art or science fiction, you see the stamp of Hemingway, of his simplicity. It's rare to say that a writer creates a style that influences at least one generation and maybe even another generation. He did that. But, you know, people are breaking away from that style. Linsey Abrams wrote a piece called "A Maximalist Novelist Looks at Some Minimalist Fiction" that I found very interesting. I love maximalist writers, the ones who are exuberant with the language. But Hemingway's important.

JEFF: Was he important to you, though?

CHARLES: No, no. Not in his storytelling. I think he gave us a major style. But his way of looking at the world is adolescent, all that bullfighting and hunting. And I never got into Faulkner. I tried. But I didn't like his stream of consciousness very much. And I'm not from the South. I just couldn't ever connect emotionally with him. Fitzgerald is important. I looked at some short stories, and the principal novel [*The Great Gatsby*], but again, I just didn't emotionally connect. I can appreciate it. There are some writers you can learn from, and you're not crazy or enthusiastic about their storytelling, but they might have something in the way of a technique or a contribution to literary culture—like we're talking about with Hemingway—that makes them important, and they should be read.

I'm of the opinion that all writers need to be readers. If you're going to know anything about your craft, you've got to know what came before, so you can ask a simple question: What can I bring to the table that nobody's ever brought to the table before? Otherwise, why do this?

NANCY: What contemporary writers excite you?

CHARLES: Well, I was a judge for the National Book Award three times and obviously I approve of our choices. One was Colum McCann's *Let the Great World Spin*. Yeah, I just admire the writing.

NANCY: That's maximalist writing for sure.

CHARLES: Now, story-wise, I'm not so sure. But that year, compared to the other books, it stood out vividly for that *performance*. Because, as I used to tell my students, I really do think when you write a book, make it your finest performance. It should be a performance novel. Your best thought, your best feeling, your best technique.

Look, I call myself an artist. I don't call myself a writer. I started out as a visual artist and a cartoonist, and some days I'm doing literary art, some days I'm doing visual art—different forms of art. But writer?

I never even thought about that; I had no interest in being a writer. But one day a novel came to me and I had to write it over the summer to get it out of my head. And then another one came to me, and okay, I'm writing these stories; let me try to get better. But I'm not writing because I wanted to be a writer, whatever the hell that is. And there's an awful lot of baggage that comes with that term, "writer," and I don't like the baggage. There's a lot of negative baggage, like "wild" and "crazy." That ain't me. I tell stories. I write books. And then I let it go.

NANCY: Why? Why do you let it go?

CHARLES: Because I learned something. The doing of it changed me: my perception, my skill level, whatever research I had to do—it all changed me. So I'm rewarded. And then you want to give that to others—the best possible gift you can give to readers is to clarify their experience. And you want to give that to others. I say to my students, "I want to laugh, I want to cry, and I want to learn something when I read a book."

NANCY: So what contemporary writers have you laughed, cried, and learned something from?

CHARLES: If we're talking about literary art, again I feel a robust and sophisticated performance of language, from one sentence to the next, is of the utmost importance, just as it is in poetry. For that reason I greatly admire the fiction of Ivan Doig. His having a PhD in history also brings a valuable rigor to his stories set in the past. I also have a lot of admiration for Ursula Le Guin, first for the elegance of her prose, secondly because of her historical significance in the field of speculative fiction, and lastly because I believe I read long ago about how Taoism (which has an important relationship to Buddhist practice in China) influenced her literary vision. I also admire James McBride because of his capacity for humor and, as a black American writer, his freedom from simplistic, preestablished political ideas and ideologies.

NANCY: How has reading influenced your spiritual practice? What books would you recommend to someone wanting to learn about Buddhism, and why those books in particular?

CHARLES: Well, I regularly read Buddhist sutras to improve my practice and understanding, because the sutras are one of the "three baskets," or [in Sanskrit] *tripitaka*, of canonical Buddhism. The other two "baskets" are *ahbidharma* literature [metaphysical writings] and *vinaya* [rules for monks and nuns]. A fun, introductory book that I have an affection for is *The Illustrated Encyclopedia of Buddhist Wisdom: A Complete Introduction to the Principles and Prac-*

tices of Buddhism by Gill Farrer-Halls. I would also recommend a text that I recently blurbed, *Musho-toku Mind: The Heart of the Heart Sutra* by Taisen Deshimaru.

NANCY: Last question: There's a beautiful picture of you and your young grandson on the cover of your book *The Way of the Writer*. What will you tell him about life? Any particular advice you're going to give him?

CHARLES: I want to tell him about all the stuff that's dark, so that he doesn't walk into a minefield, a racial minefield, and get blown up. I don't want to hide that from him, because if I don't tell him about those things, he's going to be naïve. But by the same token, I want to tell him some people have crossed that minefield and they live and they prosper and they serve others. And that's why I wrote a book about Martin Luther King, *Dreamer*. He was killed, yeah. But look at the impact he's had on our culture in that short period that he was publicly known, from the bus boycott in 1955 to his assassination in 1968. And this goes back to Gardner's *On Moral Fiction*. I think John's argument is that we have to give the next generation and young people and ourselves a vision that is positive even in the face of things that are negative. This is what I hope readers experience in my most recent book, *GRAND: A Grandparent's Wisdom for the Next Generation.*

Some Books and Authors in Chuck's Library

Samuel Delany, *Babel-17*

Taisen Deshimaru, *Mushotoku Mind: The Heart of the Heart Sutra*

Philip K. Dick, *The Man in the High Castle*

Ivan Doig

Gill Farrer-Halls, *The Illustrated Encyclopedia of Buddhist Wisdom: A Complete Introduction to the Principles and Practices of Buddhism*

John Gardner, *On Moral Fiction*

Hermann Hesse, *Siddhartha*

Ursula K. Le Guin

Sinclair Lewis, *Kingsblood Royal*

James McBride

Colum McCann, *Let the Great World Spin*

Jean-Paul Sartre, *Literature and Existentialism*

Harriett Beecher Stowe, *Uncle Tom's Cabin*

Richard Wright, *Black Boy*

Vendela Vida

Escape is a recurring theme of Vendela Vida's fiction—her protagonists always seem to be on the run from the complications and entanglements of their messy lives. In her debut novel, And Now You Can Go, *a New York college student, who barely survives an attack at gunpoint, journeys to the Philippines to put her life in perspective. In* Let the Northern Lights Erase Your Name, *a young woman discovers, in the wake of her father's death, that he was not her biological father, and travels to*

the northernmost regions of Finland in search of
her true identity. In The Lovers, a woman goes to
Turkey after her husband's sudden death in an auto
accident. And in her most recent novel, The Diver's
Clothes Lie Empty, her heroine, running away from
unnamed troubles at home, finds herself stranded
in Casablanca after the backpack containing her
passport is stolen.

In real life, Vendela has always been an ardent
traveler, but she lives in Marin County, just half
an hour from San Francisco, the city where she
was born. Her father, who owned an antique store
when she was growing up, was a second-generation
American with Hungarian roots, while her mother
was a recent immigrant from Sweden. Vendela went
to Middlebury College in Vermont, then got an
MFA in creative writing at Columbia University.
Her first book, Girls on the Verge: Debutante Dips,
Drive-Bys, and Other Initiations, was adapted from
her graduate thesis and explored the coming-of-age
rituals of young women in modern America. She
has also co-written a movie, Away We Go, with her
husband, fellow novelist Dave Eggers, and was the
longtime editor of the magazine The Believer, which
she co-founded.

We talked to Vendela at Book Passage, a Corte

Madera bookstore not far from her home. At our request, she brought along a pile of her favorite books to show us, and we talked at length about her associations with each of them.

———

NANCY: Were you a reader growing up?

VENDELA: Yes, I was. My father started an art and antique gallery in the Mission District, near where he grew up. He was really into antique furniture. One day when I was around ten, he brought this really old bookshelf home from the gallery. It was an enormous bookshelf—my parents still have it near their entranceway, in part because it's heavy and impossible to move. And then the only problem was once he bought the bookshelf, he had to fill it, and he couldn't fill it with paperbacks or books with ugly covers. So he and I went on a couple of scavenger hunts to estate sales to find books that would look appropriate in it. We found boxes of old books, the dustier the better, the older the better. And when we filled it in, the bookshelf looked beautiful. And then I started reading all the books we'd acquired.

They weren't curated in any special way; they weren't bought because of the title or the author.

They were purchased purely for aesthetics. One of the first books I read was *Of Human Bondage* by W. Somerset Maugham. He made a big impression on me, although sometimes I wonder how much of it was just based on how much I liked the name "Somerset"—I thought that was a great name. The other book I loved was a collection of Hemingway's stories, and it became a point of reference for me and my father. I would read the books in our bookshelf, he would read the books, my sister who was five years younger would read the books, and it was kind of an accidentally well-curated library.

JEFF: Are you still a fan of Somerset Maugham?

VENDELA: I reread *The Razor's Edge* a couple of years ago, and I loved it. And I was really relieved to find that my childhood taste held up. You know, sometimes you're afraid of looking back and wondering, *What was I thinking?* I also just reread this [*Bonjour Tristesse* by Françoise Sagan]. When I was maybe thirteen I decided I wanted to be a writer, and my dad gave me this book, which I devoured at the time. I just reread it last week, because the teenage daughter of a friend of mine is going to France, and she wanted recommendations of what French books to read. It was funny for me to remember what I had liked about it. After reading so much Hemingway and Somerset Maugham, I think I found the first-person voice of a young woman really appealing.

NANCY: I can see that. *Bonjour Tristesse* is a book that you have to read at exactly the right moment, I think. Those kind of books just speak to who we are at that moment, and then if you miss it by a few years—

VENDELA: It's not the right time.

NANCY: It's not the right time.

VENDELA: Well, I think about that too, because of this young woman I know who's going to France. But there's so little about France actually in it.

Bonjour Tristesse could take place anywhere, which is not really a valid critique because when you're a teenager, like the protagonist, your surroundings don't actually matter that much to you at all. It's primarily about your interior landscape, and the landscape you create with your friends, and to that extent I feel like *Bonjour Tristesse* really captures that age.

NANCY: The setting ends where your body ends. You're like a turtle, you take your shell with you wherever you go.

JEFF: Well, there's landscape, but there's also locale. Writers like Somerset Maugham and Hemingway were both always fascinated by the different customs and people in the places they traveled and set their works. Your books are like that too. You write about travelers.

VENDELA: I was always interested in travel, especially given I grew up with a mother from Sweden. She was a big advocate of travel and taking us to Sweden, but to other places too. We went to Egypt and Israel when I was around twelve, and we didn't stay in fancy accommodations by any means. She thought travel was incredibly important. She also taught us there's a difference between vacationers and travelers. We didn't do vacations, we *traveled*.

NANCY: Were you drawn to Swedish writing at all?

VENDELA: It's funny you say that—I really reacted against my Swedish upbringing when I was younger.

NANCY: So, no Selma Lagerlöf?

VENDELA: I like her now, but at the time I would have preferred to be Italian or Czech. That was where *The Unbearable Lightness of Being* [by Milan Kundera] came in. I read that and got very obsessed with the Velvet Revolution.

NANCY: When you discover an author like Maugham or Kundera, do you then go on and read all of their books? Are you a reading completist?

VENDELA: Not necessarily. In middle school I wrote all my reports on Somerset Maugham, and in high school I did every report on the Czech Republic. I went from reading Kundera to Václav Havel. I'm not a completist at all. I like the jags that reading takes you on.

JEFF: Was *Of Human Bondage* the first grown-up book that really grabbed you?

VENDELA: I would say that and *Razor's Edge* too.

JEFF: They're long books. That didn't frighten you at all when you were—how old were you?

VENDELA: Sixth grade, seventh grade.

NANCY: What do you think you got out of *The Razor's Edge*, which is my favorite Maugham, as a sixth or seventh grader, as opposed to what you might get if you read it now?

VENDELA: When I reread *The Razor's Edge* I realized that one thing I like about Maugham, is that he's very direct at times. Sometimes when I'm writing I think, *How can I make sure this quality in this character comes across?* But Maugham just comes right out and says someone is malevolent or a fool, or whatever. I appreciate the directness, and the authoritativeness, with which he can just do that.

JEFF: You don't feel you can do that? That was beaten out of you in your MFA program?

VENDELA: I feel like it was!

NANCY: Now so much is voice.

VENDELA: It is a lot more voice, which I appreciate

too. There's nothing like reading a novel with a consistently well-crafted voice—that's why I like Sally Rooney's novel *Conversations with Friends* so much. I think her first-person voice is just incredible. But of course that's the hardest thing to teach. You can encourage students to follow their own rhythm and not try to emulate someone else's, but you can't really teach voice.

JEFF: The second-person voice that you used in *The Diver's Clothes Lie Empty* was fascinating. How did you arrive at using that?

VENDELA: Do you know Jamaica Kincaid's story "Girl"? I read it in high school, and it was a big influence on me, so much so that when teaching teenage students writing I often start with this story and ask the students to do an exercise where they write something in that sort of instructional style: "Wash the white clothes on Monday and put them on the stone heap; wash the color clothes on Tuesday and put them on the clothesline to dry . . ." And with *Diver's Clothes*, I'd never done second person before.

JEFF: There's not a lot out there. *Bright Lights, Big City* by Jay McInerney—

VENDELA: And Margaret Atwood wrote part of a novel in second person, and Lorrie Moore did it, and there's a Junot Díaz story in second person. But yeah, there aren't that many. I thought for *Diver's Clothes* in particular, because it's about identity, I didn't really want to give the protagonist a name. Because I wanted her to be *anybody*, the "you" felt right for that. That said, I don't know if I could've sustained it had it been a 500-page book. I think I personally would've gotten tired of it, and I think if you as the author are getting tired of it, you can't ever expect the reader to still be interested. I don't think your reader's going to miraculously still be interested when you lose interest.

NANCY: Do you think your mother's Swedish background, and the travels that you did, led to an interest in setting your novels in different places?

VENDELA: Definitely.

NANCY: And when you were a kid, were you drawn to books set in different countries?

VENDELA: I really gravitated toward them. I pretended I was Italian for a while. And I studied Italian in college because I had this very grandiose seventeen-year-old idea of reading Dante in the original. I was already interested in trying to read things in their original.

JEFF: Do you still read in different languages?

VENDELA: I read in Italian still.

NANCY: Never giving up on that dream!

VENDELA: Never! [Laughter.]

I take Italian translation workshops every once in a while—not for any purpose, just for fun. One of the best articles I read in the *New York Times* this past year was about how people can't have hobbies anymore; everyone assumes your intention is to actually do something with your hobby. So I'm kind of shy about even mentioning the translation classes, because whenever I tell anyone I take translation classes, they say, "Oh, are you going to translate a book?"

JEFF: That was my next question!

VENDELA: And I have to say, "No, it's just for the mental exercise—it's not for the end result." I like challenging myself, trying to think in someone else's rhythm or syntax, and I think translation is the ultimate way to do that. Also, it's why I like memorizing poems, especially as I get older and feel like my memory is getting . . . weaker, shall we say? The other day I memorized an Emily Dickinson poem, and it was so much harder for me than it should've been, because her rhythm is so different from mine, and I thought that was a good thing, to try to get into that rhythm.

NANCY: Which poem?

VENDELA: It was "A Little Madness in the Spring":

> A little Madness in the Spring
> Is wholesome even for the King,
> But God be with the Clown—
> Who ponders this tremendous scene—
> This whole Experiment of Green—
> As if it were his own!

It's six lines, and it took me—I'm not going to say how long it took me to memorize that!

JEFF: I can't memorize anything anymore. Do you read a lot of poetry? Who are some of the poets you're drawn to?

VENDELA: I love Mary Oliver. For a while I was reading a poem of hers every morning. The day that she passed away, I was at the library and ran into my favorite librarian, and we were both sobbing. I respect the sense of humor that infuses her poems, and that she understands poetry doesn't have to be so serious. Which is also a problem I have with the way it's taught sometimes. It's why kids often don't relate to it, because it's like, [in a serious voice] "Now it's poetry time."

JEFF: I got into poetry by reading fiction writers who were also poets.

VENDELA: Like John Updike?

JEFF: Not Updike. I've never really liked Updike's poems. They're too formal for me. More like Raymond Carver or Denis Johnson.

VENDELA: Denis Johnson's poems are great.

JEFF: *Jesus' Son* is one of my favorite books ever: I did a stage adaptation of it in Seattle, weaving in some of his poems. They're so amazing and eye-opening. They make you realize what poetry can do, and how different it is from fiction, but also how it can be part of the same imaginative world.

VENDELA: I think *Jesus' Son* is a perfect example of how to give an arc to a short-story collection. Think of that last line of the last story ["Beverly Home"]: "I had never known, never even imagined for a heartbeat, that there might be a place for people like us." It's just that perfect ending, you almost hear a ding! The universe is in sync for a moment, and you hear the bell ringing, and you think, *Okay, that's the perfect ending not just for a short story but also for that collection of short stories.* It's all about finding your place. And it ends on this note of hope, right? Which is so important, especially for a short-story collection with a protagonist named Fuckhead. [Laughter.] Not that everything's going to be perfectly fine, but he and we are given just a little hope.

JEFF: Now we're interviewing you for our book of interviews, and you actually edited a book of interviews yourself, *The Believer Book of Writers Talking to Writers*, which is wonderful. One of the writers you interviewed for that was Shirley Hazzard. I assume she must've been an influence for you to have chosen her.

VENDELA: I deeply admired *Greene on Capri* and *The Great Fire* and I really enjoyed meeting her. I went to her apartment in New York. It was so interesting to see where she lived with her husband, Francis Steegmuller, for so many years, and it was exactly what you'd think: just books everywhere. I was also struck by meeting her at that particular time—right after she won the National Book Award. She almost didn't know what had happened to her. She had all these letters all over her apartment, all this correspondence, and she just had so much to catch up on. She was both delighted, as you might expect, but also kind of stunned. She devoted her life to literature, and it was really an honor to meet her.

JEFF: And Susan Straight? You also interviewed her for that book.

VENDELA: Yes, and she had a different kind of writer's life, because she had three girls that she was raising on her own. She would stay up very late at night working. She said that if she got up early in the morning, someone would wake up, and her writing time would be over. So she would write at night when her kids went to bed. I'm always trying to find these tips of what works for other writers.

I also remember something so funny Straight said. She teaches at UC Riverside, and she said when her students tell her they didn't have time to finish their story or their assignment before class, she would say something like "You're better off telling me you were drunk in Tijuana; I'd much rather hear that than that you didn't have time. I have three kids, a job—don't tell me you didn't have time!"

NANCY: I loved *I Been in Sorrow's Kitchen and Licked Out All the Pots.* Was there one of her books you most enjoyed?

VENDELA: I heard her do a reading for *Zoetrope[: All-Story]* magazine in San Francisco one time, and I was very taken by her voice. And then I read *Highwire Moon* and wanted to interview her. Again, she's really good about writing about place. I really admired her. I also interviewed Jennifer Egan for that book—we both grew up in San Francisco and so we have that in common.

JEFF: Are you more drawn to female writers?

VENDELA: I'm trying to think of the last few books I just read. I read a book by a Norwegian writer that I really enjoyed [*Love* by Hanne Ørstavik]—it was a National Book Award finalist for translation last year. I recently read and greatly admired Rebecca Makkai's *The Great Believers.* But no, I don't think I'm drawn to one gender more than the other.

NANCY: What do you find yourself rereading the most?

VENDELA: I reread Joan Didion a lot. A lot. Especially her essays. What else? *Disgrace* by J. M. Coetzee I've read maybe five or six times. It's such a well-done novel: it's exactly the length it should be, set in another country, and about things that really matter told through personal experiences. And it has one of my favorite first sentences: "For a man of his age, fifty-two, divorced, he has, to his mind, solved the problem of sex rather well." Well, of course, the book is in part about he hasn't solved the problem of sex at all. Last time I read it was a couple years ago when I assigned it to my grad students at the time. I regretted teaching it, because this particular group of students, who were great students, did not like it.

JEFF: The politics of it upset them too much—

VENDELA: Oh yes, the politics upset them a lot. They really didn't like David Lurie, the main character.

Finally I said, "Well, you don't read novels to make friends. You can go make friends in the real world, you know. We don't read Dostoevsky's *Crime and Punishment* or Nabokov's *Lolita*, for example, to make friends with the protagonists. You read novels to see how other people think." But they really, really objected to *Disgrace*. That's probably the book I've read the most and now will probably not read again.

JEFF: It's interesting, because it was kind of written on one side of a cultural divide, the pre-#MeToo era, and now we're on the other side, and the way it's looked at is so different. Similar to *The Human Stain* by Philip Roth.

VENDELA: Oh yeah, I like that book too.

JEFF: Well, I think a lot of Roth, unless the culture shifts back somewhat, will be really problematic.

NANCY: So when you go into the library or the bookstore, you gravitate toward . . .

VENDELA: I gravitate toward the foreign language and translation section.

JEFF: What about Graham Greene? We talked about travel.

VENDELA: I went through a whole Graham Greene phase, and I think that's why I read Shirley Hazzard's *Greene on Capri*. He wasn't a big influence, but I liked him. Paul Bowles was more of an influence; I actually wrote an introduction to his short-story collection *The Delicate Prey* that Ecco published a couple of years ago. I admire the way he uses landscape. Like it's not just a character, it's not just scenery. The landscape cannot be separated from his stories. I don't like the way people say, "Oh, the landscape's a character." That's not quite what I mean. I'm talking about when landscape actually infuses the work and affects the characters, and they embody the landscape, and they act differently than they might've somewhere else because of the landscape. That's what I love about Paul Bowles's stories.

NANCY: Another book I see here is *A Passage to India* by E. M. Forster.

VENDELA: I'm indebted to Forster. He's someone I try to read whenever I get stuck in a novel. *A Passage to India* was really influential when I was writing *The Lovers*, which is set in Turkey—in particular, the famous cave scene in that novel. I was writing about caves in Turkey, and I was thinking about what caves mean metaphorically, but also physically. What, literally, the effect is on you—the coldness and the echo of being inside one. Forster's great at showing how locale can affect someone's personality, expose their biases, and change them.

NANCY: When you're working on a book, does your reading change?

VENDELA: Yes. If I don't have patience for something, I'll give it up right away. I'm really much more focused on what's most of a service to me when I'm in the middle of writing a novel. I'm a lot more selfish about my time.

JEFF: And what about between books?

VENDELA: Then I'll read anything. I try to either read older books I haven't read before or I try to read super contemporary books. I was reading [William Makepeace Thackeray's] *Vanity Fair* recently, which I'd never read, which was just hilarious. Really funny and cutting. The narration is almost postmodern.

JEFF: What about contemporary writers? Who are some of the people you really love?

VENDELA: Lorrie Moore is one of them—I enjoy her humor a lot. Humor is incredibly important to me. That's why I read Philip Roth too. His combination of rage and humor in the same sentence, I so admire that.

NANCY: You mentioned Lorrie Moore. Do you read a lot of short stories?

VENDELA: I do like reading short stories, though I enjoy novellas just as much.

NANCY: C. S. Lewis once said something like there wasn't a cup of tea large enough or a book long enough to please him. *Vanity Fair* was always daunting to me because it's so big.

VENDELA: My perfect novel is right around 220 to 250 pages. Those are the books that I love most to read, and so I guess it's no surprise that most of the books I write hover somewhere around there. Hitchcock said the perfect movie was an hour and a half, because no one had to get up and use the restroom. I feel like for me the perfect novel is one that, in theory, you could read in the course of one day if you had time. Otherwise you could read it in two days. That's my perfect novel. Everything is in your head and you don't have to go back and think, *Who was that character?* or *What happened there?*

JEFF: What are some of your favorite novels like that?

VENDELA: I have to go back to Joan Didion. She was such a big influence on me, especially as a female writer growing up in California. She made writing feel like something I could actually do. I know that sounds strange, but when you grow up in San Francisco like I did, all the writers you hear about are the Beat Generation, who are men and writing very different kinds of stories than I was reading and writing. So just having Didion in my head, knowing you could be from California and publish a book and it didn't have to be about the things the Beats were writing about was really refreshing to me. But I liked the length of her novels as well. I remember her first novel—

NANCY: *Run, River* is such a good novel.

VENDELA: It is good. And *Play It As It Lays* is really great. So those are novels, like *Conversations with Friends*, that are my perfect length.

NANCY: When I think about Joan Didion, I also think about Renata Adler. Have you read *Speedboat*?

VENDELA: I have not. I know people whose taste I really respect who are crazy about *Speedboat*, but I haven't read it—in part, because in the copy I have, the spacing is one and a half, as opposed to two lines, and it affects my reading. I'm really particular about how words are spaced on a page because it can alter your sense of the book. But I have admired her author photos—she seems to consistently wear her hair in a long braid. Every author needs a signature hairstyle like Renata Adler. There's also the filmmaker Agnès Varda. She had a signature hairstyle.

JEFF: Susan Sontag?

VENDELA: Susan Sontag, yeah.

JEFF: Is that only for female authors?

VENDELA: Well, I just notice it more. I did get a pink streak last year, but it quickly faded, and I realized, *I can't keep this up. It's too much maintenance.* So much for my signature hairstyle.

Some Books and Authors in Vendela's Library

Paul Bowles, *The Delicate Prey*

J. M. Coetzee, *Disgrace*

Joan Didion, *Play It As It Lays*

E. M. Forster, *A Passage to India*

Shirley Hazzard, *The Great Fire*

Denis Johnson, *Jesus' Son*

Jamaica Kincaid, "Girl"

Milan Kundera, *The Unbearable Lightness of Being*

Rebecca Makkai, *The Great Believers*

W. Somerset Maugham, *The Razor's Edge*

Lorrie Moore

Mary Oliver

Hanne Ørstavik, *Love*

Sally Rooney, *Conversations with Friends*

Susan Straight, *Highwire Moon*

Donna Tartt

*D*onna Tartt is that rare American author who has managed to become a literary celebrity entirely on her own terms. She writes a novel roughly every ten years, and each of her three novels has been a bestseller. She enforces a strict zone of privacy around her personal life, but her occasional forays into the public sphere, her petite stature, and her English public schoolboy wardrobe have made her a fashion icon. She prefers canine companionship (she is a dedicated pug person) to that of New York's *literary establishment, once saying, "My dog has a number of acquaintances of his own species—as do I—but it is abundantly clear to both of us that there is little company in all the world which we enjoy so much as each other's."*

Donna was born in Greenwood, Mississippi, in 1963, attended Bennington College alongside Bret Easton Ellis and Jonathan Lethem, and became a literary sensation with the publication of her first novel, The Secret History, *in 1992. Her second novel,* The Little Friend, *is her most overtly southern work, carrying echoes of Harper Lee and Carson McCullers. Her third,* The Goldfinch, *won the 2014 Pulitzer Prize for Fiction.*

Nancy first met Donna over breakfast in 2015 at the American Library Association convention in Las Vegas, when she chaired the jury that awarded Donna the Andrew Carnegie Medal for Excellence in Fiction for The Goldfinch. *When we approached Donna's agent about interviewing her for this book, Donna readily agreed, but we were never able to align our schedules to be in the same place at the same time. In the end, our deadline upon us, we agreed to an email interview, which, while not allowing the back-and-forth of the rest of our interviews, compensates with some uniquely Tarttian turns of phrase.*

WRITER'S LIBRARY: Did you come from a reading household? How did you learn to read and at what age? Were you a voracious reader as a child? What were your favorite books as a child?

DONNA: I very much came from a reading household on my mother's side of the family . . . my maternal grandmother was a librarian; my great-aunt Frances was the head librarian at our town library; and their parents—my great-grandfather and great-grandmother—were passionate readers as well. We all lived within walking distance of each other. There were always books around all the houses, tall glass-fronted bookcases and stacks of books piled on every table. To me, as a child, the town library felt like an annex of my great-grandparents' house. I knew all the librarians and was very much at home there.

I don't remember a time when I wasn't able to read. My mother says she realized I was able to read labels off cans and boxes in the grocery before I was three, and I can remember being called upon as sort of a party trick to read aloud passages from the Jackson *Clarion-Ledger,* random articles about local elections, which I read aloud by sounding out the words and without understanding what I was reading.

So well before I started kindergarten, at four, I

remember reading simple books like Beatrix Potter or Dare Wright's Lonely Doll books to myself. I also remember reading aloud to neighborhood children my own age and younger not yet able to read. But my first really transformative reading experiences came through being read aloud to by my great-grandmother—often from the same worn 1890s editions, with haunting illustrations, from which my grandmother and great-aunts had been read to themselves as children. The fairy tales of the Grimm brothers, [Charles] Perrault, Oscar Wilde, Lafcadio Hearn, Hans Christian Andersen were my earliest intimation of transcendence in words: the cold slap of a much more beautiful sphere of existence.

Our town library was small, and though, as I said, my mother's family owned a fair amount of books, these were mostly books of the nineteenth and very early twentieth century, so with very few exceptions (*Chitty Chitty Bang Bang* [by Roald Dahl], *Bedknobs and Broomsticks* [by Mary Norton], *The Cricket in Times Square* [by George Selden], *Stuart Little* [by E. B. White]) my favorites were mostly of my great-grandmother's generation, and I read them (and had them read to me) again and again: fairy tales but also *Alice's Adventures in Wonder-*

land [by Lewis Carroll], *The Princess and the Goblin* [by George MacDonald], the Oz series [by L. Frank Baum], *Treasure Island* [by Robert Louis Stevenson], *The Wind in the Willows* [by Kenneth Grahame], *The Jungle Book* [by Rudyard Kipling], *Peter Pan* [by J. M. Barrie]. *Peter Pan* was my absolute favorite, the first book I passionately loved, and as I've said before, there's something of it in everything I've ever written.

WRITER'S LIBRARY: Do you remember the first "grown-up" book you read and loved? What about it moved you?

DONNA: When I was small, I didn't enjoy being read to if I couldn't see the page, so I was always sitting next to the person who was reading to me—most usually my great-grandmother—and following along. I remember *The Wind in the Willows*, which my mother read to me in the weeks before I started first grade, being the first "thick book" that was read to me, meaning the first book that looked like a book for adults, with word-dense pages and not too many pictures. This was another book that made its deep mark on my life and work, chiefly in its depiction of friendship. Later, in third grade, my grandmother read *Oliver Twist* [Charles Dickens] aloud to me, which I both loved and was absolutely terrorized by. I think this is the only book my grandmother ever read aloud to me, but it was surely a knockout. The idea was that, every afternoon after school, she would read me a chapter of Nancy Drew [by Carolyn Keene] for every chapter of *Oliver Twist*. This was how she had gotten my mother to read *Oliver Twist*, by holding out the enticement of Nancy Drew, but though I liked Nancy Drew all right, I got so wrapped up in Oliver's much more serious problems that soon we stopped reading Nancy Drew altogether and concentrated on Oliver.

You ask what about *Oliver Twist* moved me. Everything about it moved me, including the book itself: dating from the late 1800s, clothbound in midnight blue with the old [George] Cruikshank illustrations, the copy my great-grandfather had read as a young man and read aloud to his own daughters in the 1920s. The richness of the language stirred me deeply. At eight I was not a fluent enough reader to read *Oliver Twist* easily on my own—at one agonizing point, when I was desperate to know what happened next, I begged my grandmother to let me carry the book home for the night—which she did, making me promise to take care of it, but the words were so dense on the page and so difficult for a third grader that I had a hard time with it—I have a sharp memory of lying draped across the piano bench trying to puzzle it out. At that age I needed someone to explain to me what a beadle was, what a porringer was.

So the richness of the language, though it fascinated me, was then also largely an impediment. What gripped me at the time was the book's sense of openness and danger. The hypocrisy of Mr. Bumble and the brutality of Noah Claypole and Mr. Sowerberry, the undertaker, shocked me. I was still enough of a child to be confused by Fagin— was he good or bad? At the first, just as Oliver did, I put my trust in him, since on the surface, anyway, he was genial and friendly and a vast improvement over Oliver's previous guardians; my shock at his treachery was immense. And just when it can't get any worse . . . along comes Bill Sikes! Though it's not now my favorite Dickens—that would probably be a toss-up between *Bleak House* and *Little Dorrit*—I've since reread it numerous times. Last year I listened to an audiobook version on a long car journey, which is not really "reading" to me but which comes in handy when I don't have my hands free—it's an anxiety-provoking book, even now! And even after so many readings, there are still new things to discover. Now I see the humor of the book more; then it was pure revelation and terror. As for the first "grown-up" book that I held in my hands and read on my own, without an adult to help me—I can remember being weighed down by a volume of Sherlock Holmes stories in the third grade. That was tough reading too—I remember asking Mrs. Perry my third-grade teacher what a Jezail bullet was and getting a very blank stare.

WRITER'S LIBRARY: Was there a book that made you say, "This is what I want to do—be a writer"? If so, what was it about that book that made you feel that way?

DONNA: Who said that a writer is a reader moved to emulation? Certainly that's me. As a child I wrote the same way I drew—for fun—with no sense that my scribbles on notebook paper constituted in any way "being a writer." For me, writing things down was more a sort of focused daydreaming, and in some ways it still is. Rather than being inspired to write by any particular book, it was more that at some point I realized that writing was something I already did and that I liked to do.

WRITER'S LIBRARY: Is there a canonical writer whom you feel is a kindred spirit? Why? Which of his or her books do you particularly respond to or identify with and why?

DONNA: I think to really love a writer—any writer—is to feel in some sense in contact with a kindred spirit across culture and time. There's no writer I love to whom I don't feel akin in some way.

WRITER'S LIBRARY: What contemporary writer?

DONNA: Well, I feel kinship with almost all contemporary writers in the daily routine of getting up and making a cup of tea and going to my desk and then, later, fretting and poring through what I've done at the end of the day.

WRITER'S LIBRARY: Who is your favorite living writer and why?

DONNA: Since my earliest writing career, I've loved Don DeLillo and Joan Didion, not only as prose stylists but for what, in William Eggleston's phrase, is their constant war with the obvious. I love the work of [Thomas] Pynchon and of Edward St. Aubyn. And I am grateful to Haruki Murakami for bringing so much delight and magic to the world.

WRITER'S LIBRARY: Do you read differently when you are in the heart of the writing process?

DONNA: I don't think I do, except in the obvious way of reading more nonfiction pertaining to my subject.

WRITER'S LIBRARY: Do you classify some books you read as "escapist" reading and others as "serious" reading? If so, what are some of your favorite escapist books?

DONNA: I don't segregate books in this way. Most of the books and authors I've mentioned manage to have some strong element of both.

WRITER'S LIBRARY: Are you a fan of genre fiction? If so, what genres, and what particular writers or books, and why do you enjoy them?

DONNA: No, although I love several novelists whose works are sometimes considered (not necessarily by me) as "genre," such as Raymond Chandler, Shirley Jackson, John le Carré, and Stephen King.

WRITER'S LIBRARY: You've written three large novels and only a few short stories over the last thirty years. Are you a fan of short stories? If so, what do you particularly enjoy about them versus novels, and who are the short-story writers, past and present, you most admire?

DONNA: Short-story writers I admire: in no particular order, I love [Edgar Allan] Poe, [W.] Somerset Maugham, Katherine Mansfield, [Jorge Luis] Borges, [Vladimir] Nabokov, [Rudyard] Kipling, John Cheever, Raymond Carver, William Maxwell, Mary Robison, Tobias Wolff, Nathan Englander,

Angela Carter, Dorothy Parker, M. R. James, Barry Hannah, Isak Dinesen. But I prefer novels.

WRITER'S LIBRARY: Were there particular books that influenced each of your novels? If so, what were they and how did they particularly influence you?

DONNA: Somehow [F. Scott] Fitzgerald hasn't yet come up, nor has Evelyn Waugh, nor has George Orwell, nor has Flannery O'Connor, nor has [Fyodor] Dostoevsky, nor has [J. D.] Salinger, nor has [Joseph] Conrad. All these writers were, and are, tremendous influences. Obviously the Greek tragedies, and Homer, were a huge influence as well, particularly on my first novel, *The Secret History.* Nabokov has exercised incalculable influence on all my published work. I was already writing short stories when I first encountered him, at fourteen, and I still remember the delirious sense of possibility he opened up. I'm certainly a different writer for having read him. Dickens, however, is probably the most pervasive influence on my work, followed closely by Robert Louis Stevenson.

WRITER'S LIBRARY: Are there little-known writers or works that you wish were better known? If so, who are they and what do you love about those books/writers?

DONNA: Jane Bowles is not nearly as revered or widely read as she should be, nor is J. F. Powers.

Caroline Blackwood's *Great Granny Webster* is in its way very nearly perfect and a book to which I often return. I wish Patrick Hamilton's *Twenty Thousand Streets Under the Sky* were better known . . . I was led to Patrick Hamilton by Simon Doonan, whose memoir *Beautiful People* I must mention in passing as it's completely delightful and one of the very few books I can always rely upon to cheer me up.

WRITER'S LIBRARY: Do you reread books often? If so, why? Have you ever found that a book changed drastically upon rereading?

DONNA: I do reread books, I always have—and quite often they change for the better. I was puzzled and bored by Virginia Woolf when I first tried to read her in college. Same with Barbara Pym and Edith Wharton. Wharton, in particular, drives home such a brutal blow-by-blow account of poor Lily Bart's downfall in *The House of Mirth* that for many years I had a deep aversion to the book. To my younger self it seemed unnecessarily cruel. Now that I'm older, of course, I know she's only telling the truth. I still can't read *Ethan Frome*. Someday, maybe.

WRITER'S LIBRARY: You've been quoted as saying that *Lolita* is your favorite book. Has the current political climate changed the way you read that book? Are you still able to enjoy it as much as in the past?

If yes, what do you love about it? If no, how do you feel about your altered view?

DONNA: I don't have an altered view of it. It's a masterpiece.

WRITER'S LIBRARY: Do you need to talk to other people about the books you love, or is reading a more self-sufficient, solitary experience for you?

DONNA: My primary experience is with the book. Though, like most writers, I'm often called upon to talk about books, talking about books isn't a necessary aspect of reading for me and doesn't deepen my own enjoyment of a book.

Some Books and Authors in Donna's Library

J. M. Barrie, *Peter Pan*

Caroline Blackwood, *Great Granny Webster*

Jane Bowles

Don DeLillo

Charles Dickens, *Bleak House*, *Little Dorrit*, and *Oliver Twist*

Joan Didion

Isak Dinesen

Simon Doonan, *Beautiful People*

Kenneth Grahame, *The Wind in the Willows*

Patrick Hamilton, *Twenty Thousand Streets Under the Sky*

Shirley Jackson

Katherine Mansfield

Haruki Murakami

Vladimir Nabokov, *Lolita*

Barbara Pym

Thomas Pynchon

Edward St. Aubyn

Robert Louis Stevenson

Russell Banks

In the spring of 1998, when Nancy and her team at the Seattle Public Library were devising the program If All Seattle Read the Same Book, the inspiration for One City One Book programs across the country, she knew right away what book she wanted Seattle to read: The Sweet Hereafter by Russell Banks. She wanted a novel that had three-dimensional characters and an ambiguous ending, so that readers would be eager to debate the fates of the characters once they finished the novel. The Sweet Hereafter was perfect—a book

about community that would bring our community of readers closer together.

Over the years, Russell has remained one of Nancy's favorite writers (she especially admires Lost Memory of Skin*), and Jeff has likewise loved many of his books, especially the coming-of-age saga* Rule of the Bone *and the epic* Cloudsplitter, *his historical novel about the abolitionist John Brown.*

Our conversation took place at Russell's home in Saratoga Springs, New York, where we talked about how reading had contributed to his journey from a hardscrabble childhood in working-class New England to a career as one of America's most respected novelists.

———

NANCY: Did you grow up in a reading family?

RUSSELL: No, no. Not at all. And not really a story-telling family either. Taciturn and dour people, who mistrusted stories, which were associated with lying or manipulation or control. Especially my father's family—it was almost as if they were hiding the stories of their lives or their days, even. My mother was a storyteller. But it was a difference in personality, not a difference in family habits or ethos. My father was more typical of the rest of the family. At the end of the day, my father would come home, and I'd say, "How was your day, Dad?" He'd say it was okay, and that was the end of the discussion. But if I said to my mother, "How was your day, Mom?" She'd say, "You'll never guess who I ran into today," and that would begin a story—and it would have all kinds of exaggerations and digressions and dramatizations, because she was a storyteller by temperament. But that's not to say that they were people who read books—except for my brother and sister, my family wasn't bookish or literary in any way. They're very typical of lower-middle-class white Americans who have been in that same class situation for generations and whose education rarely exceeded high school. So I didn't grow up surrounded by books by any means.

NANCY: So where did your interest in reading come from?

RUSSELL: It's hard to pin down. I read early and read everything, in the way a precocious reader does. I remember I could read when I got to first grade. I went to a two-room school with eight grades in Barnstead, New Hampshire.

There was a fourth-grade teacher who thought that I was someone who should be encouraged to read and to know things about the larger world. This would be around 1949, in Concord, which to us was a big city. Her name was Mrs. Dougherty. She knew I was going to be trouble. A bored nine-year-old. So she had the school janitor build an eight-foot-square plywood table on sawhorses out in the hallway. She bought about fifty pounds of plaster of Paris, and she said I want you to make a map, a topographical map of Brazil, to scale, and color-code and identify the animals and the minerals and the industries and the economics and the population of this country. This is what you're going to do all year, so you don't need to come into the classroom except to check attendance, and then you go out and you work on the map. It totally engaged me in every capacity. I had to read up on the geography and geology and history of Brazil, about which I knew absolutely nothing. But by the end of the year I was an expert on Brazil. It jump-started me in a way. I credit that fourth-grade experience almost more than any other specific experience with turning my attention to books as sources of the bigger world, the world outside Concord, New Hampshire.

JEFF: Is that how you learned about Jamaica as well? Through books?

RUSSELL: Yes, initially. The history of the Caribbean always fascinated me, from adolescence forward. I started traveling there on my own when I was about eighteen. Eventually, in the middle '70s, I ended up living down there for a couple years. But books open the door to the larger world. I don't read to escape. I read to enter. To go somewhere, which is different. A very different motivation, I think.

NANCY: Do you remember any of the books you read as a child? Or as a young adult?

RUSSELL: I do, actually. Maybe the first one that was important to me, because I remember reading it to my younger brother, was *Toby Tyler* [by James Otis], the boy who ran away with the circus. Maybe that was a powerful metaphor for me as a boy. *I want to get out of here. How do I do it? Join the circus.* I remember that book very vividly, even the illustrations that went with it. Then I began the kind of reading that I think most writers have done as children and probably still do as adults, that omnivorous, haphazard, and utterly unregulated reading. I could hardly wait to get off the curriculum in those days. Because I went to school in the '40s and '50s, and it was a much more restrictive time than it is today.

JEFF: Was there a book that you read, maybe in high school or later, where you said, "This is what I want to do with my life. I want to write."

RUSSELL: That came a little later, because early on I thought I was going to be a visual artist. That was the only demonstrable talent that I had. So until I was about eighteen—that was a transitional year for me in many ways—I painted and drew whenever I had the time and the space to do it.

I had dropped out of school by then and was living in Florida, on my own, on the road, and I started hanging out at the library. That was my source for books. I think out of loneliness, boredom—because I wasn't by any means literary, nor was I in any kind of a community of literary people—I started reading. And around that time, the first book I read that made me think, *I'd love to do this, I'd love to be this person; I would do it differently, and I would invent it for myself in a way*—that book was Jack Kerouac's *On the Road.* It was right around that age, in that state of mind, where I was, without intending it, becoming sort of a late-blooming beatnik, or an early-arriving hippie. I read that book and I thought, *Yes, this is the kind of life I want to lead.* And it's also written by a working-class guy from New England, kind of a jock, kind of a roughhouse guy, and kind of an autodidact, and it was easy for me to identify with him. So I think I seized on that as a template that I thought I might use for myself. Even though it was obviously a reckless, self-indulgent, and romantic template.

NANCY: And a reckless, self-indulgent novel. [Laughter.]

RUSSELL: Yeah, right. But there you are. There's a reason those books are attractive to eighteen-year-olds. Then I started reading with intensity and with an idea of trying to find works that I could model my own after, and really began to imagine myself more clearly as a writer. I read Hemingway, of course, and Faulkner, who were both still alive then. Fitzgerald hadn't been dead very long. That triumvirate was very much the picture of contemporary literary life for a kid trying to figure out how to become a writer. They were the masters of that moment, and that was who I was reading and trying to emulate in many ways, in lifestyle as much as literary style. And their reading list becomes your reading list; you start reading their biographies and learn through them that way.

From there I thought I better read Flaubert, Dostoevsky . . . I could see in *The Paris Review* interviews, that's who I was supposed to have read. You don't need a curriculum. You don't need a canon placed in front of you. You find your own way. You cut your own path through the jungle, and you'll get there.

Eventually I went back to Boston and settled there. Not Cambridge, but Boston, over in the Back Bay area. At that time there were coffeehouses and folk singers and art galleries and art schools. The Boston Museum of Fine Arts and the New England Conservatory of Music were there as well. So it was a more bohemian quarter than, say, Harvard Square or the Cambridge side of the river.

That was where I met, for the first time, other young writers. That was the first time where I felt the kind of camaraderie and competition and education that comes when you join forces with a group. I think it's an essential part of every young artist's journey to find your peers. Then you hope you can find a living mentor too. That's where I first found my peers, and they were people who had better educations than I did, had read more widely, more deeply, and who were writing and beginning to publish work. There was one man in particular, now dead—Leo Giroux—who was very charismatic, older than I. He was about thirty; I was about twenty. He walked with a dramatic limp—he'd had polio, but it made him look like he'd suffered a war injury. And he had a big scar that came down from his forehead across his cheek. And he was handsome, very bright, and very literate. He was incredibly impressive. He'd read widely, had gone to Boston University and studied literature, and he was just wonderfully instructive. He was the person who would explicitly say, "You must read Isak Dinesen," "You must read Franz Kafka." They were outside the little canon I was building, and he was the first one who started pushing me out into a world that was more sophisticated and cosmopolitan than the one I had been shaping myself around.

I thought Giroux was a brilliant writer, but he was one of those brilliant men who is forever writing the Great American Novel and never manages to finish it. He would read parts of it in public, and I was like, *Wow, that is so brilliant! I hope someday I can write as well as that.* He could never write more than fifty, seventy-five pages or so, but implied that there were hundreds more pages waiting at home that never appeared. He never published until very late in his life, which wasn't that late actually, because he only lived to be fifty-five or so. He had a heart attack and died. He did publish one novel, which was just awful. I hate to say it, because I loved him, but it was a potboiler. I think by that point he had just decided that *I'll write anything I can to get it published.* And that Great American Novel, so lyrical and Faulknerian and Melvillian, that one never appeared.

There was one other writer there at the same time who was my age—Paul Pines, a poet. I was friends with Paul right up until his death last year. Paul was as intelligent and precocious a man as Leo, and we hung out together as peers, as equals. He was part of that group. He was at Boston University at the time, and he'd give me his reading lists for his classes in comparative literature.

NANCY: Was there a Faulkner novel that you particularly loved? It seems like you and he came from two such different places.

RUSSELL: It wasn't the southernness of Faulkner's work so much as his structural and linguistic energy and freedom that was so attractive to me at that age. Because I remember reading works that I could barely comprehend, like *Light in August*, and then those which I could partially comprehend, like *The Sound and the Fury*, and those which would overwhelm me, like *The Bear*, and some of the great stories and so on. But he could've been writing about Colombia—in fact, I responded to Gabriel Garcia Marquez much the same way I responded to Faulkner. In fact, I responded to Garcia Marquez at forty-five much the same way I responded to Faulkner at eighteen. It was the excitement of the language and the freedom, the mythmaking, the willingness to attempt the impossible, that was so attractive to me. I can't say I ever tried to imitate that same kind of energy and linguistic overflow, that kind of Thomas Wolfe-ian force. For me, writing has always been a more incremental, slow-building process. Closer probably to the way Hemingway worked.

JEFF: When you were thinking about becoming a writer, what did you think of the young, successful writers of that era—people like Updike and Cheever?

RUSSELL: The writer who was terribly important to me when I was in my early twenties was Nelson Algren. A writer of the underclass. His work had a real impact on me and made me feel that what I wanted to write about could be done at a high artistic level. An expressionistic kind of realism. Hyper-realist, if you want to call it that. But it could still be political and also literary and highly stylized. Highly refined and individualized. Almost in a Faulknerian way. But not Faulknerian. More restrained. Of all the living writers of that postwar generation, he was the one that meant the most to me. And I tracked him down.

This was in '62. I was working in New Hampshire as a plumber, and I saw an ad, probably in *The Atlantic Monthly*, for the Bread Loaf Writers'

Conference, which was then run by John Ciardi. I didn't know what a writers' conference was, or what a bread loaf was, for that matter. But I knew who Nelson Algren was, and he was going to be teaching there, which is not something he normally did. He didn't teach. I sent them a manuscript—I had written a novel, a terrible novel, which remains unpublished, but they liked it enough to give me a fellowship, and I drove my pickup truck to Bread Loaf in Vermont.

When I arrived, they sent me to Algren. He had read my manuscript, and he sat me down underneath one of those maple trees outside the main lodge, and he did this thing, which is all I ever needed for an MFA. He went through the manuscript and he'd stop at a page, and it'd be 40 pages in, and he'd say, "Now, here, this is a really good piece of exposition. You see how you set this up? And how you did that? You located us visually. That's good, kid." And then another 40 pages, he'd say, "Now, see this dialogue, this is good dialogue. Because it advances the action and it deepens our knowledge of the characters. That's all dialogue should do. It has to have a function." And another 40 pages, and he'd find another paragraph to admire and compliment me on. So he did about six of those little passages and said, "Now all you gotta do, kid, is write a whole book like those little pieces, and then you're a novelist."

And I said, "Oh, that's all it is, huh?" It was, like, 400 pages, and of those 400 pages he'd complimented about 10, and now I had to write the other 390. But that was my MFA. And then he said, "You know, kid, I hate this place. I see you've got some wheels. Let's get out of here and have a beer." And I said, "Okay, Mr. Algren, whatever you want." So we found a bar in Middlebury and we started drinking. And then he said, "You know, I have a friend who lives somewhere up here in Vermont. Let's find out where he is and give him a visit. His name is Paul Goodman." Another one of my heroes! So we go over to Paul Goodman's, and those two guys sat there telling stories. Algren was telling stories about Simone de Beauvoir, and I think, *Wow!* And he's talking about what a great guy Truman Capote is, and how he really loves *In Cold Blood.* And I just sat at their feet. We finally got back to Bread Loaf after having been gone for, like, four days, and John Ciardi fired him. [Laughter.]

So he came back to Concord with me, to my nice little apartment over a bookstore. We'd stay up late drinking and really became friends. And we stayed friends until he died. And I internalized him to such a degree that, years later, even today—and now I'm older than he was when he died—I still think, *What would Nelson do? What would Nelson say?* When he was young and in his prime, he was standing against the literary establishment, but was also a bona fide member of it. Standing against hypocrisy, speaking truth to power. He was the person who did that more deliberately than any other writer of his generation, except maybe James Baldwin, whom he admired enormously.

NANCY: Your novels are so character driven. I wonder if that three-dimensionality, that authenticity of characterization, is what you look for when you're reading other works of fiction.

RUSSELL: Yeah, I do. I wanted to reread Tolstoy's "The Death of Ivan Ilyich" because of the novel I'm writing right now. There's a character in it whose arc somewhat parallels what I could remember of Ivan Ilyich's life. I wanted to see how Tolstoy handled the transitions and the backstory, and how he could integrate it without it being a biographical novel. It's the Richard Pevear and Larissa Volokhonsky version—quite a wonderful translation, and the volume includes a whole lot of other stories that I had never read. And those characters are brutal; they're so tough. I'm totally attracted to those characters, but if you met such a person in real life, there's no way you'd be attracted to them. They're like characters out of *Affliction* or *Continental Drift*.

NANCY: Or *Lost Memory of Skin*.

RUSSELL: That's right. And Tolstoy handles them unflinchingly. He's not sentimental and doesn't soft-pedal their lives, or the world that surrounds them, and yet you have enormous sympathy for these characters. They're mean-spirited sometimes, they're ignorant, lustful, and violent, and drunks, and so on. And yet you have such compassion for them. And I thought, *Whoa, this is striking such a chord for me, I feel so happy at this point in my life to have discovered these stories.* Because yes, I read the great classics, *Anna Karenina* and *War and Peace*, but I had never read these stories. They're so moving to me right now. More than any that I have come across in contemporary writing for a long time.

I've gotten close to Toni Morrison over the years and find that her characters are also profoundly moving and beautifully embraced. She's a great, great writer. Maybe the greatest writer alive today in English. [Note: our interview was conducted the month before Morrison died.] The other thing I like about her characters, which parallels some of my ambitions in *Cloudsplitter*, is that she can humanize and contemporize historical fictional characters. In too much so-called historical fiction, the characters seem to be in costume, in stage settings. They don't feel contemporary. But her characters do. Like in her great novel *Beloved*, of course, but there are so many others. Most of her novels are set in the past. The distant past at times and sometimes the more or less recent past, like her novel *Home*. I love that novel. Set in the '50s, the Korean War, and the veteran comes home. That's historical. But it feels like he just got home from Afghanistan, you know? Iraq. It feels that contemporary.

NANCY: I loved *Jazz*. The syncopated language. It was like reading a musical score.

RUSSELL: I loved it too.

NANCY: When the world is too much with you, what do you read?

RUSSELL: I read classics. I don't go back and reread too much, because there's so much I haven't read. I found myself in the last year or so reading books from languages and cultures that I'm not very familiar with. Scandinavian or Dutch novelists, or French writers I feel I probably should've read. I want to see what's there, because I read things about 'em. Like Patrick Modiano, the French novelist: I thought, *I've never heard of him. Why have I not read him?*

JEFF: Among your contemporaries, are there some you feel especially attuned to?

RUSSELL: Yeah, there's a whole bunch of writers I feel that way about. I mean, it's a good generation, my generation of writers. I feel very close to Bill [William Kennedy] in terms of our perspective on both writing and the world generally. I feel especially close to certain aspects of Joyce Carol Oates, the kind of realism she works through, the sort of themes she works on in the mostly upstate New York region. She's a writer with whom I have a sort of sibling relationship, as I do with Toni Morrison, and Michael Ondaatje—as if we have overlapping DNA or something like that. And Don DeLillo too, even though he's a hyperrealist in a sense compared to the work I do. On the other hand, his seriousness is something that I like to think I share. And his ambition as a writer too. His scale in books like *Underworld*, and his use of historical materials. Richard Ford's work too. I think he and I feel attached to a similar kind of realism and characters.

JEFF: You've written a lot of short fiction as well as novels. Do you read one more than the other?

RUSSELL: I think I probably read more novels than books of short stories; one of the beauties of short stories as opposed to novels is that they don't demand the same commitment. So I'm always reading short stories, but I don't read as many books of short stories as I read novels. I do love the short-story form. And always have. But I use a very different part of my brain in writing them, and I think in reading them, than I do with novels. It's a very different kind of engagement, and if you put electrodes on parts of your brain, I think different lights would come on when you're reading or writing short stories as opposed to novels. And that part of the brain that is engaged by short stories is quite alive for me and always has been. In fact, a number of times I've threatened Chase [Twichell, Russell's wife], "This is the last novel I'm ever going to write. I'll finish this novel and then for the rest of my life I'm just going to write short stories." It takes three to five years for me to write a novel, and how many of them do I have left? I might have two if I'm lucky and I'm healthy, but I could write thirty short stories in that period, and they're just as valuable to me as a novel is.

NANCY: What about poetry?

RUSSELL: Well, when I first began to write, I wrote poetry right alongside fiction. I even published a couple of little books of poetry back in the '60s. It wasn't until I was a student at the University of North Carolina at Chapel Hill in 1964, where I met real poets, not just wannabes like myself, but people who had the gift. William Matthews and Robert Morgan were there, and I got to know Charles Simic and James Tate and Louise Glück—they were my contemporaries, in their twenties too, but they had something going on that I didn't have. I could read poetry well enough, I was familiar enough with the traditions and the literary context so that I could cleverly imitate it, but the next step wasn't available to me. I didn't know what it was, and I didn't know how to get it either. Also, my poems were becoming more and more narrative, and more and more housed in a character's experience and perspective and life, so I could see that if I had any gift at all then it was probably in fiction and narrative, and I better just let this dream go.

I still read and love poetry, of course, and I'm married to a very fine poet, so we share all kinds of readings back and forth. And yeah, there are many poets that I really love and admire: Charles Simic, Louise Glück, Robert Hass, Stanley Plumly, who recently died. These days I spend more time going to memorials than I do going to weddings.

I just keep track of my own generation. In an unexpected, maybe interesting development that I've had to accept, or decided to accept rather than resist,

I stopped worrying about or reading or following writers who are much younger than I am. I mean, I'm seventy-nine, I've been doing this now for sixty years, and we grew up together, most of my writer friends and I. So naturally I keep track of their work and lives and so on.

There's the first stage in your career, when you hope you're going to get a grant or a prize or something like that. Then there's the second stage, if you were lucky enough to get one or two or three along the way, you end up being asked to be a juror, and you're sitting on the juries for a while. And then there's a stage at the end where you say, "I don't want to sit on a jury. I'm not applying for any more grants or prizes—I've probably won what I'm going to win." Then you kind of withdraw, and you read the stories of Tolstoy instead.

Some Books and Authors in Russell's Library

Nelson Algren
Don DeLillo, *Underworld*
William Faulkner, *The Bear*, *Light in August*,
   and *The Sound and the Fury*

Gabriel Garcia Marquez

William Kennedy

Jack Kerouac, *On the Road*

Toni Morrison, *Beloved* and *Home*

Joyce Carol Oates

James Otis, *Toby Tyler*

Charles Simic

Leo Tolstoy, *The Death of Ivan Ilyich and Other Stories*

Acknowledgments

First and foremost, we'd like to thank the authors who agreed to be part of this project and generously shared their time and love of reading with us.

Huge thanks to our editor Tara Parsons, her team at HarperOne, and the larger HarperCollins family: Virginia Stanley and Chris Connolly in Library Marketing; A.E. Kieran, whose illustrations captured the spirits of our subjects; Terry McGrath, the book's designer; copyeditor Dianna Stirpe; and production editor Mary Grangeia, who kept the project moving forward in challenging circumstances.

Thanks to our agent, Victoria Sanders, and her associates, whose enthusiasm for the project helped us bring it to life from its earliest stages.

Grateful thanks to Anika Miller, who took the raw recordings and transcribed them into a workable format, and to Megan Muir for her eagle eye proofreading the manuscript.

Thanks to Vince Landay for helping us connect with Dave Eggers and Vendela Vida, and to Amanda Uhle for helping coordinate their busy schedules; and to Susan Mulcahy for offering us an introduction to Siri Hustvedt. Thanks as well to the agents and publicists who facilitated our interviews with their writers: Jane Beirn at HarperCollins for Louise Erdrich, Kimberly Burns at Broadside PR for Laila Lalami, Sonya Cheuse at Ecco for Jonathan Lethem, Binky Urban at ICM Partners for Jennifer Egan and Richard Ford, and Maya Solovej at The Book Group for Donna Tartt.

Finally, thanks to you, readers throughout the world, old and young, without whom this book, and all the well-loved books mentioned within its covers, would have no reason to exist.

About the Authors

Bestselling author, librarian, literary critic, and devoted reader **NANCY PEARL** regularly speaks about the pleasures of reading at libraries, literacy organizations, and community groups around the world. She can be heard on NPR's *Morning Edition* discussing her favorite books. Her monthly television show on the Seattle Channel, *Book Lust with Nancy Pearl*, features interviews with writers, booksellers, and other literary figures. Among her many honors are the 2011 Librarian of the Year Award from *Library Journal* and the 2011 Lifetime Achievement Award from the Pacific Northwest Booksellers Association. Nancy is the creator of the internationally recognized program *If All of Seattle Read the Same Book* and was the inspiration for the Archie McPhee "Librarian Action Figure." Her first novel, *George & Lizzie*, was published in 2017.

JEFF SCHWAGER is a Seattle-based writer, editor, producer, and playwright who has also had a successful career as an entertainment and media executive. He has written extensively on books, movies, music, and theater, and has interviewed many of the most esteemed artists in each of those mediums. In 2013, Book-It Repertory Theatre produced his acclaimed adaptation of Denis Johnson's *Jesus' Son*. The following year, the company's five-hour stage version of his dramatization of Michael Chabon's *The Amazing Adventures of Kavalier & Clay* won Theatre Puget Sound's prestigious Gregory Award for Outstanding Production of 2014.

HARPER LARGE PRINT